The Fig

THE BARBER OF SEVILLE
THE MARRIAGE OF FIGARO
THE GUILTY MOTHER

First published in 1993 by Absolute Classics, an imprint of
Absolute Press, 14 Widcombe Crescent, Bath, England

Cover and text design: Ian Middleton

Typesetting by Font U Like, Bath

Printed by The Longdunn Press Ltd, Bristol

ISBN 0 948230 57 6

THE BARBER OF SEVILLE
THE MARRIAGE OF FIGARO
THE GUILTY MOTHER

Three plays by
Beaumarchais

translated by Graham Anderson

absolute classics

INTRODUCTION

As all writers for the stage know, nothing is less immutable than a play text. LE BARBIER DE SEVILLE first performed at the Comédie Française on 23 February 1775 was a five-act play. Two days later, following a cool reception, Beaumarchais re-presented it as a four-acter. This version enjoyed great success and is the text of the present translation. Even before the first production, however, there had been an earlier four-act variant, and at one stage LE BARBIER had been envisaged as a comic opera.

Similar to-ing and fro-ing had attended LE MARIAGE DE FIGARO, which, although probably written as early as 1778, went through the hands of five different censors before eventually being passed fit for production, at the Comédie Française, on 27 April 1784. The performance began at half past five and ended at ten o'clock. The audience had arrived in droves, Beaumarchais's struggles to get it staged having excited frenzied anticipation amongst the Parisian theatre-goers.

By that time, aged fifty-two, Beaumarchais had earned considerable notoriety. His career had been as varied as it was vivid. Born Pierre Augustin Caron, the son of a watchmaker, in 1732, he had learnt his father's trade, won the prized title of *horloger du roi,* married the rich widow of a court functionary (taking the name Beaumarchais from one of her properties), visited Spain on a matter of family honour and used the journey to dabble in colonial dealings with the American colonies, acted as the King's agent in England and financed the provision of arms shipments to the rebel cause in the American War of Independence. At almost every stage, from watchmaker to diplomat to gun-runner, Beaumarchais found himself locked in protracted and bitter litigation. He was stripped of his civil rights and, more than once, briefly incarcerated. After the revolution, he was forced into exile in Hamburg, returning only in 1796. He was just beginning to repair his reputation and his fortune when he was felled by an apoplectic stroke in 1799, aged sixty-seven.

In the trilogy of plays presented here, the character of Figaro bears a striking resemblance to the spirit of his creator. The gaiety and wit on the one hand, and the inventive scheming on the other admittedly carry echoes of the already familiar comic-but-wise valet. They are

refined and made new, however, by the way Figaro assumes responsibility not just for the workings of his master's household, but for the
workings of society at large. Figaro is a man of the world, and of his
times. He is the spirit of enterprise, of advancement through merit,
of individual vigour set against the inertia of a system. Small wonder
that his criticism of current, ossified, pratices caused the *ancien régime*
as much alarm as amusement.

While LE BARBIER DE SEVILLE and LE MARIAGE DE
FIGARO need little introduction, the case of LA MERE
COUPABLE may be less well known. The play was first performed
at the Théâtre du Marais on 26 June 1792. Beaumarchais was sixty,
and had suffered slings and arrows (as well as earning fame and fortune) for forty years. In LA MERE COUPABLE, he returned, perhaps with a suggestion of yearning and weariness, to an earlier form
of theatre. His first two plays, EUGENIE, OU LA VERTU MAL-
HEUREUSE (1767) and LES DEUX AMIS, OU LE NEGO-
CIANT DE LYON (1770), had both been *drames bourgeois* (and had
enjoyed little success). It is hard to appreciate the extent to which
THE BARBER and FIGARO ran counter to prevailing fashion. A
moral earnestness, aimed at promoting the worthy values of the middle classes, had flavoured the bulk of serious drama in the eighteenth
century. In a zealous attempt at modernising the stage, moving away
from the remote heroes of classical tragedy, writers had fallen into the
twin traps of contrivance and sentimentality. These *comédies larmoy-
antes* and *drames bourgeois* rarely escaped the charge of stodginess and
artificiality. But Beaumarchais himself had never lost the desire to
prove the *drame bourgeois* as potent as earlier forms.

THE GUILTY MOTHER, then, takes the Almaviva household
twenty years on from Figaro's marriage, and shifts the scene from
Spain to post-revolutionary Paris. The Count and Rosine are still
together, but only just. What splits them is their own past adulteries.
The Count has an illegitimate daughter, the Countess an illegitimate
son. The parentage, in each case, remains a guilty and closely-guard-
ed secret. In this suspicious ménage thrives the interloper, Bégearss,
a former military colleague of the Count and now his adviser. It is
Bégearss whose malign influence provides the spring of the action.
And here, perhaps, lies the relative weakness of THE GUILTY
MOTHER. In the earlier plays, it had been Figaro himself who insti-
gated each stage of the intrigue and who stood to gain most from a
successful outcome. In THE GUILTY MOTHER, Figaro is still the
fixer, but now he is in a defensive mode, defying Bégearss rather than

advancing his own interests. The whole thrust of the action is conservative, where it had previously been radical and progressive. And those most dependent on a successful outcome are the two young people, Florestine and Léon. Time has caught up with both Figaro and Beaumarchais. We are suddenly aware of a generation gap, and the shifting of interest from the Almavivas to Bégearss, the model of the hissable villain. Beaumarchais called his play a "moral drama", and subtitled it "The Other Tartuffe". There is a gloomy, desperate ring about the piece, a search for security and reassurance altogether at odds with the spirit of the earlier Figaro.

If we can accept that THE GUILTY MOTHER is a different sort of play, and not expect it to cap LE MARIAGE as LE MARIAGE capped LE BARBIER, there are still some virtues to be found. Beaumarchais does not draw back from his characters' darker sides. Rosine is not the long-suffering innocent of Aguas Frescas: she has a stained and all too human history. The Count's infidelities, formerly potential, are here realised. And for the Countess's remorseful distress there is a touching and genuine sympathy. Nor is the humane element to be scorned: good and evil coexist. Evil is not ignored, but its harmful effects can be nullified by truth and forgiveness. LA MERE COUPABLE may not have the dexterity or brilliance of its forerunners, but its dramatic possibilities share with those of its fellows consecration on the musical stage. Amongst others, Paisiello, and more famously Rossini, made operas from LE BARBIER DE SEVILLE; Mozart, most famously, from LE MARIAGE DE FIGARO; LA MERE COUPABLE joins the canon in operas by Milhaud (1966) and Coriligano (1991).

THE TRANSLATION

Theatre translations date within ten years. Period pieces are dated even before the translator starts. Does the modern translator give in, and attempt cod-eighteenth century English? Or does he not so much translate as adapt? Usually, he compromises. I have tried to balance the justifiable demands of the literary student for textual faithfulness against the equally justifiable demands of the actor for speakable lines. In general, I have leaned more closely to the original in LA MERE COUPABLE than in the other two plays. Besides being more stately in tone, LA MERE COUPABLE is less well known, and I have felt duty-bound to represent the text as accurately as possible. Actors and directors will have their say in the course of production anyway. In the case of LE MARIAGE, the actor's view prevailed even in 1784, when the company objected to Marceline's "proto-feminist" outburst in Act III, Scene 16, and persuaded Beaumarchais to drop it. And at four and a half hours, the uncut MARIAGE is a trial to even the most tolerant of bottoms on seats. I have taken minor liberties with the otherwise untranslatable ou/où argument in the III/15 trial scene. The many songs are translated with similar freedom.

LE BARBIER DE SEVILLE and LE MARIAGE DE FIGARO have been translated or adapted for the stage half a dozen times in the last two hundred years. There have been some notable versions for recent productions. This is, however, the first modern translation to be generally published for thirty years. It may well be the first translation of LA MERE COUPABLE at all. It is certainly the first publication to contain all three Figaro plays in a single volume. To the translator alone, of course, must be ascribed any failings also contained.

GRAHAM ANDERSON
January 1993

CHARACTERS

COUNT ALMAVIVA (Spanish grandee, lover incognito of Rosine, appears in the first act in satin coat and breeches, and wrapped in a large brown cloak or Spanish cape; black hat, brim turned down, coloured ribbon round the crown. In the second act, cavalryman's uniform, with moustaches and boots. In the third act, tutor's costume: page-boy hair, ruff, coat, breeches and stockings of a priest. In the fourth act, he appears superbly dressed in the Spanish style with an elegant coat; over it all, the large brown cloak which he keeps wrapped round him.)

BARTHOLO (Doctor, guardian of Rosine. Short, black, buttoned coat; large wig; frilled ruff and cuffs; black belt; and when he goes outside, a long scarlet cloak.)

ROSINE (A young lady of noble origin, ward of Bartholo; dressed in Spanish style.)

FIGARO (Barber of Seville; dressed as a Spanish dandy. Head covered by a hair net; white hat with coloured ribbon round the crown; silk scarf loosely tied at his neck; satin waistcoat and knee breeches with silver-edged buttons and buttonholes; broad silk belt; garters tied with tassels hanging down each leg; coat of contrasting colour with broad lapels matching colour of waistcoat; white stockings and grey shoes.)

DON BAZILE (Organist, singing tutor to Rosine. Low-brimmed black hat, short cassock, long cloak, no ruff or cuffs.)

NIPPER (*La Jeunesse*, aged servant to Bartholo.)

SPARK (*L'Eveillé*, Bartholo's other servant, a sleepy

simpleton. Both of them dressed as men from Galicia: hair in pony tails; buff-coloured waist-coats; broad leather belts with buckles; blue breeches and coats whose sleeves, cut at the shoulder to leave the arms free, trail behind them.)

A LAWYER

AN ALCADE (Officer of the law; holds a long white baton.)

NUMEROUS (Spanish policemen.)
ALGUAZILS

SERVANTS (with torches.)

The setting is Seville, in the street and beneath Rosine's windows in the first act; and, for the remainder of the play, inside the house of Doctor Bartholo.

THE BARBER OF SEVILLE

ACT ONE

SCENE ONE

A street in Seville, with grills across all the windows.

COUNT

(Alone, dressed in a flowing brown cloak and a hat with down-turned brim. He pulls out his watch as he paces up and down.) It is earlier than I thought. Every day she comes and stands at her window, but her usual time is still some way off. Never mind. Better to arrive too early than miss the chance of seeing her. If any of the dashing gentlemen at court imagined they'd ever find me here, hundreds of miles from Madrid, hanging around each morning under the windows of a woman I've never spoken to, they'd take me for a Spaniard from the good old days of Queen Isabelle... Why not? Every man chases happiness. For me it lies in the heart of Rosine... All the same, pursuing a woman to Seville when Madrid and the court offer such easy pleasures everywhere you look?... And that's exactly what I'm running away from. Self-interest, vanity, convention supply us with an endless series of conquests, and I'm tired of them. It's so good to be loved as a real person! And if this disguise could help me find out for certain... Damn! Who's this, getting in my way?

SCENE TWO

Figaro and the Count, hidden.

FIGARO

(A guitar slung over his back on a broad ribbon; happily humming and singing, pencil and paper in hand)
  To banish grief, which makes us pine,
        I venture this remark:
  Without the fires of good strong wine
        To thrust away the dark,

> Man to languish would be forced,
> Man, from pleasures all divorced,
>   Would see his foolish life slip by,
> And all too soon that man would die

Not too bad so far, eh? Eh?

> And all too soon that man would die...

>   For me good wine and idleness
>   Battle for my heart so fervent.

No they don't! They don't battle for it, they reign
there together as peacefully as you could wish...

> Embrace ... in this heart so fervent.

Do you say: embrace?... Ah, for God's sake, come
on! You don't get writers of musicals worrying
about that sort of detail. Anything not worth saying, musicals is exactly where it belongs, nowa-
days. *(Sings)*

> For me good wine and idleness
> Embrace in this heart so fervent.

I want to end on something good, something brilliant and striking, something with the feel of an
epigram. *(Lowers one knee to the ground and writes
as he sings.)*

>   Embrace in this heart so fervent.
>   If one shows all my tenderness...
>   The other is no less emergent.

Bloody hell! Flat as a pancake. That's no good...
I need a contrast, an antithesis:

>   The one.. I make my dear mistress,
>   And the other..

.Yes, damn it, I've got it:

And the other is my humble servant.

Bloody good, Figaro! *(Writes as he sings.)*

> For me good wine and idleness
> Embrace in this heart so fervent;
> The one I make my dear mistress,
> And the other is my humble servant.
> And the other is my humble servant.
> And the other is my humble servant.

Ha, ha, when that's got a backing underneath it, then we'll see, you gossip column critics, whether I know what I'm about... *(Catches sight of the Count.)* I've seen that priest somewhere before. *(Gets to his feet.)*

COUNT   *(Aside)* I know that man.

FIGARO   Ah, no! He's no priest! That lofty, noble air...

COUNT   That grotesque turnout...

FIGARO   I'm not wrong: it's Count Almaviva.

COUNT   I do believe it's that rascal Figaro.

FIGARO   The very man, my lord Count.

COUNT   You scoundrel! If you say a word...

FIGARO   Yes, I recognise you all right; the friendly way you greet me just as you always used to.

COUNT   Well, I didn't recognise you. So sleek and well-fed...

FIGARO   What can I do, sir, that's poverty for you.

COUNT   You poor little thing. But what are you doing in Seville? I thought I gave you a testimonial for a job some time ago, in a government department.

FIGARO   I got the job, sir; and I'm grateful...

COUNT   Call me Lindor. Can't you see from my disguise
              I'm trying to avoid being recognised?

FIGARO   I'll slip away.

COUNT   On the contrary. There's something I'm waiting
              for here, and two men chatting look less suspicious
              than one man walking up and down. Let's look as
              if we're chatting. So, then, that job?

FIGARO   The minister, bearing in mind Your Excellency's
              recommendation, had me immediately appointed
              apprentice apothecary.

COUNT   In the hospitals of the army?

FIGARO   No, in the stud farms of Andalusia.

COUNT   *(Laughs)* A fine debut!

FIGARO   It was not a bad position to have, because being in
              charge of dressings and drugs, I was often able to
              sell to the men some excellent horse remedies.

COUNT   Which killed the king's subjects!

FIGARO   Ah, well now, there's no such thing as a universal
              remedy - but from time to time they made very
              effective cures for Galicians, or Catalans, or
              Irishmen.

COUNT   Why did you leave, then?

FIGARO   Leave? I was forcibly ejected. Someone got at the
              powers-that-be:
              "Hook-fingered envy, with his pale and livid
              mask"...

COUNT   Oh, spare me, spare me, friend! Don't tell me
              you're a poet as well. I saw you singing away there
              just now and scribbling on your knee.

FIGARO The exact cause of my downfall, Excellency. When it was reported to the minister that I was composing, very prettily I might add, garlands to Chloris; that I was sending riddles and puzzles to the papers; and that madrigals of mine were in circulation; in short, when he found out that I was coming hot off the presses, he made a tragedy out of a drama and had my position removed, on the theory that a love of letters is incompatible with the spirit of business.

COUNT A powerful argument! And you didn't defend yourself?

FIGARO I was glad to get off that lightly. Men in power are doing you a good enough turn if they're not actively doing you harm.

COUNT You're not telling me the whole story. When you were in my service I seem to remember you made a pretty bad servant.

FIGARO Well, sir, heavens above! People expect the poor to have no faults at all.

COUNT Lazy, unreliable ...

FIGARO Judging by the virtues they demand in a servant, does Your Excellency know many masters fit to do the job?

COUNT (Laughs) Not bad! And so you retired to this town?

FIGARO No, not straight away.

COUNT (Stops him.) Just a moment... I thought that was her... Go on, I'm still listening.

FIGARO Back in Madrid, I wanted to try my literary talents again; and the theatre seemed to me to be a field of honour...

COUNT   Ah! For pity's sake!

FIGARO   *(While he speaks, the Count watches the window
               closely.)*   To tell you the truth, I can't understand
               why I didn't have a major triumph, because I'd
               filled the stalls with the most excellent workers.
               Hands... like carpet beaters. I'd rejected gloves,
               sticks and everything that makes the applause
               sound muffled. And, honestly, before the perfor-
               mance, the café critics had seemed to be with me
               all the way. But the professional show-busters...

COUNT   Ah! The hacks and gossips! And our distin-
               guished author came a cropper!

FIGARO   I'm not the first one to suffer. What could I do?
               They whistled me. But if ever I get them all
               together...

COUNT   You'll bore them to death in revenge?
FIGARO   Ah, but it gets to me still, damn them!

COUNT   I can see it does! You know you've only got twen-
               ty-four hours in a court of law to fight the sentence
               against you?

FIGARO   In the theatre you have twenty-four years. Life
               isn't long enough to get over the resentment I feel.

COUNT   It gladdens my heart to see you in such joyous
               anger. But you haven't told me what made you
               leave Madrid.

FIGARO   My guardian angel, Excellency, since I am fortu-
               nate enough to run into my former master.
               Seeing in Madrid that the republic of letters is a
               republic of wolves, always up in arms against each
               other, and seeing how this ludicrous harassing of
               everybody just leaves the whole lot of them
               buzzing with contempt, all the insects, the mos-
               quitos, the cousins, the critics, the blood-suckers,
               the envious, the gossip columnists, the booksellers,
               the censors, and everything that attaches itself to

the hide of the unfortunate man of letters and sucks out what little substance they have left; weary of writing, bored with myself, disgusted by the others, crushed by debts and hard up for cash; eventually convinced that the useful income from wielding the razor is preferable to the empty honour of wielding the pen, I left Madrid. And with my baggage on my back I trod a philosopher's path through the two provinces of Castille, through La Mancha, Estramadura, Sierra-Morena, Andalusia. Welcomed in one town, thrown into gaol in another, and everywhere rising above such events; praised by these men, condemned by those; giving help in good times, bearing up in bad; scorning fools, braving villains; laughing at my poverty and giving a close shave to anyone I met; here you find me finally settled in Seville, and ready to serve Your Excellency once more in any and every task he might desire of me.

COUNT   Who has given you such a cheerful philosophy?

FIGARO   My loyal companion Misfortune. I make a point of laughing at everything, for fear of having to cry. What is it you keep looking at over there?

COUNT   Let's get out of here.

FIGARO   Why?

COUNT   Just come on, you wretch! You'll give me away.

They hide.

SCENE THREE

Bartholo, Rosine.
The lattice on the first floor opens, and Bartholo and Rosine stand at the window.

ROSINE   Oh, it's lovely to breathe the fresh air!...This window is opened so rarely.

BARTHOLO   What is that paper you're holding there?

ROSINE   It's a song from "The Futile Precaution", which
                my singing master gave me yesterday.

BARTHOLO   What is this "Futile Precaution"?

ROSINE   It's a new play.

BARTHOLO   Yet another bourgeois drama! Some new-fangled
                piece of idiocy!

ROSINE   I don't know anything about it.

BARTHOLO   Ha! Well, the newspapers and the authorities will
                sort that out for us. What a barbaric age we live
                in!...

ROSINE   You are always insulting this poor century of ours.

BARTHOLO   Pardon me for living! What has it produced that
                we should praise it for? Idiocies of every variety:
                freedom of thought, the laws of gravity, electricity,
                religious tolerationism, vaccination, quinine, the
                Encyclopedia, and plays...

ROSINE   *(The paper slips from her fingers and falls into the
                street.)* Oh! My song! I dropped my song while I
                was listening to you. Oh, run, sir, run! My song
                will be lost!

BARTHOLO   In this world, damn it, you hold on to what you've
                got.

                Leaves the balcony.

ROSINE   *(Glancing inside the room, makes a signal down into
                the street)* Psst! Psst! *(Count appears.)* Pick it up,
                quickly, and get out of sight.

                *Count darts forward, snatches up the paper and
                withdraws.*

BARTHOLO	*(Emerging from the house and searching)* Where is it, then? I can't see anything.
ROSINE	Under the balcony, down by the wall.
BARTHOLO	This is a ridiculous errand to be sent on! Are you sure nobody has come by?
ROSINE	I didn't see anyone.
BARTHOLO	*(To himself)* And I'm generous enough to come down here searching...! Bartholo, my friend, you're a fool: this will teach you never to open windows on to the street.

> *He goes back in.*

ROSINE	*(Still on the balcony)* My excuse is my unhappiness. Lonely, shut up, victim of a horrid man's persecution, is it a crime to attempt to break the chains of slavery?
BARTHOLO	*(Appearing on the balcony)* Senora, go back inside. It is my fault if you have lost your song, but it is a misfortune you will not suffer again, I promise you.

> *He closes the lattice and turns the key.*

SCENE FOUR

Count, Figaro.
They enter cautiously.

COUNT	Now they've gone in, let's have a look at this song. There's sure to be some mystery folded up in it. It's a letter!
FIGARO	And he wanted to know what "The Futile Precaution" was!
COUNT	*(Reads eagerly.)* "Your attentiveness excites my

curiosity. As soon as my guardian has gone out,
sing something to the tune of this familiar song,
but sing it casually, and make the words tell me at
last the identity, the position and the intentions of
the man who seems to be so unswervingly
attached to the unfortunate Rosine."

FIGARO
(Imitating Rosine's voice) Oh! My song! I've
dropped my song! Oh, run, sir, run! *(Laughs)*
Ha, ha, ha! Oh, these women! You want to teach
the most innocent of them how to be sly? - Lock
her up.

COUNT
My sweet Rosine!

FIGARO
Sir, now I understand the reason why you're in
disguise. You've got a love affair in prospect.

COUNT
So now you know. But if you breathe a word...

FIGARO
A loose tongue, me? I will spare you the grand
declarations of honour and devotion people constantly sound off with: all you need to know is this:
my self-interest is your guarantee. Think about it
that way, and...

COUNT
All right. And all you need to know is this: six
months ago, quite by chance, I met on the Prado a
young lady of such beauty!... Well, you've just
seen her. I sent out search parties through the
whole of Madrid, but without success. I only discovered a few days ago that she is called Rosine,
she comes from a well-born family, she's an
orphan, and she's married to an old doctor named
Bartholo who lives in this town.

FIGARO
A pretty bird too, my word! And a tough cage to
unfasten! But who told you she was married to the
doctor?

COUNT
Everybody.

FIGARO
It's a story he cobbled together when he arrived

from Madrid, to throw young men off the scent and keep them away. She's only his ward, so far, but soon...

COUNT

(Energetically) Never!... Ah! What wonderful news! I was ready to risk anything just to let her know what a loss she was, and I find she's free! There's not a moment to lose. I must make her fall in love with me, and rescue her from the appalling match he's planning. Do you know this guardian, then?

FIGARO

Like my own mother.

COUNT

What sort of man is he?

FIGARO

(Energetically) He's a fine portly, squat, young old codger, grey in patches, scratchy, shaven, craven, spying, prying and whining all at the same time.

COUNT

(Impatient) All right! I've seen him. I want to know his character.

FIGARO

Brutish, mean, infatuated, and wildly jealous of his ward, who hates him to death.

COUNT

In other words, his good points are...

FIGARO

Nil.

COUNT

Excellent. His integrity?

FIGARO

The bare minimum to keep him from being hanged.

COUNT

Excellent. To punish a villain and make oneself happy at the same time...

FIGARO

Is to combine personal gain with public service. A masterpiece of morality, sir, and that's the truth!

COUNT

You say he keeps his door locked for fear of young men?

FIGARO	Locked and bolted. And if he could stop up the cracks...
COUNT	Ah, damn him. That's a blow. Do you have any access?
FIGARO	Do I just! For a start, the house I live in belongs to the doctor, who has settled me there free of charge.
COUNT	Ah! Ah!
FIGARO	Yes. And to mark my gratitude, I have promised to pay him ten gold pistoles per annum, also free of charge.
COUNT	*(Impatient)* You are his tenant?
FIGARO	More than that, I'm his barber, his surgeon, his apothecary. In his household there's not a stroke of the razor, a jab of the lance or a plunge of the syringe that isn't performed by the hand of your humble servant.
COUNT	*(Embraces him.)* Ah! Figaro, my friend, you will be my guardian angel, my liberator, my guiding light.
FIGARO	Hell, being useful doesn't half bring down the barriers! Talk about people with passions!
COUNT	Lucky Figaro, you are going to see my Rosine! You are going to see her! Can you conceive your own good fortune?
FIGARO	There's the remark of a lover for you! Am I the one who's mad about her? Pity you can't take my place!
COUNT	Ah, if only we could get rid of all the servants who watch her.
FIGARO	I was just thinking about that.

COUNT	Twelve hours would be enough!

FIGARO	The way to stop people minding others' business is to get them to mind their own.

COUNT	Absolutely. Well then?

FIGARO	*(Thinking)* I'm wondering if a touch of the pharmaceuticals might just provide a little harmless…

COUNT	You scoundrel!

FIGARO	Do I mean them any harm? They all need my ministrations. It's simply a question of giving them their medicine all at the same time.

COUNT	But our doctor would suspect something was up.

FIGARO	We need to work so quickly that suspicion hasn't time to stir. I have an idea: the regiment of the Prince-Royal is arriving here in town.

COUNT	The Colonel is a friend of mine.

FIGARO	Good. Present yourself at the doctor's house in cavalry uniform, and show him a billeting order. He'll have no choice but to take you in; and I'll see to the rest.

COUNT	Excellent!

FIGARO	Come to that, it wouldn't be a bad idea if you turned up looking a bit the worse for wear…

COUNT	What's the point of that?

FIGARO	And led him a bit of a dance while you're in a bad state.

COUNT	What for?

FIGARO	So that he won't get upset, so that he'll think you want sleep and not trouble.

COUNT   Crafty thinking! But why shouldn't you take me
               in yourself?

FIGARO   Oh, yes! Me! We'll be happy enough if he fails to
               recognise you, a man he's never set eyes on before.
               And how could I get you in again after that?

COUNT   You're right.

FIGARO   Because perhaps you may not be able to keep up a
               difficult act. The cavalryman... with a drop too
               much inside him...

COUNT   You're joking. *(Putting on a drunken voice)* Is this
               the house of doctor Bartholo, my friend?

FIGARO   Not bad, I admit. Just a little more wine in the
               legs. *(An even more drunken voice)* Is this the
               house...?

COUNT   Come off it! That's the way a common street
               drunkard sounds.

FIGARO   And it's the right way to be drunk. Drunk for fun.

COUNT   Someone is opening the door.

FIGARO   That's our man. Step aside until he's gone.

SCENE FIVE

Count and Figaro, hidden; Bartholo.

BARTHOLO   *(Talking as he leaves the house)* I shall be back
               straight away. Don't let anybody in. How stupid
               of me to have gone down! I should have suspected
               as soon as she started pleading... And Bazile still
               hasn't arrived! He was supposed to have been
               making arrangements for me to get married in
               secret tomorrow: and not a word of news! I have
               to go and see what's holding him up.

SCENE SIX

Count, Figaro.

COUNT   Did I hear right? Tomorrow he marries Rosine in secret!

FIGARO   Sir, the difficulty of the task only increases the necessity of taking it on.

COUNT   And who is this Bazile who's fixing his marriage?

FIGARO   A feeble wretch who gives his ward music lessons. A small-time rogue, besotted by his art, paid in peanuts and ready to crawl for a couple of quid. He'll give us no trouble, sir... *(Looks up at the lattice window.)* There she is, there she is.

COUNT   Who?

FIGARO   Behind her window, there she is, there she is. Don't look, whatever you do, don't look!

COUNT   Why not?

FIGARO   Didn't her letter say: "Sing casually"? That means, sing as if you were singing... simply for the sake of singing. Oh! There she is, there she is!

COUNT   Since I've begun to interest her without her knowing who I am, let's keep to my assumed name of Lindor. It'll add all the more charm to my success. *(Unfolds Rosine's paper.)* Here's the tune, but what am I going to do for words? I'm no good at making up songs.

FIGARO   Any old thing that comes to mind, sir, will be just spot-on. In matters of love, the heart is not fussy about the products of the intellect... And take my guitar.

COUNT   What am I supposed to do with this? I can hardly play the thing!

FIGARO   Is there anything a man of your station can't do?

Just use the back of your hand: vrumm, vrumm,
vrumm... Sing in Seville without a guitar? They'd
soon recognise you, believe me, they'd have you
flushed out in no time.

*Figaro flattens himself against the wall, under the
balcony.*

COUNT   *(Wanders up and down, singing and accompanying
             himself on his guitar.)*
                   By your command I name myself and sing,
                 Though still unknown I dared you to adore:
                   How could a name bring any hope for more?
                 What can I do but kneel as to my king?

FIGARO   *(Aside)* Bloody hell, good stuff! Keep it going,
             sir!

COUNT   My name's Lindor, my birth is very low,
                   My status that of simple undergrad;
                   The trappings of a knight I wish I had:
                 A brilliant rank and fortune'ld suit you so.

FIGARO   The man's a genius, damn it! I couldn't do better
             myself, and I'm a dab hand at this stuff.

COUNT   Every morning here in tender song,
                   I'll sing again a love hopeless but true.
                   It's joy enough to set my eyes on you:
                 Yet might your heart, to hear me, beat more
                                 strong?

FIGARO   Oh, let's hear it for that one!...

             *He creeps over and kisses the hem of his master's
             cloak.*

COUNT   Figaro?

FIGARO   Excellency?

COUNT   Do you think she heard me?

ROSINE	*(In her room, sings.)*

                Lindor pleases me in every part,
             I love him truly now with all my heart...

The closing of a window bar cuts her off with a crash.

FIGARO   Now do you think she heard you?

COUNT   She shut her window. Someone must have come into the room.

FIGARO   Ah! The poor little thing! You could hear her voice tremble when she was singing. Sir, she's in love!

COUNT   She gives her own answer back the same way. "Lindor pleases me in every part." What grace! What intelligence!

FIGARO   What slyness! That's love!

COUNT   Figaro, do you think that means she's given herself to me?

FIGARO   If she had to jump off the balcony to give herself, she'd jump.

COUNT   That's it then, my Rosine has me for her own... for life!

FIGARO   Sir, I think you're forgetting that she can't hear you any more.

COUNT   Mister Figaro! Let me tell you just this one thing: she is going to be my wife. And if you help my plans along by keeping quiet about my name... You understand what I mean, you know me...

FIGARO   I'm all yours. Here you go, Figaro, fly onward to fortune, my son.

COUNT   Now let's get away before we're noticed.

FIGARO	*(Energetically)* Not me, I'm going into the house, where, by the sheer power of my arts, and with a single wave of my wand, I shall send the watch-keepers to sleep, stir love to wakefulness, lead jealousy a false trail, send plotters barking up the wrong tree, and overturn every obstacle in our path. You sir, to my house to arm yourself with the soldier's uniform, the billeting order, and enough gold to fill your pockets.
COUNT	Gold? Who for?
FIGARO	*(Sharply)* Gold, good God, gold: it's the key to the whole thing.
COUNT	Don't get excited, Figaro. I'll bring more than enough.
FIGARO	*(Moving off)* I'll see you very soon.
COUNT	Figaro?
FIGARO	What?
COUNT	Your guitar?
FIGARO	*(Coming back.)* I forgot my guitar! Me! I'm losing my grip!

He moves off.

COUNT	And your house, scatterbrain? Where do I find it?
FIGARO	*(Coming back.)* Ah! Truly, I'm going demented! - My shop, a dozen yards from here, blue paint, leaded window, shop sign three drip trays for blood spills and an eye held in a hand, "consilio manuque", clever as well as handy, "FIGARO".

He rushes off.

END OF ACT ONE

ACT TWO

SCENE ONE

Rosine's apartment. The window at the back is screened by an iron grille.

Rosine, alone, holding a candlestick. She takes a sheet of paper on the table and begins to write.

ROSINE   Marceline is unwell; the servants are all busy; and no one can see me writing. I don't know if these walls have ears and eyes, or if my all-seeing keeper has an evil genie who tells him as soon as anything happens; but I can't say a word or take a single step without his guessing my intentions at once. ... Ah, Lindor! *(She seals the letter.)* I'll seal my letter anyway, although I don't know when or how I shall be able to deliver it. I saw him through the window, having a long conversation with the barber Figaro. He's a good fellow, and I can see he sometimes feels sorry for me. If I could just talk to him for a minute!

SCENE TWO

Rosine, Figaro.

ROSINE   *(Surprised)* Ah! Mister Figaro, you can't tell how glad I am to see you!

FIGARO   Are you not feeling well, madame?

ROSINE   Not very, Mister Figaro. The boredom is killing me.

FIGARO   I can believe that. Only fools thrive on it.

ROSINE   Who was that you were having such an animated talk with down in the street? I couldn't hear anything, but...

FIGARO   A young relative of mine, a student, with great
                prospects; full of wit, fine feelings, talent, and
                strikingly handsome.

ROSINE   Oh! Very striking, I assure you! And his name?...

FIGARO   Lindor. He's penniless: but if he hadn't left
                Madrid suddenly he could have found an excellent
                position there.

ROSINE   *(Rashly)* He will do, Mister Figaro, he will do. A
                young man like the one you describe cannot
                remain unrecognised for long.

FIGARO   *(Aside)* Good stuff. *(Aloud)* But he has one major
                failing which is always going to hinder his
                progress.

ROSINE   A failing, Mister Figaro? A failing! Are you sure?

FIGARO   He is in love.

ROSINE   In love! And you call that a failing?

FIGARO   Only in combination with his lack of money, I
                admit.

ROSINE   Ah, fate is so unjust! And does he say who this
                person is that he loves? I'm terribly curious...

FIGARO   You are the last person, madame, with whom I
                would wish to share a confidence of that nature.

ROSINE   *(Eagerly)* Why, Mister Figaro? I can keep a
                secret. This young man is a relation of yours, he
                interests me greatly,... so do tell me.

FIGARO   *(Looking at her slyly)* Picture the prettiest little
                creature, gentle, loving, comely and fresh, exciting
                the appetite; light of foot, supple and slender of
                waist, rounded arms, rosy lips, and her hands!
                Her cheeks! Her teeth! Her eyes!...

ROSINE   Who lives in this town?

FIGARO   In this district.

ROSINE   In this street, perhaps?

FIGARO   Not two strides away from me.

ROSINE   Ah! How delightful... for your young relation.
                And the young lady is...?

FIGARO   Did I not say her name?

ROSINE   *(Excitedly)* It's the only thing you have forgotten,
                Mister Figaro. Tell me, tell me quickly. If some-
                one were to come in now, I might never know...

FIGARO   You absolutely insist, madame? Well, then! That
                young lady is... the ward of your guardian.

ROSINE   The ward...?

FIGARO   Of Doctor Bartholo; yes, madame.

ROSINE   *(Overwhelmed)* Ah! Mister Figaro!... I don't
                believe you're telling me the truth, truly.

FIGARO   And that is why he is burning to come and per-
                suade you of it himself.

ROSINE   Mister Figaro, you are making me tremble all
                over.

FIGARO   What's this trembling! Not a good idea, madame.
                When you begin to fear evil, you're already giving
                way to the evils of fear. Besides, I've just put all
                your servants out of harm's way until tomorrow.

ROSINE   If he loves me, he must prove it by keeping
                absolutely calm.

FIGARO   What! Madame! Can calmness and love reside in
                a single heart? The poor youth of today is un-

happily trapped in a terrible dilemma: love without calm, or calm without love.

ROSINE   *(Lowering her eyes)* Calm without love... seems...

FIGARO   Ah, very flat. It seems indeed that love without calm is a better bet. And for my part, if I were a woman...

ROSINE   *(Embarrassed)* It is surely the case that a young lady cannot prevent an honest man from thinking well of her.

FIGARO   Therefore my relative thinks infinitely well of you.

ROSINE   But if he were to do something rash, Mister Figaro, we would be lost.

FIGARO   *(Aside)* We would be lost! *(Aloud)* If you were to expressly forbid him, by means of a little letter... A letter carries great weight.

ROSINE   *(Giving him the letter she has just been writing)* There isn't time to start this one again; but when you give it to him, tell him... tell him carefully...

          She listens.

FIGARO   Nobody there, madame.

ROSINE   That everything I am doing is done out of pure friendship.

FIGARO   That goes without saying. Heavens above, love is something quite different!

ROSINE   Only out of pure friendship, do you understand? I'm only worried that he might be put off by all the difficulties...

FIGARO   Yes, some weak wimps... Remember, madame, that the wind which blows a candle out sets an inferno blazing, and that we are that inferno. Just talking about it is enough to bring me out in a heat rash, it's as if I've caught the fires of his own passion, and I've got nothing to do with it!

ROSINE   Oh, my God! I can hear my guardian. If he found you here... Go into the music room, and take the stairs down as quietly as you can.

FIGARO   Don't worry. *(Aside, showing the letter)* This is worth more than anything I could say.

He goes into the music room.

SCENE THREE

Rosine, alone.

ROSINE   I'll be worried to death until he's safely outside... I like that Figaro, he's so good! He's a really honest man, so kind to his relations! Ah! Here comes my gaoler. Time to get back to work.

She blows out the candle, sits, and takes up an embroidery hoop.

SCENE FOUR

Bartholo, Rosine.

BARTHOLO   *(In a rage)* Ah! Damn the man! That mad, rascally bandit, that Figaro! I can't leave the house for a second without being sure that when I get back...

ROSINE   This is a furious rage, sir: who could have caused it?

BARTHOLO   That damned barber. He's put my entire household out of action at a stroke. He's given Spark a sleeping draught and Nipper sneezing powder. He's bleeding Marceline's foot. And he

hasn't even spared my mule... a poor blind beast
of burden, and he's slapped a poultice over its
eyes! Because he owes me a hundred crowns, he's
making sure he's got plenty of bills to come in.
Ah! Just let him try presenting them!... And no
one guarding your anteroom! Getting to your
apartment is like crossing an empty parade
ground.

ROSINE   And who else but you could possibly get in, sir?

BARTHOLO   Better to be fearful without cause than make
myself vulnerable by taking no precautions at all.
The world is full of bold and shameless men...
Didn't someone snatch up that letter of yours this
morning pretty smartly while I was on my way
down to look for it? Oh, I...

ROSINE   You give the worst interpretation to the smallest
trifles. It could have been blown away by the wind,
or picked up by whoever came along; how should
I know?

BARTHOLO   The wind, whoever came along!... There is no
wind, madame, no whoever came along, they
don't exist. It is always someone stationed there
for the express purpose who picks up the papers
which a woman makes it appear that she dropped
out of carelessness.

ROSINE   Makes it appear, sir?

BARTHOLO   Yes, madame, makes it appear.

ROSINE   *(Aside)* Oh! The evil old man!

BARTHOLO   But that kind of mishap will not happen again.
Because I am going to have this grille sealed fast.

ROSINE   You can do better than that. Why not wall up the
windows altogether? From house arrest to prison
cell, what's the difference?

BARTHOLO	As far as the street windows go, that may not be such a bad idea... That barber didn't come in here at any rate?
ROSINE	Are you even worried about him as well?
BARTHOLO	Just as much as any other man.
ROSINE	There speaks the voice of a true gentleman!
BARTHOLO	Ah! Trust the whole world, and you'll soon find you're housing a fine wife bent on deceiving you, fine friends ready to steal her away and fine servants eager to help them.
ROSINE	What! Do you imagine I have so few principles I'd allow the advances of Mister Figaro?
BARTHOLO	Who the devil looks for any truth in the weird minds of women? How many times have I seen these principled virtues in action...!
ROSINE	*(Angry)* But, sir, if the only qualification for not being despicable is to be a man, why do I despise you so much?
BARTHOLO	*(Stunned)* Why?...Why?...You're avoiding my question about that barber.
ROSINE	*(Beside herself)* All right, yes. The man came into my room; I saw him, I spoke with him. And I won't conceal the fact that I found him very likeable: and I hope you choke on your own bile!

Exits.

SCENE FIVE

Bartholo, alone.

BARTHOLO	Oh! My servants, the Jews, the dogs! Nipper! Spark! Spark, damn you!

SCENE SIX

Bartholo, Spark.

SPARK	*(Arrives yawning and half asleep.)* Aah, aah, ah, ah...
BARTHOLO	Blasted oaf, where were you when that barber got in here?
SPARK	Sir, I was.. ah, aah, ah...
BARTHOLO	Planning some monkey trick, no doubt? And you didn't see him?
SPARK	Obviously I saw him, since he's the one who found me looking so ill, that's what he said. And he must have been right, because I started to feel pains all over my body just listening to him tal... Ah, ah, aah...
BARTHOLO	*(Mimicking)* Just li-listening to him!... Where's Nipper, the useless clown? Giving this young lad drugs without my prescription! There's some mischief at the bottom of all this.

SCENE SEVEN

As before, plus Nipper. Nipper arrives, an old man walking with the aid of a crutch; he sneezes several times.

SPARK	*(Still yawning)* Nipper?
BARTHOLO	You can do your sneezing on your day off.
NIPPER	That's fifty times... more than fifty... in a minute! *(Sneezes)* I'm sneezed to pieces.

BARTHOLO	Look! I'm asking the pair of you if anyone went in to Rosine's apartment, and you refuse to tell me that that barber...
SPARK	*(Still yawning)* Does he count as anyone, then, Mister Figaro? Aah, ah...
BARTHOLO	You cunning dog, I bet you're in the plot with him.
SPARK	*(Bursting into an idiot's tears)* Me... Me a plot!
NIPPER	*(Sneezing)* But, sir, that's not...that's not fair!...
BARTHOLO	Fair! What's fairness got to do with wretches like you? I am your master, and that makes me always right.
NIPPER	*(Sneezing)* But, God's truth, when a thing is true...
BARTHOLO	When a thing is true! When I state that a thing is not true, I mean it to be not true. Allow all those scoundrels to be right, and you'd soon see what happens to authority.
NIPPER	*(Sneezing)* I'd be better off getting the sack. This is a rotten place, they run you round like a blue-arsed fly.
SPARK	*(Crying)* A poor honest boy treated like a worm.
BARTHOLO	Get out then, poor honest worm! *(Mimics them.)* Atchoo, atchoo! One sneezes in my face, the other yawns in it.
NIPPER	Ah, sir, without Miss Rosine there'd be... there'd be no way a man would stay in this household.
	Exits, sneezing.
BARTHOLO	Just look at the state they're in! That man Figaro!

I can see what he's up to; the villain's trying to
write off the hundred crowns he owes me without
touching his wallet...

SCENE EIGHT

*Bartholo, Don Bazile; Figaro, hidden in the music room, appears from
time to time, listening.*

BARTHOLO   *(Continuing)* Ah! Don Bazile, time for Rosine's
                music lesson?

BAZILE   That's the least important of our concerns.

BARTHOLO   I called at your house but couldn't find you.

BAZILE   I had gone out to see to your affairs. I picked up a
                piece of bad news.

BARTHOLO   Bad for you?

BAZILE   No, for you. Count Almaviva is in town.

BARTHOLO   Keep your voice down. The man who was search-
                ing for Rosine all over Madrid?

BAZILE   He's in lodgings on the main square, and goes out
                every day in disguise.

BARTHOLO   That's bad news all right, no doubt about that.
                What are we to do?

BAZILE   If he was just some ordinary citizen and not a
                nobleman, we could find a way of getting rid of
                him.

BARTHOLO   Yes, an ambush in the dark, knives and daggers...

BAZILE   *Bone Deus!* And compromise ourselves? Instigate
                a scandal, now, that's another matter. And while
                the rumour is brewing, spice it and spread it with

our inside knowledge. If you adopt that kind of plan, then *concedo*, I am with you.

BARTHOLO   A curious way of disposing of a man!

BAZILE   Ah, calumny, sir! Do not disdain so powerful a weapon. I have seen the most upright men brought to the brink of collapse. Believe me, there is not a simple elementary lie, no horror stories, no fantastical tale that you can't make the chattering classes repeat if you set about it the right way, and in this town we have some highly skilled operators! First a faint breath, skimming the ground like a swallow before the storm, *pianissimo*, whispers and winds its way, sowing the poisoned word. A mouth here gathers it up to savour, and, *piano, piano*, slides it into an ear there. The harm is done; it takes root, it crawls, it spreads, and *rinforzando* from mouth to mouth, it accelerates at an amazing rate; then, all of a sudden, I can't explain how, you see the calumny rear up, whistle and fill like a gathering wind, grow before your very eyes. It hurtles outwards, takes flight, tumbles and turns, envelops you, tears you up, carries you along, bursts and thunders until it becomes, praise be, a general cry, a public *crescendo*, a universal *chorus* of hatred and ostracism. Is there a man in the world who could survive?

BARTHOLO   What are you drivelling about, Bazile? What has all this *piano-crescendo* to do with my situation?

BAZILE   What has it to do with it? It's what the whole world does to shake off its enemies, and it's what you must do here if you want to prevent yours from getting close.

BARTHOLO   Get close? I intend to marry Rosine before she even knows this Count exists.

BAZILE   In that case, you haven't a moment to lose.

BARTHOLO   And on whom does that depend, Bazile? I

entrusted you with all the arrangements of the affair.

BAZILE   Yes, but you have been skimping the expenses; if we are to have a well-orchestrated composition, then a marriage crossing the generations, an iniquitous settlement, a clear abuse of privilege, are all discords which one should always resolve and smooth away with the perfect harmony of gold.

BARTHOLO *(Giving him money)* Do it your way, if there's no other. But let's get it done.

BAZILE   Now you're talking like a businessman. Tomorrow, it will all be finished; your job, today, is to prevent anyone informing your ward.

BARTHOLO You can trust me for that. Will you be coming this evening, Bazile?

BAZILE   Don't count on it. Just fixing your marriage will keep me busy all day: don't count on it.

BARTHOLO *(Accompanying him towards the door)* I'm much obliged to you.

BAZILE   That's all right, doctor, no need to show me out.

BARTHOLO Oh, but yes. I want to lock the street door behind you.

SCENE NINE

Figaro, alone, emerging from the music room.

FIGARO   Ah, a wise precaution! Go on, lock the street door; and when I go out myself I'll leave it open for the Count. What a villain, that Bazile! Luckily he's an even bigger fool. You need status, a family, a name, a title; if you want to make a scandal in society by telling tales, you need to be a

man of substance. But a Bazile! He could lie his
head off and they'd never believe him!

SCENE TEN

Rosine, hurrying in; Figaro.

ROSINE   What! Are you still here, Mister Figaro?

FIGARO   Fortunately for you, Miss Rosine. Your guardian
                and your singing tutor thought they were alone
                here, and have just been talking openly...

ROSINE   And you listened to them, Mister Figaro? Don't
                you know that's a very bad thing to do?

FIGARO   Listen? But it's the very best thing to do if you
                want to hear properly. I have to tell you that your
                guardian is making preparations to marry you
                tomorrow.

ROSINE   Ah! Oh, my God!

FIGARO   Never fear. We'll give him so many other worries
                to think about, he won't have time to consider that
                one.

ROSINE   He's coming back. Go out by the little servants'
                staircase. Now you've filled me with terror.

                Figaro runs off.

SCENE ELEVEN

Bartholo, Rosine.

ROSINE   Were you here just now, talking to someone, sir?

BARTHOLO   Don Bazile, I've just shown him out, and with

good reason too. No doubt you'd have preferred it
if it had been Mister Figaro?

ROSINE   It's a matter of complete indifference to me, I
          assure you.

BARTHOLO All the same, I'd be most interested to know what
          that barber had to tell you that was so urgent.

ROSINE   Do you want me to be serious? He was reporting
          back on the health of Marceline, which is not
          entirely good, from what he says.

BARTHOLO Reporting back! I'll take a bet that he was passing
          on some letter.

ROSINE   And who might that be from, if you please?

BARTHOLO Oh! Who from! From the sort of person women
          never give a name to. How should I know? An
          answer to the paper you dropped at the window,
          perhaps.

ROSINE   (Aside) He doesn't miss a thing! (Aloud) You'd
          deserve it if it had been.

BARTHOLO (Looking at Rosine's hands) It was. You have been
          writing.

ROSINE   (Awkwardly) It would be a fine thing if you
          thought you had any way of making me admit it.

BARTHOLO (Taking her right hand) Make you? Me?
          Certainly not. But with an ink stain on your fin-
          ger, what about that? Eh, cunning senora?

ROSINE   (Aside) The man is evil!

BARTHOLO (Still gripping her hand) Women always think
          they're perfectly safe when they're left by them-
          selves.

ROSINE   Ah! Is that so... Here's the proof!... You can let me go now, sir, you're twisting my arm. I burnt myself holding my work too near the candle. I've always heard that the thing to do is to bathe a burn at once in ink: so that's what I did.

BARTHOLO   So that's what you did? Let's see if a second witness can corroborate the evidence of the first. I refer to this pad of paper which I know contains six sheets, because I count them every morning, including today.

ROSINE   *(Aside)* Fool! I never thought...

BARTHOLO   *(Counting)* Three, four, five...

ROSINE   The sixth one...

BARTHOLO   I can see very well that the sixth one is not there.

ROSINE   *(Eyes lowered)* The sixth one? I used it to make a twist for some sweets I sent to Figaro's little girl.

BARTHOLO   Figaro's little girl? What about the pen here, which was a new one? How has it come to be all black? Writing the address for Figaro's little girl?

ROSINE   *(Aside)* The man's jealousy, he's got a natural instinct for it! *(Aloud)* I needed the pen to redraw the outline of a flower for that coat of yours I'm embroidering.

BARTHOLO   How edifying! If you wish me to believe what you say, my child, you'd do better not to blush redder and redder at every truth you try to cover up. But that's a tip you have yet to learn.

ROSINE   Oh! Who wouldn't turn red, sir, when she sees the most wicked constructions placed on the most innocent of acts?

BARTHOLO   Oh well, I'm wrong then. Burn your finger, dip it in ink to soothe it, make paper twists for sweets to give to Figaro's little girl, and draw my coat on the embroidery frame: what could be more innocent! The lies you heap on each other in order to conceal a single fact!... I AM ALONE, I AM UNSEEN: I CAN LIE MY HEAD OFF. But the tip of your finger remains black, the pen has been used, paper is missing! You can't be expected to think of everything. One thing that is for sure, senora: when I next have business that takes me into town, I'll see you're honestly answered for by a double lock on all the doors.

SCENE TWELVE

Count, Bartholo, Rosine.

Count, dressed in cavalryman's uniform and seemingly half-cut, enters, singing "Réveillons-la" (ie "Wake the girl up") or some suitable soldiers' drinking song.

BARTHOLO	But who's this man? What's he doing here? A soldier! Retire to your room, senora.
COUNT	*(Singing "Réveillons-la", and striding over towards Rosine)* Which of you ladies is called Doctor Barrelo? *(Aside, to Rosine)* I am Lindor.
BARTHOLO	Bartholo!
ROSINE	*(Aside)* He said Lindor.
COUNT	Barrelo, Bordello: I couldn't give that for it. *(Snaps his fingers.)* All I need to know is which of you two ladies... *(To Rosine, showing her a paper)* Take this letter.
BARTHOLO	Two ladies! It's perfectly obvious you want me! Two ladies! Come, Rosine, go to your room; this man appears to be the worse for wear.
ROSINE	A good reason to stay, sir. You are alone. A woman's presence can sometimes bring them to their senses.
BARTHOLO	To your room, to your room. I can look after

myself.

SCENE THIRTEEN

Count, Bartholo.

COUNT   Ah! I recognised you straight away from your
             specification.

BARTHOLO   *(To the Count, who is stuffing the letter away)*
             What's that you've got there, hiding it in your
             pocket?

COUNT   I am hiding it in my pocket so that you don't know
             what it is.

BARTHOLO   My specification! These people talk to everyone
             as if they were in the army as well.

COUNT   Do you think a specification such as yours is diffi-
             cult to draw up?

                    Sings to the tune of "Ici sont venus en personne":

                        Doddering head and bald of pate,
                         Eyes a-squint and wild of gaze,
                         His fierce look says Red Indian;
                          Figure lumpy like a boulder,
                       Up one side a hunched right shoulder;
                      The pock-marked skin says Moroccan,
                        The beak-like nose says pelican;
                          Burly legs bent circumflex,
                        Surly words and voice perplexed;
                        Destructive in his every lust:
                       The perfect doctor... ain't he just!

BARTHOLO   What is the meaning of all this? Are you here in
             order to insult me? Remove yourself at once.

COUNT   Remove yourself! Shame on you! What a way to
             talk! Can you read, doctor... Beetlebrow?

BARTHOLO	Another preposterous question!

COUNT — Oh, don't let that embarrass you, for even I, who am just as much a doctor as you are,...

BARTHOLO — How is that?

COUNT — Am I not doctor to the regimental horses? That is why I have been billeted with a fellow practitioner.

BARTHOLO — He dares to compare a blacksmith!...

COUNT — *(To the tune "Vive le vin". First 3 lines spoken, last 4 sung:)*

> No, doctor, I do not claim
> That our art is of greater fame
> Than that of your Hippocrates.

> My friend, your knowledge holds the keys
> To triumphs on a larger scale:
> To kill disease may not prevail,
> But kills a man with greatest ease.

Isn't that just about right?

BARTHOLO — It suits you ill, ignorant navvy, to thus debase the first, the greatest and the most useful of all the arts!

COUNT — Useful, I agree, for those who practise it.

BARTHOLO — An art whose successes the sun is proud to shine upon.

COUNT — And whose blunders the earth is swift to be shovelled upon.

BARTHOLO — It is clear, dunce, that you are only used to talking to horses.

COUNT — Talk to horses! Ah, doctor! For a doctor so well-informed... Is it not a well-known fact that the vet always cures his patients without saying a word, whereas the doctor says many a word to his...

BARTHOLO   Without curing them, you were going to say?

COUNT   You're the one who said it.

BARTHOLO   Who the devil sent this damned drunkard here?

COUNT   I do believe you're trying to flirt with me, my pretty!

BARTHOLO   Enough of this, what do you want, what are you after?

COUNT   *(In feigned rage)* So that's it! Flying off the handle now! What do I want? Have you no eyes in your head?

SCENE FOURTEEN

Rosine, Count, Bartholo.

ROSINE   *(Running in)* Mister Soldier, please don't get angry! *(To Bartholo)* Sir, speak to him gently: a man out of his senses...

COUNT   You are right. That man is out of his senses. But we are sensible, we two. Me dutiful, and you beautiful... so, enough. In fact, there's no one else I want to deal with in this household.

ROSINE   How can I be of service, Mister Soldier?

COUNT   A mere trifle, my child. But if my words fail to make my meaning clear...

ROSINE   I can read between them.

COUNT   *(Showing her the letter)* No, follow them to the letter, to the letter. The only thing I... Let me put it straight and say that I want you to give me a bed for the night.

BARTHOLO   Is that all?

COUNT   That's all. Read this little love letter that our
            quarter- master has written you.

BARTHOLO   Let me see. *(The Count hides the letter, and gives
            him another. Bartholo reads:)* "Doctor Bartholo is
            required to receive, feed, house, offer a bed..."

COUNT   *(Emphasising it)* Offer a bed.

BARTHOLO   "For one night only, to the above-named Lindor,
            known as The Scholar, cavalryman in the regi-
            ment of..."

ROSINE   It's him, it's him.

BARTHOLO   *(Sharply, to Rosine)* What's the matter?

COUNT   Well, am I still in the wrong, Doctor Barbarous?

BARTHOLO   The man seems to take a vicious pleasure in twist-
            ing me round every way he can. To hell with your
            Barbarous, Beetlebrow! Go and tell your imperti-
            nent quartermaster that since my trip to Madrid I
            have been exempt from having soldiers billeted in
            my house.

COUNT   *(Aside)* God, this is a disaster!

BARTHOLO   Aha! That's put our friend out, and sobered him
            up a bit too! But don't let it prevent you from
            removing yourself straight away.

COUNT   *(Aside)* I thought I'd given the game away.
            (Aloud) Remove myself! You may be exempt
            from lodging soldiers, but you're not exempt from
            being polite, I presume? Remove myself! Show
            me your exemption order; I may not be able to
            read, but I'll soon see.

BARTHOLO	By all means. It is in that desk.
COUNT	*(While Bartholo goes over to it, Count speaks without moving from where he stands.)* Oh, my beautiful Rosine!
ROSINE	What! Lindor, is it really you?
COUNT	You must at least have this letter.
ROSINE	Be careful, he's watching us.
COUNT	Take out your handkerchief. I'm going to drop it.

He moves towards her.

BARTHOLO	Steady, soldier, steady. I don't like people looking at my wife from so close.
COUNT	She's your wife?
BARTHOLO	What about it?
COUNT	I took you for her great grand-father, paternal, maternal, sempiternal; there are at least three generations between her and you.
BARTHOLO	*(Reading from a sheaf of documents)* "Pursuant to the excellent and loyal attestations with which we have been furnished..."
COUNT	*(Flicking his hand up under the documents and scattering them on the floor)* What do I want with all this verbiage?
BARTHOLO	Do you realise, soldier, that if I call my servants I can soon have you dealt with as you deserve?
COUNT	A battle? Ah, yes please, a battle! That's a trade I know about. *(Showing the pistol in his belt)* And here's something that'll send up a pretty smoke-screen for them. Perhaps you've never seen a battle, madame?

ROSINE   And I don't wish to.

COUNT   But there's nothing quite so much fun as a battle.
                Imagine first of all *(Pushing the Doctor back)* that
                the enemy is on one side of the ravine, and our
                friends on the other. *(To Rosine, showing her the let-
                ter)* Get your handkerchief out. *(He spits on the
                floor.)* There's the ravine, all right?

                *Rosine pulls out her handkerchief; the Count lets
                his letter fall between them.*

BARTHOLO   *(Stooping)* Ah, ah!

COUNT   *(Picking it up again)* Listen to me...very nearly
                giving away my professional secrets... Here's a
                discreet lady, to be sure. Isn't that a love letter
                she's spilling from her pocket on to the floor?

BARTHOLO   Give, give.

COUNT   Dulciter, dulciter! Easy now, granddad! Everyone
                to their own business. What if a prescription for
                rhubarb had fallen from yours?

ROSINE   *(Reaching out a hand)* Ah! I know what this is,
                Mister Soldier.

                *She takes the letter and hides it in her apron pock-
                et.*

BARTHOLO   Right, you. On your way.

COUNT   Fine, I'm just going. Farewell, Doctor; no hard
                feelings. Grant me one little favour, my sweet one:
                pray that death might spare me for a few cam-
                paigns yet. Life has never been so dear to me.

BARTHOLO   Just keep walking. If I had any influence over
                death...

COUNT   Influence over death? Aren't you a doctor?

You've done death so many favours, it can't possi
bly refuse.

Exit.

SCENE FIFTEEN

Bartholo, Rosine.

BARTHOLO   *(Watching him go)*   At last he's gone!   *(Aside)*
            Now I must be more subtle.

ROSINE   All the same, sir, you'll agree he's an amusing
            man, that young soldier! One can see through his
            drunkenness that he doesn't lack wit, nor a certain
            education.

BARTHOLO   I am only too happy, my love, to have been able to
            rid ourselves of him! But aren't you just a little
            curious to read together the paper he passed to
            you?

ROSINE   What paper?

BARTHOLO   The one he pretended to pick up so that he could
            give it to you.

ROSINE   Ah, yes! That was the letter from my cousin the
            officer. It had dropped from my pocket.

BARTHOLO   It was my impression that he pulled it out from
            his.

ROSINE   I knew what it was straight away.

BARTHOLO   What's the harm in just having a little look at it?

ROSINE   Only I can't seem to remember what I did with it.

BARTHOLO   *(Pointing to her pocket)* You put it in there.
ROSINE   Oh, oh, I must be getting absent-minded.

BARTHOLO   Ah! Of course. It'll be some piece of silliness, you'll see.

ROSINE   *(Aside)* Unless I make him lose his temper, there's no way I can refuse.

BARTHOLO   So give it to me, dear heart.

ROSINE   But why this insistence, sir? Do you still not trust me?

BARTHOLO   What about you? Why should you not want me to see it?

ROSINE   I repeat, sir, that this paper is nothing more than my cousin's letter which you gave me yesterday with the seal already broken. And since we're on the subject, I can tell you plainly that I take exception to such liberties.

BARTHOLO   I don't understand you.

ROSINE   Do I go about examining the letters which arrive for you? What makes you think you have the right to interfere with ones addressed to me? If you do it out of jealousy, then I take it as an insult; if you are abusing an ill-founded authority, then I am all the more in revolt.

BARTHOLO   In revolt! What do you mean! You have never spoken to me like this.

ROSINE   If I have been restrained until today, it was not meant to give you the right to exploit me as you pleased.

BARTHOLO   What is this exploitation?

ROSINE   I mean that it is unforgivable to take it on yourself to open another person's letters.

BARTHOLO	Not even one's wife's?
ROSINE	I am not yet your wife. But why should she be the one subjected to an indignity no one else has to suffer?
BARTHOLO	You are trying to change the subject, and deflect my attention from the letter, which is doubtless a message from some lover. But I intend to see it, believe me.
ROSINE	You shall not see it. If you take a single step towards me, I shall run from this house and seek refuge from the first person I meet.
BARTHOLO	Who will not take you in.
ROSINE	That remains to be seen.
BARTHOLO	This is not France, where they always take the woman's side. But, to remove the fantasy from your mind, I will lock the door.
ROSINE	*(While he goes to do so)* Oh, God! What am I to do?...I'll exchange it for my cousin's letter, and make sure he has an easy chance to read that one.
	She makes the switch, and puts the cousin's letter in her pocket, ensuring part of it shows.
BARTHOLO	*(Returning)* Ah! Now I shall see it, I hope.
ROSINE	By what right, may I ask?
BARTHOLO	By the universally acknowledged right of the stronger over the weaker.
ROSINE	You'll have to kill me before I'll let you have it.
BARTHOLO	*(Stamping his foot)* Madame! Madame!
ROSINE	*(Collapsing into an armchair and pretending to feel ill)* Ah! The indignity of it!...

BARTHOLO	Hand over that letter, or fear my wrath.
ROSINE	*(Overwhelmed)* Poor Rosine can take no more!
BARTHOLO	What is wrong with you?
ROSINE	What an appalling life the future holds!
BARTHOLO	Rosine!
ROSINE	I can't breathe for fury!
BARTHOLO	She isn't well.
ROSINE	I'm feeling weak, I'm dying.
BARTHOLO	*(Reaching for her pulse - aside)* Good God! The letter! It's my chance to read it without her knowing.

He continues to feel her pulse, takes the letter, and tries to read it, twisting round to see.

ROSINE	*(Still in a state of collapse)* A tragic woman! Ah!...
BARTHOLO	*(Lets go of her arm - aside)* What an insane craving this is, to find out the one thing you go in fear of knowing!
ROSINE	Ah! Poor Rosine!
BARTHOLO	Using strong perfumes... sometimes brings on these fainting fits.

He reads over the back of the chair, feeling her pulse again. Rosine raises herself slightly, glances at him slyly, nods her head, and lies back without speaking.

| BARTHOLO | *(Aside)* Good God! It's the letter from her cousin. Damn my suspicious mind! How am I going to appease her now? At least she needn't know I've read it. |

He pretends to help her sit up, and slips the letter back in her pocket.

ROSINE   *(Sighing)* Ah!...

BARTHOLO   Well, now. That was nothing, my child; a touch of the vapours, that's all. Your pulse never wavered.

He goes to fetch a flask from the table.

ROSINE   *(Aside)* He's put the letter back! Excellent.

BARTHOLO   My dear Rosine, won't you take a little of these spirits?

ROSINE   I want nothing from you. Leave me alone.

BARTHOLO   I admit I was over-zealous about that paper.

ROSINE   The paper is the least of it! It's your way of demanding things which revolts me.

BARTHOLO   *(On his knees)* Forgive me. I saw I was wrong at once. Here I am at your feet, ready to repair my faults.

ROSINE   Oh, yes, forgive you! When you believe that letter isn't from my cousin!

BARTHOLO   Whether it is from him or from someone else, I don't wish to know anything about it.

ROSINE   *(Holding out the letter)* You see, if you go about it the right way, I'll do anything you ask. Read it.

BARTHOLO   Such straightforward behaviour would dissipate my suspicions, were I so wretched a man as to harbour any.

ROSINE   Then read it, sir.
BARTHOLO   *(Backing away)* God forbid that I should do you

any such insult!

ROSINE   You would insult me by refusing.

BARTHOLO   Let me make amends by showing you how much I
                trust you. I am going to visit poor Marceline,
                whom Figaro, for reasons best known to himself,
                has bled in the foot. Will you come as well?

ROSINE   I will come up in a moment.

BARTHOLO   Since we have made our peace, my sweet, give me
                your hand. If only you could love me, ah! How
                happy it would make you!

ROSINE   (*Lowering her gaze*) If only you could make me
                happy, ah! How I would love you!

BARTHOLO   Make you happy? I'll make you happy! Just see
                how happy I'll make you!

                Exit.

SCENE SIXTEEN

ROSINE   (*Watches him go*) Ah! Lindor! He says he will
                make me happy!... It's time I read this letter,
                which nearly caused me so much trouble. (*She
                reads, then exclaims.*) Ah!... I should have read it
                before. He tells me to pick a quarrel with my
                guardian, and I've just let such a good one go to
                waste. I could feel myself blushing to the eyebrows
                when he passed me the letter. Ah, my guardian is
                right: I'm far too inexperienced in the ways of the
                world, which, as my guardian often tells me, is
                what allows women to keep up appearances even
                in the worst of circumstances! But an unjust man
                would turn innocence herself into cunning incar-
                nate.
                    END OF ACT TWO

ACT THREE

SCENE ONE

Bartholo, alone, dismayed.

BARTHOLO   The woman's moods! Her whims! I thought I'd calmed her down... I wish someone would tell me who the devil put it into her head to refuse to take any more lessons from Don Bazile. She knows he is involved in my marriage... *(A knock at the door)* You bend over backwards to please a woman; if you miss a single point... I say one single point... *(Another knock at the door)* Who's that?

SCENE TWO

Bartholo, the Count, dressed as a student.

COUNT   May peace and joy ever inhabit this house!

BARTHOLO   *(Abruptly)* I never heard a more timely wish. What do you want?

COUNT   Sir, I am Alonzo, a qualified graduate...

BARTHOLO   I do not need a private tutor.

COUNT   ... pupil of Don Bazile, organist at the great convent and whose honour it is to give musical instruction to madame your...

BARTHOLO   Bazile! Organist! Whose honour it is!... I know that; get to the point.

COUNT   *(Aside)* What an appalling man! *(Aloud)* A sudden indisposition which has obliged him to take to his bed...

BARTHOLO   Take to his bed! Bazile! It's a good thing he sent word; I am on my way so see him now.

COUNT   *(Aside)* Hell! *(Aloud)* When I say bed, sir, what I mean is... he is confined to his room.

BARTHOLO   Let's hope it's nothing serious. Go on ahead, I'll come at once.

COUNT   *(Embarrassed)* Sir, he commanded me... Can anyone hear us?

BARTHOLO   *(Aside)* What mischief is this fellow up to? *(Aloud)* Certainly not, Mister Mystery-Maker! Talk openly, if you know how.

COUNT   *(Aside)* Surly old fool! *(Aloud)* Don Bazile commanded me to inform you...

BARTHOLO   Speak up, I'm deaf in one ear.

COUNT   *(Raising his voice)* Ah! Certainly....that Count Almaviva, who was staying in the Main Square,...

BARTHOLO   *(Horrified)* Not so loud! Not so loud!

COUNT   *(Louder)* ...moved out this morning. Seeing that it was through me that he learned Count Almaviva...

BARTHOLO   Hush, talk quietly, I beg you.

COUNT   *(As loud as before)* ...was visiting this town, and since I found out that Señora Rosine has written to him...

BARTHOLO   Written to him? My dear friend, lower you voice, I entreat you! Come, sit over here, we can chat more easily. You say you found out that Rosine...

COUNT   *(Proudly)* Beyond a doubt. Bazile, worried on your behalf by this correspondance, requested me to show you her letter; but the way you're taking the news...

BARTHOLO   My God, I'm taking it very well! But don't you
             think it might just be possible for you to speak less
             loudly?

COUNT   But you are deaf in one ear, you said.

BARTHOLO   Forgive me, Señor Alonzo, forgive me if I struck
             you as suspicious or harsh; but I am so thoroughly
             surrounded by plots and traps...; and then your
             appearance, your age, your manner... Forgive me,
             forgive me. Well! You have the letter?

COUNT   Now you sound like a man I can deal with, sir!
             But I'm worried we may be overheard.

BARTHOLO   Eh? Who by? All my servants dropping like flies!
             Rosine locking her door in a rage! The devil's got
             into my house. All the same, I'll go and check
             again...

             He goes over to Rosine's door and opens it gently.

COUNT   *(Aside)* I've gone and dug a hole for myself out of
             sheer annoyance. How am I going to hang on to
             the letter now? I'll have to turn tail and run: bet-
             ter if I hadn't come at all... Wait! Show it to
             him!... If I can warn Rosine in advance, showing
             it to him would be a stroke of genius.

BARTHOLO   *(Tip-toeing back)* She's sitting at her window with
             her back to the door, reading a letter from her
             cousin the officer which I had unsealed for her...
             So let's have a look at hers.

COUNT   *(Handing over Rosine's letter)* Here it is. *(Aside)*
             It's my letter she's re-reading.

BARTHOLO   *(Reads)* "Ever since you told me your name and
             what you are..." Ah! The traitress! This is her
             handwriting all right!

COUNT   *(Horrified)* Keep your voice down yourself!

BARTHOLO	My dear fellow, this puts me in your debt!...
COUNT	When all this is over, you can decide for youself what you think you owe me. Don Bazile is presently working something out with a lawyer...
BARTHOLO	With a lawyer, about my marriage?
COUNT	Would I have imposed on you for anything else? He instructed me to tell you that everything can be made ready for tomorrow. Then, if she resists...
BARTHOLO	She'll resist.
COUNT	*(Reaches to take the letter; Bartholo clutches it tightly)* That's the moment when I can help you: we'll produce her letter, and if necessary *(More mysteriously)* I'll even tell her I obtained it from some woman the Count gave it away to. You can imagine how embarrassment, shame and rage will instantly give her away...
BARTHOLO	*(Laughing)* This is what they mean by calumny! My dear friend, I can see now that you are here on Bazile's behalf! But if this isn't to resemble a conspiracy, wouldn't it be better if she had already met you?
COUNT	*(Suppressing a gesture of elation)* Don Bazile is of a similar opinion. But how are we to arrange it? It's late... there's little time left...
BARTHOLO	I'll tell her you are coming in his place. You can give her a lesson, can't you?
COUNT	I would do anything to oblige you. But beware of all those stories about tutors in disguise, it's a well-known ruse, an old stage trick. What if she begins to suspect...?
BARTHOLO	What could she suspect, if you were introduced by me? You look less like one of my allies, and more like a lover in disguise.

COUNT   Yes? Do you think my appearance could help the
               deception, then?

BARTHOLO   The slyest of men would be hard put to guess the
               truth. She's in a terrible mood this evening. But
               she'd only have to see you... Her harpsichord is
               kept in this study. I'll leave you to amuse yourself
               while you wait: it'll take all my powers to per-
               suade her to come out.

COUNT   Take care not to mention the letter.

BARTHOLO   Before the crucial moment? It would lose all its
               effect. You don't need to tell me things twice: you
               don't need to tell me twice.

                    He goes off.

SCENE THREE

Count, alone.

COUNT   Saved! Phew! He's a tough devil to handle, that
               man! Figaro knows him well all right. I could see
               myself standing there telling lies; it made me
               appear awkward and dull; and he's got eyes like a
               hawk!... My God, without that sudden brainwave
               about the letter, I was on my way out, I have to
               admit, like a complete idiot. Oh Lord, they're
               arguing in there! What if she refused to come out?
               Let's see if I can hear... If she won't come out, the
               whole point of the trick is lost. *(He goes to listen
               again.)* Here she comes; let's stay out of sight for
               a moment.

                    He goes into the study.

SCENE FOUR

Count, Rosine, Bartholo.

ROSINE	*(Pretending to be angry)* Nothing you can say will do the slightest good, sir. I have made up my mind. I do not wish to hear any more talk of music.
BARTHOLO	But listen, my child. It is Señor Alonzo, the friend and pupil of Don Bazile, chosen by him to be one of our witnesses... And music will calm you down, I guarantee.
ROSINE	Oh! If that's your idea, you can forget it now. You think I feel like singing tonight?... So where is this tutor you're afraid to send packing? I'll settle his account with a couple of well-chosen words, and Bazile's too. *(She catches sight of her lover; gives a cry.)* Ah!...
BARTHOLO	What's the matter?
ROSINE	*(Both hands clutched to her heart, speechless with shock)* Ah! Oh God, sir... Oh God, sir...
BARTHOLO	She's still unwell! Señor Alonzo!
ROSINE	No, I don't feel ill... But when I turned round... Ah!...
COUNT	You twisted your ankle, madame?
ROSINE	Ah! Yes, I twisted my ankle. It hurts terribly.
COUNT	I noticed.
ROSINE	*(Staring at the Count)* The pain went right to my heart.
BARTHOLO	A seat, a seat. Isn't there a comfortable chair anywhere?
	He goes to fetch one.
COUNT	Ah! Rosine!

ROSINE   This is madness!

COUNT   I've a hundred things to say to you, all vital!

ROSINE   He'll never leave us on our own.

COUNT   Figaro is coming to help us.

BARTHOLO   *(Bringing an easy chair)* Here you are, my sweet,
              sit down. It doesn't look possible, Mister Tutor,
              that she'll be taking any lesson this evening. It will
              have to be another day. Farewell.

ROSINE   *(To Count)* No, wait. The pain has eased a little.
              (To Bartholo) I feel I have been unjustly harsh with
              you, sir. I want to imitate you, and repair at
              once...

BARTHOLO   Oh! The sweet little disposition of a woman! But
              after a shock like that, my child, I won't have you
              strain yourself in the smallest way. Farewell,
              farewell, Mister Tutor.

ROSINE   *(To Count)* Just a moment, please! *(To Bartholo)*
              I will begin to believe that you have no regard for
              my wishes, sir, if you prevent me from proving
              how sorry I am by having my lesson.

COUNT   *(Aside, to Bartholo)* Better not to oppose her,
              that's my view.

BARTHOLO   We'll say no more, my lovebird. The very last
              thing I want to do is go against your wishes. In
              fact, I'd like to stay with you to hear every minute
              of your lesson.

ROSINE   No, sir. I know that music holds no charm for
              you.

BARTHOLO   I assure you that tonight I shall find it enchanting.

ROSINE   *(Aside, to Count)* This is torture!

COUNT   *(Taking a sheet of music from the desk)* Is this what you wish to sing, madame?

ROSINE   Yes, it's a most delightful piece from "The Futile
                Precaution".

BARTHOLO   This "Futile Precaution" again!

COUNT   It's the very latest thing just now. It's an image of
                spring, in quite a lively style. If madame cares to
                try it...

ROSINE   *(Staring at the Count)* With great pleasure: a por-
                trayal of springtime is the subject I like best of all.
                It is nature in youth. As a person emerges from
                winter, it seems that the heart acquires a higher
                level of sensitivity; the way a slave, locked up for a
                long time, savours with heightened pleasure the
                charm of the new freedom which has just been
                offered him.

BARTHOLO   *(Muttering to the Count)* Her head is forever full of
                romantic ideas.

COUNT   *(Murmuring back)* Don't you see their meaning?

BARTHOLO   Good Lord!

                He goes and sits in the chair Rosine has left.

ROSINE   *(Sings)*
                When in the plains
                Returns again
                The springtime,
                The lovers' favourite fling-time,
                Then life returns;
                Its fire burns
                Budding parts
                Of flowers' and lovers' hearts.
                All the little lamblets
                Are sent out from the hamlets,
                All the grassy hillsides
                Are full of happy lamb-cries
                Ringing out;

They frisk about;
All ferments,
Grows intense;
The young ewes crop
The flower-tops,
While faithful hounds
Protect their bounds.
But Lindor's lost in passion,
His head's a whirl:
Might she his gladness fashion,
His shepherd girl?

(Same tune)
From mother's nest
That shepherdess
Goes singing
Where Lindor lurks, heart ringing:
A cunning ruse
For her abuse.
But can song
Protect a girl from wrong?
Sweet the pipes do play,
And bird song fills the day;
Sweet sixteen or under,
Her charms are ripe for plunder:
All agitates
Her heated state;
The poor thing's flurried,
Growing worried.
From where he hides,
Lindor espies;
She closer creeps;
Out Lindor leaps:
He dares his worst and kisses;
The girl, well pleased,
Feigns anger; - why? - she wishes
To be appeased.

(Reprise)
The sighings,
The oaths and the caresses,
The eager tendernesses,
Desires,

The sly words of flirtation,
All find their destination,
And soon the angry shepherdess
Finds her anger growing less.
If some jealous other
Should seek such joy to smother,
Our lovers find a fashion,
They make a willing plot...,
To conceal their secret passion;
Though when love's hot,
Troubles add an extra ration
To pleasure's pot.

> *While listening to this, Bartholo has dozed off. The Count, during the Reprise, ventures to take a hand, which he covers with kisses. Her emotion causes Rosine's singing to slow down, grow faint, and even ends up cutting her off altogether in mid phrase, on the words "willing plot". The orchestra follows the singer, playing more faintly, and stopping when she does. The absence of the sounds which had sent Bartholo off to sleep wakes him up again. The Count stands up, Rosine and the orchestra suddenly pick up the song and continue to the end. If the Reprise is repeated, the same thing happens a second time.*

COUNT   Indeed, it is a charming piece. And madame interprets it so well.

ROSINE   You flatter me, Señor. The glory belongs entirely to the teacher.

BARTHOLO   *(Yawning)* I think I nodded off for a second during the charming piece. I have my patients to see to. I run about all day, hither and thither, I turn like a top, and no sooner do I sit down than...oh, my poor legs!

> *He gets to his feet and pushes the chair away.*

ROSINE   *(Whispering, to Count)* Figaro hasn't arrived!

COUNT   We must play for time.

BARTHOLO   But listen, scholar, what I'm always telling that old
                 Bazile is this: why can't the girl be set to study
                 tunes with a bit more life to them than all these
                 grand arias, which seem to go up high, go down
                 low, go on and on, HI, HO, A, A, A, A, and
                 sound to me like so many funeral dirges? What
                 about those catchy little tunes they used to sing
                 when I was a lad, which everyone could remember
                 easily? I used to know some once... For instance...
                 (During the refrain, he gropes in his memory, scratch-
                 ing his head, and sings with much clicking of fingers
                 and old man's bent-kneed dancing.)
                 Do you wish, my Rosinette,
                 To take the chance to get
                 The prince of husbands while you may?...
                 (Laughing to Count)
                 It says Fanchonnette in the song, but I've changed
                 it to Rosinette to make it nicer for her, and
                 because it fits the situation. Ha, ha, ha, ha! Very
                 neat, don't you agree?

COUNT   *(Laughing)* Ha, ha, ha! Yes, a good touch!

<u>SCENE FIVE</u>

Figaro, entering in the background; Rosine, Bartholo, Count.

BARTHOLO   *(Sings)*
                 Do you wish, my Rosinette,
                 To take the chance to get
                 The prince of husbands while you may?
                 I may not be the dish of the day;

                 But in the shadows, in the night,
                 I'm worth whatever you have to pay;
                 For when you come to put out the light,
                 In the dark all cats are grey.

                 (He repeats the last five lines, dancing. Figaro
                 appears behind him, imitating his movements.)

I may not be the dish of the day.

(Notices Figaro.) Ah! Mister Barber, come in, come in, what a fine fellow you are!

FIGARO   *(Bowing)* Sir, my mother once told me so, it's true. But I have gone to seed a little since then. *(Aside, to Count)* Well done, my lord!

> *Throughout this scene, the Count attempts to speak with Rosine, but the suspicious and watchful eye of her guardian prevents him, making a dumb play between all the actors outside the argument between the Doctor and Figaro.*

BARTHOLO   Have you come to do some more purging, bloodletting and doping? Are you planning to have all my household laid up again?

FIGARO   Sir, we can't have a party every day. But as sir can see, quite apart from my daily ministrations, when they need it, my helping hand does not idly wait for their summons...

BARTHOLO   Your helping hand! What are you going to say, Mister Handyman, to that wretch yawning and asleep on his feet? And to that other one, who's been sneezing fit to blow his head open for the last three hours, and spread his brains all over the house? What are you going to say to them?

FIGARO   What am I going to say to them?

BARTHOLO   Yes!

FIGARO   I'll say... Well, damn it, to the one who's sneezing I'll say "Bless you!"; and "Go to bed!" to the one who's yawning. There's nothing there that's going to add to the bill.

BARTHOLO   I should think not. But the bleedings and the prescriptions will add to it, if I know anything. And was it also a helping hand which bandaged the eyes of my mule? Is your poultice going to give it back its sight?

FIGARO

My poultice may not make your mule see again, but on the other hand my poultice isn't what stops it from seeing in the first place.

BARTHOLO

Just let me find that on the bill!... I've never heard of such extravagance!

FIGARO

Believe me, sir, since man is left with little to choose from except foolishness or madness, if I can't see any profit in a thing, at least I want some pleasure from it. Happiness is the only thing! Who knows if the world will last another three weeks?

BARTHOLO

You would do better, Mister Philosopher, to pay me my hundred crowns plus interest without further delay. I warn you.

FIGARO

Do you doubt my integrity, sir? Your hundred crowns? I would sooner owe you them all my life than deny them for a single second.

BARTHOLO

And tell me, how did your little daughter like the sweets you took her?

FIGARO

What sweets? What do you mean?

BARTHOLO

Yes, sweets. The ones in the sweet-cone made from a twist of that notepaper, this morning.

FIGARO

I'm damned if I...

ROSINE

(Interrupting) Surely you didn't forget to tell her they were a present from me, Mister Figaro? I did ask you.

FIGARO

Ah! Ah! The sweets from this morning? I'm such a fool! I'd put it quite out of mind... Oh, excellent, madame! Delicious!

BARTHOLO	Excellent! Delicious! Oh, yes, I'm sure they were, Mister Barber. Cover your tracks if you can! This is a fine trade you ply, sir!
FIGARO	What's the matter with it, sir?
BARTHOLO	And a fine reputation it will earn you, sir!
FIGARO	I'll try to live up to it, sir.
BARTHOLO	You mean you will have to live *with* it, sir.
FIGARO	As you please, sir.
BARTHOLO	Don't take that haughty tone with me, sir! I warn you, when I cross swords with a pretentious fool, I never allow him to have the last word.
FIGARO	*(Turning his back)* In that, sir, we differ. I always do.
BARTHOLO	Eh? What's he say, scholar?
FIGARO	Do you think you're dealing with some village barber whose only accomplishment is to wield the razor? Let me tell you, sir, that I have lived in Madrid by wielding the pen, and if certain envious parties...
BARTHOLO	Well, why didn't you stay there, instead of coming here and changing your profession?
FIGARO	One must do the best one can. Put yourself in my shoes.
BARTHOLO	Put myself in your shoes! My God, I'd be saying some pretty stupid things!
FIGARO	Sir, you are doing well already. Your day-dreaming colleague over there will confirm it.
COUNT	*(With a start)* I... I am not this gentleman's colleague.

FIGARO

No? Seeing you together here in consultation, I imagined you must be pursuing the same goal.

BARTHOLO

(Angry) Enough of this. What have you come here for? Another letter you're delivering to madame this evening? Tell me, should I withdraw?

FIGARO

What a sarcastic tongue you keep for the poor of this world! Well, for heaven's sake, I've come to shave you, of course. Isn't today your day?

BARTHOLO

You'll have to come back later.

FIGARO

Oh, yes! Come back later! The whole garrison is due for its treatment tomorrow morning, I got the contract through my connections. That gives me plenty of time on my hands, doesn't it? Would sir care to go through to his own room?

BARTHOLO

No, sir would not care to go through to his own room. Well then... what's to stop you shaving me here?

ROSINE

(Disdainfully) What a charming man! Why not in my bedroom?

BARTHOLO

You're angry! Forgive me, my child, you're about to finish your lesson. I just didn't want to miss a second of your delightful singing.

FIGARO

(Whispering, to Count) We'll have to get him away from here! *(Aloud)* Spark, where are you? Nipper? Bring the basin, bring some water, and everything else sir will need!

BARTHOLO

Call them, by all means! Exhausted and drained and worn down by your kind attentions, I had to send them to bed, didn't I!

FIGARO

Very well! I'll fetch everything myself. It's all in your bedroom, isn't it? *(Whispering, to Count)* I'll make him follow me out.

BARTHOLO   *(Thoughtfully, unhooking his bunch of keys)* No, no,
                I'll go myself. *(Whispering to Count)* Keep an eye
                on them, whatever you do.

SCENE SIX

Figaro, Count, Rosine.

FIGARO   Ah! What an opportunity missed! He was going
                to give me the whole bunch. The key to the shut-
                ter is there, isn't it?

ROSINE   It's the newest one of all.

SCENE SEVEN

Bartholo, Figaro, Count, Rosine.

BARTHOLO   *(Coming back, aside)* Really, I don't know what
                I'm doing, leaving that blasted barber here. *(To
                Figaro)* Here. *(Gives him the bunch of keys.)* In my
                study, under the desk; but don't touch anything.

FIGARO   Serve you right if I did, seeing what a suspicious
                type you are. *(Aside, as he goes off)* See how prov-
                idence protects the innocent!

SCENE EIGHT

Bartholo, Count, Rosine.

BARTHOLO   *(Whispering to Count)* He's the comedian who
                passed the letter to Almaviva.

COUNT   *(Whispering)* He looks like a rascal to me.

BARTHOLO   He won't catch me again.

COUNT   As far as that goes, I think the worst is already done.

BARTHOLO   On second thoughts, I considered it wiser to send him to my room than leave him alone with her.

COUNT   They couldn't have said a word without my over-hearing.

ROSINE   Is it polite, gentlemen, to keep on talking in whispers like that? What about my lesson?

A crash is heard, as of breaking china-ware.

BARTHOLO   *(Gives a cry.)*   What's that noise? The malicious barber has gone and dropped everything down the stairs, and my toilet set all of the best pieces!...

He runs out.

SCENE NINE

Count, Rosine.

COUNT   Figaro has engineered us a moment together, let's not waste it. Madame, grant me, I entreat you, a minute's vital interview this evening. I mean to rescue you from the slavery that threatens to trap you.

ROSINE   Ah! Lindor!

COUNT   I can climb up to your window. And about the letter I had from you this morning, something happened which forced me to...

SCENE TEN

Rosine, Bartholo, Figaro, Count.

BARTHOLO   I wasn't wrong. Everything is smashed, shattered.

FIGARO	What a fuss, it isn't such a disaster as all that! You can't see a thing on that staircase. *(He shows the Count the key.)* I caught myself on a key carrying it all up...
BARTHOLO	Most people watch what they're doing. Caught yourself on a key! And you such a clever man!
FIGARO	Well then, sir, find a cleverer one if you can!

SCENE ELEVEN

As before, and enter Don Bazile.

ROSINE	*(Aside, horrified)* Don Bazile!...
COUNT	*(Aside)* Oh, my God!
FIGARO	*(Aside)* That's the last thing we need!
BARTHOLO	*(Coming forward to meet him)* Ah! Bazile, my friend, welcome back to health. So your illness wasn't serious? Truly, Señor Alonzo gave me a real fright about you; ask him, I was about to come and see you, and if he hadn't detained me...
BAZILE	*(Surprised)* Señor Alonzo?
FIGARO	*(Stamping his foot)* What's this! Still more hold-ups? Two hours to shave a rotten beard... This is a hell of a way to run a business!
BAZILE	*(Staring at everybody)* Will you do me the kindness of explaining, gentlemen...?
FIGARO	You can talk to him when I've gone.
BAZILE	I repeat, it's only right that I...
COUNT	It's only right that you should keep quiet, Bazile. Do you imagine you're telling sir something he doesn't already know? I have told him you

instructed me to come and give the music lesson in your place.

BAZILE   *(More surprised)* The music lesson!... Alonzo!...

ROSINE   *(Aside, to Bazile)* Hush! Will you be quiet!

BAZILE   Her as well!

COUNT   *(Aside, to Bartholo)* Tell him we've got things all fixed.

BARTHOLO   *(Aside, to Bazile)* Don't tell her he isn't your pupil, Bazile, you'll ruin everything if you don't back us up.

BAZILE   Ah! Ah!

BARTHOLO   *(Aloud)* I tell you the truth, Bazile, there isn't a more talented musician than your pupil.

BAZILE   *(Stupefied)* My pupil!... *(Whispering)* I was coming to tell you that the Count has moved out of his lodgings.

BARTHOLO   *(Whispering)* I know. Shut up.

BAZILE   *(Whispering)* Who told you?

BARTHOLO   *(Whispering)* He did, obviously.

COUNT   *(Whispering)* Me, of course. Just listen.

ROSINE   *(Whispering, to Bazile)* Can you really not shut up?

FIGARO   *(Whispering, to Bazile)* Hey! Great beanpole! Are you deaf?

BAZILE   *(Aside)* Who do they think they're deceiving? They're all in the secret together: there's no one left!

BARTHOLO	*(Aloud)* Well, Bazile, how did you get on with your lawyer?
FIGARO	You've got the rest of the evening to talk about the lawyer.
BARTHOLO	*(To Bazile)* A quick word: just tell me if you are happy with the lawyer?
BAZILE	*(Dismayed)* The lawyer?
COUNT	*(Smiling)* Did you not see him, the lawyer?
BAZILE	*(Impatient)* Well, no! I didn't see him, the lawyer.
COUNT	*(Aside, to Bartholo)* Do you want him to discuss your plans in front of this girl? Send him away.
BARTHOLO	*(Whispering, to Count)* You're right. *(To Bazile)* This illness that struck you down so suddenly, what was it?
BAZILE	*(Angry)* I fail to understand your meaning.
COUNT	*(Slipping a purse into his hand)* Yes, the gentleman is asking you what you are doing here in your present state of health?
FIGARO	He's as pale as a corpse!
BAZILE	Ah! Now I get it ...
COUNT	Take yourself off to bed, my dear Bazile: you aren't well, and you're killing us with worry. Go home to bed.
FIGARO	His face has gone all baggy. Go home to bed.
BARTHOLO	Take my word, you can feel his fever a mile off. Go home to bed.
ROSINE	Why did you ever leave the house? I've heard it's contagious. Go home to bed.

BAZILE	*(Stunned)* You want me to go home to bed?
ALL TOGETHER	That's right.
BAZILE	*(Looking at them all)* Indeed, gentlemen, I believe I might be wise to retire; I don't feel quite my usual self here.
BARTHOLO	Tomorrow, then; if you are feeling better.
COUNT	Bazile, I'll be round to see you first thing.
FIGARO	Take my advice, stay wrapped up and warm in your bed.
ROSINE	Good night, Mister Bazile.
BAZILE	*(Aside)* Damned if I've a clue what's going on! If it wasn't for this purse...
ALL TOGETHER	Good night, Bazile, good night.
BAZILE	*(Going off)* Well! Good night, then. Good night.

They all accompany him, laughing.

SCENE TWELVE

As before, except for Bazile.

BARTHOLO	*(Pompously)* That man is not at all well.
ROSINE	His eyes are wild.
COUNT	He must have caught something in the street.
FIGARO	Did you see the way he was talking to himself? What a poor creature a man is! *(To Bartholo)* Right, then: have you made your mind up this time?

> *He pushes a chair to the far side of the room from the Count, and holds up a towel.*

COUNT	Before we finish, madame, there is one point I must make, essential to your progress in the art which it is my honour to teach.

He approaches and whispers in her ear.

BARTHOLO	*(To Figaro)* Hey, what's this! I believe you're doing this on purpose to get close and stand in front of me so I can't see...
COUNT	*(Whispering, to Rosine)* We have the key to the window grille. We'll be here at midnight.
FIGARO	*(Arranging the towel round Bartholo's neck)* See what? If she was having a dancing lesson, there'd be something to see, but singing!... Ow, ow!
BARTHOLO	What's the matter?
FIGARO	Something in my eye. I don't know.

He thrusts his head closer.

BARTHOLO	Well, don't rub it.
FIGARO	It's the left one. Could you be very kind and blow into it sharply?

> *Bartholo takes Figaro's head between his hands, looks over the top of it, pushes him violently back, and scurries round behind the lovers to hear their conversation.*

COUNT	*(Whispering, to Rosine)* And as for your letter, it was so hard to find an excuse for staying here at first...
FIGARO	*(Across the room, trying to warn them)* Ahem! Ahem!...
COUNT	And alarmed to find my disguise no use again.

BARTHOLO	*(Passing between them)* Your disguise no use.

ROSINE	*(Horrified)* Ah!...

BARTHOLO	Very good, madame, please don't trouble yourself. How dare you! Before my very eyes, in my very presence, you have the audacity to perpetrate such an outrage!

COUNT	But what is the matter, Señor?

BARTHOLO	Alonso, ha! You traitor!

COUNT	Señor Bartholo, if you are frequently given to the sort of mad fantasies we are being forced to witness now, then I cease to be surprised at the señorita's distaste for becoming your wife.

ROSINE	His wife! Me! Spend my days with a jealous old man when the only happiness he has to offer my young womanhood is a state of abominable slavery!

BARTHOLO	Ah! What am I hearing!

ROSINE	Yes, I'll shout it out loud. I shall give my heart and my hand to the man who can release me from this horrible prison, where my person and my possessions are held against all justice.

Rosine exits.

SCENE THIRTEEN

Bartholo, Figaro, Count.

BARTHOLO	I'm choked with rage.

COUNT	In truth, Señor, it is difficult for a wife when she is only a young woman...

FIGARO	Yes, young wives and great age, that's a recipe

guaranteed to cause trouble in an old man's head.

BARTHOLO   What! When I catch them in the act! Damned barber! I've a good mind to...

FIGARO   I'm leaving, he's crazy.

COUNT   Me too; you're right, he is crazy.

FIGARO   Crazy, crazy...

They exit.

SCENE FOURTEEN

Bartholo, alone, chasing them out.

BARTHOLO   Crazy! Filthy seducers! Devil's agents, doing the devil's work, the devil cart the lot of you off to hell!... I am going crazy!... I saw them as clear as I see this desk... to have the nerve to pretend...! Ah! I'm forgetting none of my servants is here... A neighbour, someone walking by, anyone. It's enough to send a man mad! It's enough to send a man mad!

Between the acts, the theatre goes dark; the sound of a storm; the orchestra plays the music - number 5 -from the "Barber" score.

END OF ACT THREE

ACT FOUR

SCENE ONE

The stage is in darkness.

Bartholo, Don Bazile holding a paper lantern.

BARTHOLO   What do you mean, Bazile, you don't know him! I can't believe what you're saying.

BAZILE   Ask me a hundred times, and I'll give you the same answer. If he brought back the letter Rosine wrote, then he must be one of the Count's messengers. Though from the magnificence of the present he gave me, he could even be the Count himself.

BARTHOLO   Is that very likely? And as it happens, what about that present, eh? Why did you accept it?

BAZILE   You looked as if you were all in it together; I didn't understand what was going on. And in cases where it is difficult to come to a balanced conclusion, a purse of gold always strikes me as an irrefutable argument. And then, as the proverb says, one man's meat...

BARTHOLO   I know, is another man's...

BAZILE   ... caviar.

BARTHOLO   *(Surprised)* Ah! Ah!

BAZILE   Yes, I have rearranged a few proverbs like that, with my own variations. But let's get down to business: what's your plan now?

BARTHOLO   If you were in my shoes, Bazile, wouldn't you do everything you possibly could to possess her?

BAZILE	Believe me, Doctor, no. Whatever the merchandise in question, possession counts for little: it's the enjoyment of it that makes a man happy. In my opinion, marrying a woman who doesn't love you is laying yourself open...
BARTHOLO	You fear there could be accidents?
BAZILE	Ha, ha, sir... we have seen plenty of them happen this year. I wouldn't risk doing violence to her feelings.
BARTHOLO	Excuse me, Bazile. Better that she should cry for having me than I should die for not having her.
BAZILE	So it's a matter of life or death? Well, in that case, marry her, marry her.
BARTHOLO	Which is what I intend to do; and what's more, I intend to do it tonight.
BAZILE	Then goodbye until later... And remember, when you speak with your ward, to paint them all as black as pitch.
BARTHOLO	You are right.
BAZILE	Calumny, Doctor, calumny! You must always come back to that!
BARTHOLO	Here is Rosine's letter, which that Alonzo passed on. And he inadvertently showed me how to make best use of it with her.
BAZILE	Goodbye: we will all meet again here at four o'clock.
BARTHOLO	Why not earlier?
BAZILE	Impossible: the lawyer has another appointment.
BARTHOLO	Another marriage?

BAZILE   Yes, at the barber Figaro's house. It's his niece's
                wedding.

BARTHOLO   His niece? He hasn't got a niece.

BAZILE   That's what they told the lawyer.

BARTHOLO   That clown is in the plot: what the devil's going
                on!...

BAZILE   You wouldn't be thinking...?

BARTHOLO   Believe me, I wouldn't put anything past those
                people. Listen, my friend, I don't feel easy. Go
                back to the lawyer's house. Tell him to accompa-
                ny you here immediately.

BAZILE   It's pouring with rain, it's a terrible night; but if
                it's to serve you, you can count on me. What are
                you going to do?

BARTHOLO   I'll show you out. They arranged for Figaro to put
                all my servants out of action, didn't they? I'm all
                on my own here.

BAZILE   I have my lantern.

BARTHOLO   Look, Bazile, here's my master-key. I'll wait for
                you, I'll keep watch. And apart from the lawyer
                and you, not a soul shall set foot in here tonight.

BAZILE   If you take all the necessary precautions, you have
                nothing to fear.

SCENE TWO

Rosine (alone, emerging from her bedroom)

ROSINE   I thought I heard people talking. The clock has
                already struck midnight; Lindor hasn't come! And
                this bad weather couldn't have been better for his

plan. He wouldn't have met anyone about... Ah!
Lindor! If you have deceived me!... What's that
noise?... Heavens, it's my guardian. I must go
back.

SCENE THREE

Rosine, Bartholo.

BARTHOLO   *(Holding a light)* Ah! Rosine, since you haven't
             gone to bed yet...

ROSINE   I was about to retire.

BARTHOLO   You won't get any sleep in this awful weather, and
             there are some urgent things I need to say.

ROSINE   What do you want of me, sir? Isn't it enough to
             be tormented all day?

BARTHOLO   Rosine, listen to me.

ROSINE   I'll hear what you have to say tomorrow.

BARTHOLO   Give me a moment, please!

ROSINE   *(Aside)* What if he were to arrive now!

BARTHOLO   *(Showing her the letter she wrote)* Do you recognise
             this letter?

ROSINE   *(Recognises it)* Ah! Oh, my God!...

BARTHOLO   It is not my intention, Rosine, to reproach you: at
             your age a girl can make a mistake. But I am your
             friend; listen to me.

ROSINE   This is too much.

BARTHOLO   This letter which you wrote to Count Almaviva!...

ROSINE   *(Amazed)* To Count Almaviva!

BARTHOLO	This Count is an evil man. Look: no sooner did he receive the letter than he showed it off like some trophy. I got it from a woman he gave it to.
ROSINE	Count Almaviva!...
BARTHOLO	You find it difficult to believe such a horrible thing. Lack of worldliness, Rosine, makes women a trusting and credulous race. But you should know the trap they were preparing for you. This woman told me all about it, apparently to rid herself of a rival as dangerous as you. It makes me shudder to think of it! It was the most vile plot, hatched by Almaviva, Figaro and that Alonzo who claimed to be Bazile's pupil. That isn't his real name, and he's nothing more than the Count's agent of corruption. They were about to sink you in a pit beyond all reach of human aid.
ROSINE	*(Shattered)* I'm appalled! I can't believe it!... What, Lindor!... What, that young man!...
BARTHOLO	*(Aside)* Ah! So it's Lindor!
ROSINE	He was doing it all for Count Almaviva... He was doing it for someone else...
BARTHOLO	That's what I was told when I was given the letter.
ROSINE	*(Overwhelmed)* Oh! The indignity of it!... The man must be punished! ... Sir, you have been wishing for some time to make me your wife?
BARTHOLO	You know how strong my feelings are.
ROSINE	If you can still have any such feelings, I am yours.
BARTHOLO	Well! I'll have the lawyer come this very night!
ROSINE	That is not all. Oh, God, am I not already humiliated enough! ... I have to tell you that at any moment the traitor is going to have the temerity to enter this room by the window, having tricked you

into giving them the key.

BARTHOLO   *(Examining his bunch of keys)* Ah! The criminals!
                My child, I'll never let you out of my sight again!

ROSINE   *(Taking fright)* Ah, sir! What if they are armed?

BARTHOLO   You are right. My vengeance would come to
                nothing. Go up to Marceline: lock yourself in her
                room and bolt the door too. I'm going for help;
                the police will surround the house. If we can
                arrest him as a burglar, we'll have the double plea-
                sure of getting our revenge and getting rid of him
                at a single stroke! And you can count on my love
                for your compensatiion...

ROSINE   *(In despair)* All I ask is that you should forgive
                what I've done! *(Aside)* Ah! I'm punishing myself
                more than enough!

BARTHOLO   *(Going off)* Let's get this ambush set up. After all
                my troubles, I've got her at last!

                Exit.

SCENE FOUR

Rosine, alone.

ROSINE   His love will be my compensation!... Unhappy
                girl!... *(She takes out her handkerchief and weeps.)*
                What am I to do? ... He'll be here soon. I want
                to stay and face him out, see him for an instant as
                the evil man he really is. The vile way he's acted
                will protect me from... Ah! I need protecting.
                That noble face, that gentle manner, and a voice
                so tender!... And he's nothing but the base go-
                between of a seducer! Ah! Unhappy girl!
                Unhappy girl!... Oh, God, there's someone at the
                window!

                She runs off.

SCENE FIVE

The Count, Figaro who, wrapped in a cloak, appears at the window.

FIGARO	*(Outside)* There's somebody running away. Shall I go in?
COUNT	*(Outside)* A man?
FIGARO	No.
COUNT	It's Rosine. Your ugly mug has scared her away.
FIGARO	*(Jumping into the room)* You're very probably right... Here we are at last, then, in spite of the rain and the thunder and the lightning.
COUNT	*(Wrapped in a long cloak)* Give me a hand. *(Jumps into the room.)* Victory!
FIGARO	*(Throwing off his cloak)* We're soaked to the skin. Delightful weather for an adventure! What do you think of the night so far, my lord?
COUNT	For a lover, superb.
FIGARO	Yes, but for his assistant?... And what if someone caught us here?
COUNT	You're with me, aren't you? Anyway, I've got more important things on my mind: how to persuade her to abandon the Doctor's house on the spot.
FIGARO	You've got three all-powerful passions working for you, when it comes to the fairer sex: love, hatred and fear.
COUNT	*(Peering in the darkness)* How am I going to spring it on her suddenly that we've got the lawyer round at your house now, waiting to marry us? She's

going to find my plan bold, to say the least. She'll
accuse me of being reckless.

FIGARO   If she accuses you of being reckless, you must
           accuse her of being cruel. Women like it very
           much when a man calls them cruel. And anyway,
           if her love is as powerful as you hope, you must
           tell her who you are: that'll put an end to any
           doubts she has.

SCENE SIX

Count, Rosine, Figaro. Figaro lights all the candles on the table.

COUNT   Here she is. - My beautiful Rosine!...

ROSINE   *(Stiffly)* I was beginning to fear, sir, that you
           might not come.

COUNT   Isn't that wonderfully touching!... Señorita, it
           would not be fitting for me to abuse the situation
           by suggesting that you throw in your lot with that
           of a miserable fellow like me; but wherever you
           should decide to seek shelter, I swear on my hon-
           our...

ROSINE   Sir, if the gift of my hand were not automatically
           to have followed the gift of my heart, you would
           not be here. If there is anything improper in this
           meeting, let it be justified in your own eyes by
           necessity.

COUNT   But you, Rosine! The partner of a wretch with no
           fortune, no background!...

ROSINE   Background, fortune! I have no interest in such
           tricks of chance. If you can assure me your inten-
           tions are pure...

COUNT   *(Kneeling at her feet)* Ah! Rosine! I adore you!

ROSINE   *(Indignant)* Stop there, you lying dog!... How

dare you insult the word!... You adore me!...
That's it, the spell is broken! That's all I needed to
hear to hate you. Before I leave you to the bitter
remorse that's coming, *(Beginning to weep)* you
should know this: I was in love with you; sharing
your impoverished fate was to be my happiness.
Evil Lindor! I was going to abandon everything in
order to follow you! But your cowardly abuse of
my goodness, and the scandalous effrontery of this
dreadful Count Almaviva you were selling me to
have enabled this piece of evidence to fall into my
hands. Do you recognise this letter?

COUNT   *(Eagerly)* Which was handed over to you by your
               guardian?

ROSINE   *(Haughtily)* I am obliged to him for it, yes.

COUNT   God, you've made me happy! I'm the one who
               gave it to him! When I was in difficulties yester-
               day, I had to use it to gain his confidence; and I
               wasn't able to find a moment to warn you. Ah,
               Rosine! So it's true you really love me!

FIGARO   My lord, you were looking for a woman who
               would love you for yourself...

ROSINE   My lord!... What is he saying?

COUNT   *(Throwing aside his cloak to reveal his finery)* Oh,
               my most beloved of women! The time for decep-
               tion is over: the lucky man you see at your feet is
               not Lindor. I am Count Almaviva, who is dying
               for love of you and who has been vainly searching
               for you for six months!

ROSINE   *(Collapsing into Count's arms)* Ah!...

COUNT   *(Alarmed)* Figaro!

FIGARO   Nothing to worry about, my lord: joy is such a
               wonderful emotion, it never brings on any harm.
               There, look! See, she's recovering her senses. My

word, she's beautiful!

ROSINE   Ah, Lindor!... Ah, sir, I've been so wicked! I was
about to give myself to my guardian this very
night.

COUNT   Rosine, you weren't!

ROSINE   Look how I would have been punished! I would
have spent my whole life hating you. Ah, Lindor,
isn't it the worst torture a person can suffer, to
hate when you know you are made to love.

FIGARO   *(At the window)* My lord, our escape is cut off.
The ladder has gone.

COUNT   Gone!

ROSINE   *(Abashed)* Yes, that was me... it was the Doctor.
This is the result of my gullibility. He tricked me.
I confessed everything, betrayed all our plans. He
knows you are here, and is bringing a squad of
men.

FIGARO   *(Still looking out at the window)* My lord! They are
opening the street door.

ROSINE   *(Rushing terrified into the Count's arms)* Ah,
Lindor!...

COUNT   *(Resolutely)* Rosine, you love me! I fear nobody;
and you shall be my wife. So now I will punish
that despicable old man with relish!...

ROSINE   No, no; be kind to him, dear Lindor! My heart is
too full to have any place left in it for revenge.

SCENE SEVEN

As before, plus the lawyer and Don Bazile.

FIGARO My lord, it is our lawyer.

COUNT And friend Bazile with him!

BAZILE Ah! What do I find here?

FIGARO Well! What chance, friend...?

BAZILE What stroke of fate, gentlemen...?

LAWYER Are these people here the prospective couple?

COUNT Yes, sir. You were due to conduct the marriage for Rosine and myself tonight at the barber Figaro's house; but we preferred it to be done here, for reasons you will learn shortly. Have you brought our contract?

LAWYER Do I have the honour then of addressing His Excellency the Count Almaviva?

FIGARO You certainly have.

BAZILE *(Aside)* Maybe this is why he gave me the master-key...

LAWYER The thing is, my lord, I have two marriage contracts. We must not get them confused: here is yours; and this one is for the marriage of Señor Bartholo and Señorita... Rosine as well? The young ladies are apparently two sisters who share the same name.

COUNT Let us sign anyway. Don Bazile will be kind enough to act as our second witness.

They sign.

BAZILE	But, Your Excellency... I don't understand...
COUNT	My dear Master Bazile, the merest trifle embarrasses you, and absolutely everything astonishes you.
BAZILE	My lord... but if the Doctor...
COUNT	*(Throwing him a purse)* Don't be such a baby! Get on and sign.
BAZILE	*(Astonished)* Ah! Ah!...
FIGARO	What's so difficult about signing your name?
BAZILE	*(Weighing the purse)* Nothing, not now. It's just that, you know me, once I've given my word, it takes a weighty reason...

      He signs.

SCENE EIGHT

As before, plus Bartholo, a magistrate, some policemen, some servants with torches. Bartholo sees the Count kissing Rosine's hand, and Figaro grotesquely kissing Don Bazile. He launches himself at the lawyer's throat and yells.

BARTHOLO	Rosine with these villains! Arrest them all! I've collared one of them.
LAWYER	You've collared your lawyer.
BAZILE	It's your lawyer. What's the matter with you?
BARTHOLO	Ah! Don Bazile! How did you come to be here?
BAZILE	What about you? How did you come not to be?
MAGISTRATE	*(Indicating Figaro)* Wait a moment! I know this man. What do you think you're up to, in this

house, at this time of night?

FIGARO   This time of night? Sir can see very well that it's as close to morning as it is to evening. Besides, I am in the service of His Excellency My Lord the Count Almaviva.

BARTHOLO   Almaviva!

MAGISTRATE   So these men are not burglars?

BARTHOLO   Never mind that. - Everywhere else, my lord Count, I am your Excellency's humble sevant; but you will appreciate that in my household your superiority of rank has no force. Have the good-ness, if you please, to withdraw.

COUNT   Yes, rank should have no force here. But what does carry a great deal of force is the preference the young lady has just accorded me over you, by freely giving herself to me.

BARTHOLO   What is he saying, Rosine?

ROSINE   The truth. Why are you surprised? Wasn't this the night I was going to take my revenge on the man who had deceived me? Well, I've just done so.

BAZILE   Remember I warned you it could be the Count himself, Doctor?

BARTHOLO   What do I care? The marriage is a joke! Where are the witnesses?

LAWYER   Everything has been done properly. I have had the assistance of these two gentlemen.

BARTHOLO   What, Bazile! You signed?

BAZILE   What else could I do? This fiend of a man always has his pockets full of irresistible arguments.

BARTHOLO	To hell with his arguments. I call upon my authority as her guardian.
COUNT	You forfeited that when you abused it.
BARTHOLO	The girl is still a minor.
COUNT	As my wife, she has just become an adult.
BARTHOLO	Who's wants your opinion, upper-class gangster!
COUNT	The lady is noble and beautiful; I am a man of breeding, young and rich; she is my wife: in those circumstances, and in our new state, which honours both of us equally, do you still imagine you have any claim on her?
BARTHOLO	You will never succeed in taking her away from me.
COUNT	She is out of your power already. I place her under the authority of the law; and the gentleman you brought along yourself will protect her from the violence you wish to inflict on her. The true magistrate is the supporter of the oppressed.
MAGISTRATE	Quite so. And this pointless resistance to a most honourable marriage provides a clear enough indication of his justifiable fright concerning the mis-administration of his ward's wealth, for which he will be required to give me a full account.
COUNT	Ah! Let him just give his consent in this matter, and I ask nothing more of him.
FIGARO	... except the receipt for my hundred crowns: let's not get carried away.
BARTHOLO	*(Exasperated)* They were all in it against me. I've stuck my head into a wasps' nest.
BAZILE	Wasps' nest? Who's stung you? You didn't get the woman, but just think, Doctor, you've kept the

money. Oh, yes, you keep it!

BARTHOLO   Oh, leave me in peace, can't you, Bazile! All you
                can think about is money. A fat lot I care for the
                money! Well, all right, I'll keep it; but do you
                imagine it's an argument that carries any weight
                with me?

                    He signs.

FIGARO   *(Laughing)* Ha, ha, ha, my lord! They're both
                from the same stable!

LAWYER   But, gentlemen, I still don't understand what's
                going on. Are there not two young ladies sharing
                the same name?

FIGARO   No, sir, they are only the one!

BARTHOLO   *(Bemoaning his fortune)* And I was the one who
                took the ladder away to make the marriage safe!
                Ah! I lost through lack of sufficient pains.

FIGARO   Lack of sufficient brains. But let's be honest,
                Doctor: when youth and love are working hand in
                hand to foil an old man, even the very best he can
                do to prevent them can only be called, as it has
                turned out to be, a "Futile Precaution".

                            THE END

THE MARRIAGE OF FIGARO

CHARACTERS

COUNT ALMAVIVA	(Governor of Andalusia)
THE COUNTESS	(His wife)
FIGARO	(The Count's valet, and steward of the castle)
SUZANNE	(The Countess's principal maid, and engaged to Figaro)
MARCELINE	(Housekeeper)
ANTONIO	(Head gardener, uncle of Suzanne and father of Fanchette)
FANCHETTE	(Daughter of Antonio)
CHERUBIN	(The Count's principal page)
BARTHOLO	(A doctor from Seville)
BAZILE	(Music master to the Countess)
DON GUZMAN BRID'OISON	(A judge)
DOUBLE-MAIN "CLAWFINGERS"	(Lawyer's clerk, secretary to Don Guzman)
AN OFFICER OF THE LAW AND CLERK OF THE COURT	
GRIPE-SOLEIL	(A young shepherd)
A YOUNG SHEPHERDESS	
PEDRILLO	(The Count's huntsman)

SERVANTS, PEASANTS, WOMEN AND GIRLS from the Count's estates

Scene: the Castle of Aguas-Frescas, three leagues from Seville.

ACT ONE

SCENE ONE

A bedroom with the furniture partially removed. A large high-backed chair in the middle. Figaro is measuring the floor with a six-foot rule. Suzanne is standing before a mirror trying on the garland of orange blossom known as the bride's crown.

Figaro, Suzanne.

FIGARO	Nineteen feet by twenty-six.
SUZANNE	Look, Figaro, my little crown: do you think it suits me like this?
FIGARO	*(Taking her hands)* You couldn't look better, my darling. Ah, that pretty, virginal garland; worn on her wedding morning by a beautiful woman, you can't imagine how sweet it looks to the loving eyes of a husband!
SUZANNE	*(Stepping from his clutches)* So what are you measuring there, my love?
FIGARO	I'm seeing if that magnificent bed the Count is giving us, my little Suzanne, will fit nicely here.
SUZANNE	In this room?
FIGARO	This is the one he's letting us have.
SUZANNE	Well, I don't want it.
FIGARO	Why not?
SUZANNE	I don't want it.

FIGARO   Yes, and why?

SUZANNE   I don't like it.

FIGARO   People sometimes have reasons.

SUZANNE   And what if I don't want to give one?

FIGARO   Oh! When a woman knows she's got you!

SUZANNE   If I had to prove I was right, it would suggest I
              could be wrong. Are you my devoted servant, or
              aren't you?

FIGARO   You've decided you don't like the most convenient
              room in the whole castle, slap between the two
              apartments. If the Countess needs you in the
              night, she can ring from her side; zip! in two
              strides you are at her side. The Count wants
              something? He only has to go jingle-jangle from
              his side: zap! in a single bound I am there.

SUZANNE   Extremely convenient! But when he's jingle-jan-
              gled in the morning to send you off on some useful
              and lengthy errand, zip! in two strides he is at my
              door, and zap! in a single bound ...

FIGARO   What are you trying to say?

SUZANNE   Listen calmly and I'll tell you.

FIGARO   Tell me what, for God's sake?

SUZANNE   Just this: the fact is, my love, that the Count has
              grown tired of exploring the beauties of the neigh-
              bourhood and wants to return to the pleasures of
              the castle. But not with his wife in mind. His
              sights are set on *your* wife, and he hopes that
              installing us here will not exactly impede his view,
              if you get my meaning. And that's the tune which
              the loyal Bazile, honest broker of the Count's plea-
              sures, and my noble singing tutor, hums in my ear
              every day to accompany my lesson.

FIGARO   Bazile! Oh, my little cherub! If ever a man need-
              ed his spine stiffening with a good whippy cane
              across the back...

SUZANNE   There's a clever lad! You didn't think, did you,
              that the dowry I'm getting was a tribute to your
              own shining merits?

FIGARO   Considering all I've done for the Count, it is a
              reasonable hope.

SUZANNE   The sharpest-witted men are often the most stu-
              pid!

FIGARO   There are people who say that.

SUZANNE   But some people refuse to believe it!

FIGARO   And some people are quite wrong.

SUZANNE   If you want to understand the dowry, it's meant to
              persuade me to give him a quarter of an hour
              alone, in secret, for the exercise of an ancient droit
              du seigneur ... you know all about that sorry
              story.

FIGARO   I know enough about it to tell you that the Count
              abolished that shameful right on his own wedding
              day; and if he hadn't done so, I would never have
              married you while in his service.

SUZANNE   Well, abolish it he may have, but he's regretting it
              now. And your betrothed is the one he means to
              reinstate it with today.

FIGARO   *(Rubbing his head)* My brain is turning soft with
              pure astonishment. My head is bulging...

SUZANNE   I shouldn't rub it, then!

FIGARO   What?

SUZANNE   *(Laughing)* If a little horn-like bump were to grow, you know how superstitious people can be...

FIGARO

You can laugh, you evil creature! Oh, if only I could find a way to catch the master in his treachery, snare him properly in a trap and still pocket the dowry!

SUZANNE

Money and intrigue - now you're in your element.

FIGARO

It isn't the shame that holds me back.

SUZANNE

What, then? Fear?

FIGARO

Taking on a dangerous adventure is nothing. But to bring it off successfully while escaping the consequences... Creeping into a man's bedroom at night, stealing his wife and getting a hundred lashes for your pains, nothing could be easier. A thousand stupid villains have done it. But ...

A bell rings from the Countess's room.

SUZANNE

That's the Countess awake. She insisted I should be the first person to speak to her on my wedding day.

FIGARO

I suppose there's some secret meaning behind that as well?

SUZANNE

According to the old shepherds' saying, it brings good luck to deserted wives. Goodbye, my little fi-, fi-, Figaro. Concentrate you mind on our little problem.

FIGARO

A little kiss would help me concentrate better.

SUZANNE

Kiss my lover today! Thank you very much! What would my husband say tomorrow! *(Figaro embraces her.)* All right, all right!

FIGARO

You don't know how much I adore you.

SUZANNE

(Smoothing herself down) You tell me so from

morning to night. When are you ever going to
stop, you fool?

FIGARO   *(Mysteriously)* When I can prove it to you from
night to morning.

The bell rings again.

SUZANNE   *(Moving away, tips of her fingers to her lips)* Here's
your kiss back, Sir. That's all you're getting from
me.

FIGARO   *(Running after her)* Ah, but that's not the way I
gave it to you.

<u>SCENE TWO</u>

Figaro, alone.

FIGARO   What a girl! Always laughing, fresh as spring, full
of gaiety and humour, loving and delightful! But
a good girl! *(He strides back and forth, rubbing his
hands.)* Ah, my lord Count! My dear Count! So
this is how your gift is given: still warm from your
own sticky hands? And there I was, wondering
why his being appointed ambassador necessitated
my appointment as his accompanying messenger.
Particularly when I've just been made steward of
the castle. Now I understand, my lord Count!
Three promotions at one fell swoop: you, the
Ambassador with full powers; me, the diplomatic
trouble-shooter; and Suzon, the lady of the party,
and pocket Ambassadress! And then, whip up
your horse, messenger! While I gallop off in one
direction, you lead my beauty a pretty dance in the
other. While I cover myself in filth and break my
back for the greater glory of your family, you kindly work towards the greater increase of mine!
What a generous way of sharing the burden! But,
my lord Count, you are abusing your powers.
Travelling all the way to London, to manage your
master's affairs and your valet's, all at the same

time! Simultaneously standing in for the King
and me, at a foreign court, it's too much by half,
it's too much altogether. - As for you, Bazile,
when it comes to playing tricks you're an infant at
my knee! By the time I've finished with you,
you'll be limping with the club-footed. I'll... No,
let's keep this all hidden, better to use each of
them to destroy the other. Look to the day's
business, Master Figaro! To begin with, have
your marriage ceremony take place earlier than
planned, just to make sure it does take place.
Head off the broody Marceline; she's got her heart
set on you like a devil with a pitchfork. Get your
hands on the dowry and the presents. Put up a
false scent for the Count's little infatuation. Give
Master Bazile a sound beating, and ...

SCENE THREE

Marceline, Bartholo, Figaro.

FIGARO   *(Interrupting himself)* ... Aaaah! And here comes
                the stout Doctor. Now our ceremonies will be
                complete. Ah, good day, my dearest Doctor. Is it
                my marriage with Suzanne that brings you to the
                castle?

BARTHOLO   *(Disdainful)* Oh, my dear Sir, certainly not.

FIGARO   That would be all too generous of you.

BARTHOLO   It would indeed, and all too stupid.

FIGARO   Remembering how I had the misfortune to ruin
                your own wedding day.

BARTHOLO   Is there anything else you wish to say to us?

FIGARO   Are they looking after your mule all right?

BARTHOLO   *(Angry)* You raving lunatic! Leave us!

FIGARO   Angry, Doctor? Men of your status are so hard.
                They feel no more sympathy towards poor animals
                than if - well, to tell the truth of it - than if ani-
                mals were mere humans! Goodbye, Marceline.
                Still determined to have me up in court? "For
                want of loving others, must one hate oneself?" I
                am relying on the Doctor.

BARTHOLO   What's all this?

FIGARO   She'll tell you all you want - and probably more.

                Exit Figaro.

SCENE FOUR

Marceline, Bartholo.

BARTHOLO   *(Watching him go)* That clown never changes!
                Unless someone flays him alive, I tell you he'll die
                the most thick-skinned, insolent, cock-sure...

MARCELINE   *(Turning him round)* There you are, now. Come
                on. Still the same old Doctor, always so serious
                and stuffy, a person could die waiting for you to
                do anything to help them. Just as a certain couple
                married each other not long ago in spite of all your
                useless precautions.

BARTHOLO   Still just as bitter and provocative! Well then,
                what makes my presence at the castle so neces-
                sary? Has the Count had some accident?

MARCELINE   No, Doctor.

BARTHOLO   Rosine, his treacherous Countess, is she unwell,
                praise God?

MARCELINE   She is suffering.

BARTHOLO   In what way?

MARCELINE   Her husband neglects her.

BARTHOLO   *(Pleased)* Ah, the noble husband. He avenges me!

MARCELINE   The Count's behaviour is difficult to explain. He is unfaithful and jealous at the same time.

BARTHOLO   Jealous out of self-regard, unfaithful out of boredom. That much goes without saying.

MARCELINE   Today, for example, he is giving our Suzanne in marriage to his servant Figaro, and rewarding him generously to celebrate their union...

BARTHOLO   Already made necessary by the Count himself!

MARCELINE   Not quite, but a union the Count is keen to celebrate further and in his own way with the bride...

BARTHOLO   With Master Figaro's? He's a man you could fix that sort of deal with easily enough.

MARCELINE   Not so, according to Bazile.

BARTHOLO   Is that villain here too? It's a real thieves' cave. What is he doing here?

MARCELINE   As much harm as he can manage. But the worst of it is he still harbours that ridiculous passion for me he's had since years back.

BARTHOLO   I would have beaten him off a dozen times over.

MARCELINE   How?

BARTHOLO   By marrying him.

MARCELINE   That's a feeble and cruel joke to make. You could have beaten me off in the same way, at least a dozen times over. Don't you owe it to me? Remember your promises? And where is your memory of our little Emmanuel, that fruit of a for

gotten love which was to have led us into marriage?

BARTHOLO   *(Removing his hat)* Did you bring me all the way
from Seville to listen to this rubbish? You've had
a relapse, a bad attack of marriage...

MARCELINE   Very well, let's drop the subject. But if there's no
way of making you do the right thing by marrying
me, at least give me your help in marrying someone else.

BARTHOLO   Ah, with all my heart! Tell me about it. But what
man on earth, God-forsaken and woman-forsaken,
...

MARCELINE   Aha! Who could he be, Doctor, if not the handsome, the spirited, the kindly Figaro?

BARTHOLO   That rascal?

MARCELINE   Never angry, always in a sunny mood, devoting
himself to the joy of the moment, worrying about
the future as little as he sorrows for the past.
Dashing, generous! Generous...

BARTHOLO   As only a thief can be.

MARCELINE   As only a nobleman can. In short, a charmer. But
he's a complete monster!

BARTHOLO   What about his Suzanne?

MARCELINE   She won't get him, the cunning litle cat, if you
help me hold him, my dear Doctor, to a promise
he gave me.

BARTHOLO   But she is marrying him today.

MARCELINE   Marriages are broken off later than that. And if I
weren't afraid to give away a little women's
secret!...

BARTHOLO   Are there any secrets a woman holds back from a
                doctor?

MARCELINE   Ah! You know there are none I have held back
                from you! My sex is fiery, but fearful. We might
                be attracted to the charms of pleasure, but even
                the most adventurous of women hears a voice
                inside that says: "Be beautiful if you can, be good
                if you wish, but be of good reputation you must."
                Now, since we must at least preserve our reputa-
                tion, and every woman understands the impor-
                tance of that, we must first of all make Suzanne
                thoroughly frightened that the offers she has been
                receiving are about to be disclosed.

BARTHOLO   How will that help us?

MARCELINE   She will keep on refusing the Count's advances,
                the shame would be too great. And the Count, in
                revenge, will back me up in opposing her mar-
                riage. Which in turn will make mine all the more
                certain.

BARTHOLO   She's right. And damn me if it isn't a good trick
                to marry off my old housekeeper to the villain
                responsible for the loss of my young mistress.

MARCELINE   *(Rapidly)* The man who thinks he can double his
                fun by destroying my own hopes.

BARTHOLO   *(Rapidly)* And the man who once robbed me of a
                hundred crowns, a matter still close to my heart.

MARCELINE   Ah! What a wonderful joy...!

BARTHOLO   To punish a scoundrel...

MARCELINE   To marry him, Doctor, to marry him!

SCENE FIVE

Marceline, Bartholo, Suzanne.

SUZANNE   *(Carrying in her hand a woman's nightcap with a broad ribbon and over her arm a woman's dress)* Marry him, marry him! Marry whom? My Figaro?

MARCELINE   *(Bitter)* Why not? *You're* going to!

BARTHOLO   *(Laughing)* Ah, the unbeatable reasoning of an angry woman! We were discussing, pretty Suzon, Figaro's pleasure in having you for his own.

MARCELINE   Not to mention the Count's, which we won't mention.

SUZANNE   *(Curtseys)* Your servant, Madame. Every time you speak you betray your own bitterness.

MARCELINE   *(Curtseys)* Yours, to be sure, Madame. But where is the bitterness? It is only fair that a liberal-minded master should share a little of the pleasure he procures for his dependants.

SUZANNE   Procures?

MARCELINE   Yes, Madame.

SUZANNE   Fortunately the strength of Madame's jealousy is as renowned as the feebleness of her claims on Figaro.

MARCELINE   They might have been made stronger had they been sealed in the manner Madame likes to employ.

SUZANNE   Oh! That manner, Madame, is the preserve of experienced ladies like yourself.

MARCELINE   Whereas our little girl has no such knowledge at all? Innocent as an old judge!

BARTHOLO   *(Drawing Marceline away)* Goodbye, our Figaro's
                  pretty bride.

MARCELINE   *(Curtseys)* Accepter of the Count's secret favours.

SUZANNE   *(Curtseys)*   Who holds you in the highest regard,
                  Madame.

MARCELINE   *(Curtseys)* But can she honour me with any tiny
                  display of warmer feelings, Madame?

SUZANNE   *(Curtseys)*   I assure Madame that in that respect
                  she wants for none.

MARCELINE   *(Curtseys)* And Madame is such a pretty young
                  lady!

SUZANNE   *(Curtseys)*   Ah, yes, Madame must be quite sick!

MARCELINE   *(Curtseys)* With such an unimpeachable reputa-
                  tion!

SUZANNE   *(Curtseys)*   They are more the province of old
                  duennas.

MARCELINE   *(Outraged)* Old duennas! Old duennas!

BARTHOLO   *(Holding her back)* Marceline!

MARCELINE   Come, doctor, let us go, before I lose all restraint.
                  Madame, good day. *(Curtseys)*

Exeunt Marceline and Bartholo.

SCENE SIX

Suzanne, alone.

SUZANNE   Go, madame!   On your way, starchy old crow!
                  I'm not scared of you and I couldn't give a damn
                  for your insults. The old hag thinks she can run

the whole castle, just because she once had an
education and used to make the Countess's life a
misery when she was a girl. *(She throws the dress
over a chair.)* Now I can't remember what I came
here to find.

SCENE SEVEN

Suzanne, Cherubin.

CHERUBIN   *(Running in)* Oh, Suzon! I've been hanging about
               for two hours, waiting for the chance to catch you
               alone. It's awful! You are getting married, and I
               have to leave the castle.

SUZANNE   How can my wedding cause the Count's head
               page to have to go away?

CHERUBIN   *(Piteously)* Suzanne, he's throwing me out!

SUZANNE   *(Mimicking)* Cherubin, what have you been up
               to?

CHERUBIN   He caught me last night in your cousin
               Fanchette's room. I was helping her rehearse her
               part for the ceremony this evening. He flew into a
               terrible rage when he saw me! "Get out of here,"
               he said, "you little..." I daren't repeat the shock-
               ing word he used, in front of a lady. "Get out, and
               tomorrow you won't be spending the night in this
               castle." If the Countess, my beautiful godmother,
               doesn't succeed in calming him down, it's all over,
               Suzon. I shall never have the joy of seeing you,
               ever again.

SUZANNE   Of seeing me! It's me now, is it? So your secret
               sighs are no longer for my mistress?

CHERUBIN   Oh, Suzon! She is so noble and so beautiful. But
               so awe-inspiring!

SUZANNE   Meaning that I'm not, and so you can still hold out hopes for me...

CHERUBIN   You know perfectly well, you wicked woman, I
                hold out no hopes of hoping. But you are so
                lucky! Every minute of the day you see her, you
                talk to her, you dress her in the morning and
                undress her at night, pin by pin... Ah, Suzon, I'd
                give... What have you got there?

SUZANNE   *(Teasing)* Woe is me! The fortunate nightcap and
                the privileged ribbon which spend the night
                embracing the hair of that lovely godmother.

CHERUBIN   *(Excited)* The ribbon from her nightcap! Give me
                it, my darling Suzon!

SUZANNE   *(Pulling it away)* Most certainly not. His 'darling'
                indeed! The familiarity of the boy! As if he
                weren't a pimply youth of no account. *(Cherubin
                snatches the ribbon.)* Hey, the ribbon!

CHERUBIN   *(Dodging round the big armchair)* Tell her it's lost,
                spoiled. Say you mislaid it. Tell her anything you
                like.

SUZANNE   *(Chasing after him)* Oh! Three or four years time,
                and I prophesy you'll be the biggest little good-for-
                nothing!... Will you give that ribbon back?

                She tries to take it from him.

CHERUBIN   *(Pulls a sheet of paper from his pocket.)* Leave me
                alone! Oh! let me keep it, Suzon! I'll give you the
                song I've written. When the memory of your beau-
                tiful mistress saddens every moment for me, I'll
                look to your memory as the one shaft of joy that
                can lighten my heart.

SUZANNE   *(Snatching the song)* Lighten your heart, you little
                villain! You must think you're talking to your
                Fanchette. First they catch you in her room, then
                you start panting for the Countess, and now on
                top of all that you're giving the line to me!

CHERUBIN   *(In a state of exaltation)* It's true, you're perfectly
                right! I don't know what I am any more. For
                months I've been getting these great bursting feel-
                ings inside. I only have to look at a woman, and
                my heart skips wildly. Words like *love* and *bliss*
                make it flutter and hurt. And in the end the need
                to say to someone: "I love you", has become so
                urgent I say it all alone running up and down in
                the park. I shout it to your mistress, to you, to the
                trees, to the clouds, to the wind that carries them
                away with my words, lost on the air. - Yesterday,
                I met Marceline...

SUZANNE   *(Laughing)* Ha, ha, ha, ha!

CHERUBIN   Why not? She's a woman, she's female! Female,
                woman! Ah, don't the words sound gentle!
                Don't they sound exciting!

SUZANNE   He's going mad!

CHERUBIN   Fanchette is sweet. At least she listens to me.
                You're not sweet at all!

SUZANNE   Oh, dear, what a shame! Listen to the man!

                She tries to snatch the ribbon.

CHERUBIN   *(Twists and dodges away.)* Oh, no you don't!
                You'll have to kill me first! But if the bargain isn't
                good enough for you, I'll throw in a thousand kiss-
                es.

                He gives chase in his turn.

SUZANNE   *(Runs to escape.)* You'll get a thousand kicks if you
                take a step closer. I'll complain to my mistress.
                And you can forget about getting any help from
                me with the Count. I'll go to him myself and tell
                him: "Quite right, Sir. Send the little thief away.
                Send him back to his family. He's an evil little
                pageboy who fancies himself as the Countess's
                lover and tries to give me kisses when he's jilted."

CHERUBIN   *(Sees the Count coming; hurls himself behind the arm-
                chair in terror.)*   I've had it! I've had it!

SUZANNE   What a fuss!

SCENE EIGHT

Suzanne, the Count, Cherubin (hidden).

SUZANNE   *(Sees the Count.)*   Oh!

                Crosses to the chair to conceal Cherubin.

COUNT   *(Coming into the room)* All excited, Suzon? You
                were talking to yourself, and your little heart looks
                quite stirred up... Not to worry, perfectly under-
                standable on a day like today.

SUZANNE   *(Confused)* Sir, what do you want with me? If
                someone found you here...

COUNT   I would be most upset if anyone were to find me
                here. But you know how deep an interest I take in
                you. Bazile has not left you unaware of my love
                for you. I have only a second to explain myself.
                Listen.

                He sits in the chair.

SUZANNE   *(Sharply)* I refuse to listen to a word.

COUNT   *(Takes her hand.)* Not even one? You know the
                King has made me his ambassador in London. I
                am taking Figaro with me: I have given him an
                excellent position. And, since the duty of a wife is
                to follow her husband ...

SUZANNE   Oh, if I had the nerve to speak out!

COUNT   *(Pulling her towards him)* Speak freely, my dear,
                speak freely.   Exercise today the lifelong power
                you have over me.

SUZANNE   *(Frightened)* That's not what I want, Sir, that's not what I want. Leave me now, I beg you.

COUNT   But tell me first.

SUZANNE   *(Angry)* I don't remember what I was going to say.

COUNT   We were talking about the duties of a wife.

SUZANNE   All right, then! When the Count won his wife from under the Doctor's nose and took her from his house, he married her for love. And when he abolished that terrible droit du seigneur ...

COUNT   *(Cheerfully)* Causing a lot of hardship to the girls. Oh, Suzette! It is such a charming custom! If you would just come down to the garden when it's dark tonight and have a little talk about it, I would set such a price on that small favour...

BAZILE   *(His voice is heard outside.)* The Count is not in his apartment.

COUNT   *(Standing up)* Whose voice is that?

SUZANNE   Ah, this is terrible!

COUNT   Leave the room, someone might come in...

SUZANNE   *(Alarmed)* You want me to leave you in here?

BAZILE   *(Outside, shouting)* The Count was with the Countess, but he has gone. I'll go and see.

COUNT   And nowhere to hide! Ah! Behind this chair ... not very good. But get rid of him as quick as you can.

> *Suzanne bars his way. He pushes her gently; she steps back, thus coming between him and the little page. But while the Count crouches and moves into his place, Cherubin dodges away and jumps in*

terror on to the seat of the chair where he huddles
up in a ball. Suzanne picks up the dress she
brought in and covers the page with it. She stations
herself in front of the armchair.

SCENE NINE

The Count and Cherubin (hidden), Suzanne, Bazile.

BAZILE	You wouldn't by any chance have seen His Lordship, would you, Miss?
SUZANNE	*(Sharply)* Why should I have seen him? Go away.
BAZILE	*(Coming closer)* If you were more sensible you would find nothing unusual in my question. Figaro is looking for him.
SUZANNE	You mean he's looking for his worst enemy, apart from you?
COUNT	*(Aside)* Now we're seeing how well my servant serves me.
BAZILE	To be well-disposed towards a wife does not mean one wishes harm to her husband.
SUZANNE	No, not by your disgraceful principles, you sower of corruption.
BAZILE	What are you being asked to give here that you weren't going to give freely to some other man anyway? Thanks to the charming rites of marriage, what you were forbidden to do yesterday will be expected of you tomorrow.
SUZANNE	That's a shocking thing to say!
BAZILE	Out of all the things that people take seriously, marriage is quite the most farcical. And so I imagined ...

SUZANNE   *(Furious)* Just what a despicable mind would
               imagine. Who allowed you in here?

BAZILE   Now, now, temper! Calm down: good will to all
               men! You shall have it your own way. But don't
               deceive yourself that I take Figaro for the obstacle
               in His Lordship's way. What about the little page ...

SUZANNE   *(Faltering)* Cherubin?

BAZILE   *(Mimicking)*   *Cherubino di amore*, the little cherub
               himself, who hangs around you all the time. Even
               this morning he was on the prowl, waiting for me
               to leave so that he could get in to see you. Try
               telling me that isn't true.

SUZANNE   It's a complete lie! Get out of here, you evil man!

BAZILE   A man is evil because he can see straight, is that it?
               And that song he's been composing so mysterious-
               ly, are you telling me that's not for you as well?

SUZANNE   *(Angry)* What? Oh, yes! Just for me!

BAZILE   Unless of course he wrote it for Her Ladyship!
               Indeed, they do say, when he serves at table his
               eyes are out on stalks for her!... But I warn you,
               don't let him overstep the mark. When it comes
               to that kind of thing His Lordship is positively *bru-
               tal*.

SUZANNE   *(Furious)* And you're a sneaking rat to go about
               spreading tales like that to discredit a poor child
               who's already in disgrace with his master.

BAZILE   Am I making it up? I'm only saying what every-
               body is saying.

COUNT   *(Springing to his feet)* What do you mean, every-
               body is saying!

SUZANNE   Oh, my God!

BAZILE   Ah, ah!

COUNT   Away, Bazile, and have the wretch thrown out!

BAZILE   Ah! What a mistake to have come in here!

SUZANNE   *(Alarmed)* Oh, my God! Oh, my God!

COUNT   *(To Bazile)* She's having a fit. Sit her down in this armchair.

SUZANNE   *(Pushing Bazile away vigorously)* I don't want to sit down. Barging his way in here like that, it's a disgrace!

COUNT   But there are two of us with you now, my dear. There's not the slightest danger!

BAZILE   I must apologise for speaking so facetiously about the page, I didn't know you could hear. I only talked in that way to see what she really thought. The truth is ...

COUNT   Give him fifty crowns and a horse, and send him packing to his own family.

BAZILE   My Lord, for a little harmless banter?

COUNT   He's a dissolute little scoundrel. Only last night I caught him again with the gardener's daughter.

BAZILE   With Fanchette?

COUNT   In her bedroom.

SUZANNE   *(Outraged)* Doubtless the Count had a reason to be there himself!

COUNT   *(Cheerfully)* I like the drift of that remark.

BAZILE   It's a good sign!

COUNT   *(Cheerfully)* Unfortunately, no. I was on my way to give some orders to your uncle Antonio, my drunkard of a gardener. I knock on the door. There's a long pause before it opens. Your cousin seems ruffled. I grow suspicious, I speak with her, and while I talk, I look round. Behind the door is a sort of curtain, screening off a wardrobe, she hangs her clothes there, I don't know. Pretending all is well, I edge over, softly, softly, and lift the curtain *(He demonstrates by lifting the dress from the armchair.)* and I find ... *(He sees Cherubin.)* Ah!...

BAZILE   Ah, ah!

COUNT   He's done it again!

BAZILE   An even better one this time.

COUNT   *(To Suzanne)*   Young lady, I'm amazed! Hardly a bride yet and already organising this sort of thing! Is that why you wanted to be alone, to entertain my page? And you, Sir, whose behaviour never changes. Showing no respect for your godmother, you seek out her personal maid, the only woman you haven't yet turned your attentions to, and the wife of Figaro your friend! But I refuse to allow Figaro, a man I both respect and love, to be victim of such a deception. Bazile, was he with you just now?

SUZANNE   *(Outraged)*   There is no deception and no victim! He was there all the time you were talking to me.

COUNT   *(Furious)*   I hope for your sake that's a lie!   His worst enemy wouldn't wish it on him if it's not!

SUZANNE   He was here to see if I could persuade the Countess to ask you to spare him.   He was so frightened when you came in, he hid in the chair.

COUNT   *(Angry)*   Another lie! I sat down in it straight away.

CHERUBIN   Ah, Sir! I was crouched in fear behind it.

COUNT	The devil you were! Where do you think I just sprang from?
CHERUBIN	Excuse me, but that's when I jumped round and huddled up on the seat.
COUNT	*(Even more furious)* So this little viper is a ... a snake in the grass! He was listening to us!
CHERUBIN	Oh, no, Sir. I did everything I could not to hear.
COUNT	The treachery! *(To Suzanne)* You can give up any hope of marrying Figaro.
BAZILE	Sir, restrain yourself. People are coming.
COUNT	*(Dragging Cherubin from the chair and planting him on his feet)* He'd stay there for the whole world to see!

SCENE TEN

Cherubin, Suzanne, Figaro, Countess, Count, Fanchette, Bazile. A crowd of servants and countryfolk all dressed in white.

FIGARO	*(Holding a woman's hat decorated with white feathers and white ribbons. He is speaking to the Countess.)* You are the only person, Madame, who could secure us this favour.
COUNTESS	Look at them all, Sir: they imagine I have an influence which I altogether lack. But since their request is not unreasonable...
COUNT	*(Embarrassed)* I'm sure it would have to be quite exceptionally so ...
FIGARO	*(Aside, to Suzanne)* Back me up while I try.
SUZANNE	*(Aside, to Figaro)* You won't do any good.

FIGARO	*(Aside)* All the same...
COUNT	*(To Figaro)* What do you want?

FIGARO   Sir, your loyal subjects, touched that your love for the Countess should have inspired you to abolish a certain unwelcome privilege, ...

COUNT   Yes, all right, the privilege no longer exists. What do you want?

FIGARO   *(Slyly)* It is high time the virtuousness of so good a master should be publicly acclaimed. It is of such benefit to me today, that I desire to be the first to celebrate it at my own wedding.

COUNT   *(Increasingly embarrassed)* I think you must be joking, my friend. To abolish a shameful privilege like that is no more than paying off a debt to decent behaviour. A Spaniard may hope to win a beautiful woman by paying her his honourable attentions. But to demand that she should yield to him the first and sweetest enjoyment of that beauty out of slavish subservience, ah! that is the bullying of a Vandal. It is not the acknowledged right of a noble Castilian.

FIGARO   *(Taking Suzanne by the hand)* Then permit this young lady, her honour intact thanks to your wisdom, to receive publicly and from your own hand, this bride's crown of chastity, decorated with white feathers and ribbons. It is the symbol of the purity of your intentions. Let it become part of the ceremonial for all marriages, to be remembered for ever in the hymns of the wedding choir...

COUNT   *(Embarrassed)* I know that writing verses, composing music and being in love are three excuses for all manner of silly practices, ...

FIGARO   My friends, I need your support!

EVERYONE
TOGETHER   My Lord! My Lord!

SUZANNE   *(To the Count)* Why be embarrassed to accept a
               tribute you deserve so much?

COUNT   *(Aside)* Treacherous woman!

FIGARO   Just look at her, Sir. You couldn't ask for a pretti-
               er bride to mark the greatness of your sacrifice.

SUZANNE   Leave my looks out of it and let's just praise his
               virtue.

COUNT   *(Aside)* This whole thing has been put up!

COUNTESS   I am on their side, Sir. It will be a ceremony I
               shall always treasure because of its origins in the
               wonderful love you had for me.

COUNT   Which I have now, Madame; and because of
               which I yield.

EVERYONE
TOGETHER   Long live His Lordship!

COUNT   *(Aside)* I've been had. *(Aloud)* I only ask, so that
               the ceremony can be prepared to maximum effect,
               that it be put off until a little later. *(Aside)* And in
               the meantime, let's find Marceline, quickly!

FIGARO   *(To Cherubin)* What's up, you monkey? Not
               cheering?

SUZANNE   He's in the pits of despair. The Count is sending
               him away.

COUNTESS   Oh! Sir, I ask for his pardon.

COUNT   He doesn't deserve it.

COUNTESS   But he's so young!

COUNT   Not as young as you imagine.

CHERUBIN	*(Trembling)* The privilege you abolished when you married Madame was not the right of generous forgiveness.
COUNTESS	He only gave up the one which harmed you all.
SUZANNE	If the right to pardon his subjects *had* been the one His Lordship had abolished, that, surely, would be the first one he would try secretly to restore.
COUNT	*(Embarrassed)* Absolutely.
COUNTESS	What need is there to restore anything?
CHERUBIN	*(To the Count)* My behaviour was foolish, Sir, it is true. But nothing indiscreet has ever passed my lips...
COUNT	*(Embarrassed)* Very well, enough of that...
FIGARO	Indiscreet, what does he mean?
COUNT	*(Sharply)* That's enough, that's enough. Everybody demands his pardon: I grant it. And I'll go further than that: I give him a company to command in my regiment.
EVERYONE TOGETHER	Long live His Lordship!
COUNT	But on condition that he leaves immediately to join them in Catalonia.
FIGARO	Oh! Sir, make it tomorrow.
COUNT	*(Insisting)* Today. Those are my orders.
CHERUBIN	Then I obey.
COUNT	Say goodbye to your godmother, and ask her protection.

Cherubin kneels before the Countess, but is unable

to speak.

COUNTESS *(Moved)* Since we cannot keep you even for today, go on your way, young man. A new life calls you. Live it as befits you. Bring honour to your benefactor. Remember this house, and the affectionate indulgence of your youth here. Be obedient, honest and brave. We shall rejoice in your triumphs.

Cherubin rises and returns to his place.

COUNT You seem very moved, Madame!

COUNTESS I don't deny it. Who knows what fate lies in store for a child thrust into such a dangerous career? He is a relation of my family; he is also my god-son.

COUNT *(Aside)* I see that Bazile was right. *(Aloud)* Young man, you may embrace Suzanne ... for the last time.

FIGARO Why, Sir? He can come and spend his winters here. A hug for me too, Captain! *(He embraces Cherubin.)* Goodbye, my little Cherubin. It's a very different life you'll follow now, my lad. Oh, yes! No more roaming round the women's apart- ments all day. No more hot drinks and cream cakes. No more games of tag or blind-man's-buff. Proper soldiers, heavens above! Swarthy faces, ragged clothes; a great heavy rifle; left turn, right turn, forward march, onward to victory and don't flinch on the way... Unless a well-aimed shot! ...

SUZANNE Oh! What a horrible idea!

COUNTESS What a terrible thing to suggest!

COUNT And where is Marceline? It's strange that she's not with you.

FANCHETTE Sir, she went off towards the town by the little path through the farm.

COUNT	And she'll be returning?...
BAZILE	God knows.
FIGARO	If only God didn't know he knew!
FANCHETTE	The Doctor was accompanying her.
COUNT	*(Sharply)* The Doctor is here?
BAZILE	She pounced on him straight away...
COUNT	*(Aside)* He couldn't have come at a better time.
FANCHETTE	She looked very excited about something. She was talking loudly all the time and kept stopping and going like this, waving her arms ... And the Doctor kept doing this, with his hand, calming her down. She seemed so angry! She kept saying my cousin Figaro's name.
COUNT	*(Taking her under the chin)* Your cousin ... to be.
FANCHETTE	*(Indicating Cherubin)* Sir, have you forgiven us for yesterday?
COUNT	*(Cutting her off)* Oh, come along, come along, my girl.
FIGARO	It's her amorous claws she's sharpening up. She'd like to make trouble at our wedding...
COUNT	*(Aside)* Believe me, she will. *(Aloud)* Come, Madame, let us go in. Bazile, I need to see you.
SUZANNE	*(To Figaro)* Are we going to be able to have a word?
FIGARO	*(Aside, to Suzanne)* Have we trussed him up well enough for you?
SUZANNE	*(Aside)* Clever boy!

They all begin to go off.

SCENE ELEVEN

Cherubin, Figaro, Bazile.

As the others are leaving, Figaro stops Cherubin and Bazile and brings them back.

FIGARO
Well now, you two. With that part of the ceremony settled, my plans for tonight's festivities follow next. We need to be properly organised. I don't want us to be like actors who reserve their worst performance for critics' night. There'll be no run afterwards to pull everything together, not for us. So let's get used to our parts today.

BAZILE
(Slyly) Mine is harder than you imagine.

FIGARO
(Gesturing, unseen by Bazile, as if to thump him) Ah, but little do you know the prize it will bring you.

CHERUBIN
My friend, you're forgetting that I have to go.

FIGARO
Oh, so you'd be willing to stay!

CHERUBIN
Oh, would I!

FIGARO
We need to be cunning. Make no fuss about leaving. Pack your bags openly, put on your travelling cloak, and let them see your horse at the gates. A quick gallop as far as the farm, then come back on foot and in through the rear of the castle. The Count will think you have gone. Just make sure you keep out of his sight, and I'll smooth it all over with him after the celebrations.

CHERUBIN
But Fanchette doesn't know her part yet!

BAZILE
You've been closeted with her for a week. What

FIGARO

the devil have you been teaching her, then? You have nothing to do all day. For heaven's sake, give her a lesson.

BAZILE

Take care, young man, take care! Her father Antonio is not happy. She's had her ears boxed already: whatever she's doing with you, it isn't studying. Ah, Cherubin, Cherubin, you're only making trouble for her. "You can take a horse to water..."

FIGARO

Ah, listen to our old fool and his hoary proverbs! Well, ancient pedant, what does the wisdom of nations say? "You can take a horse to water..."

BAZILE

And one day it'll drink.

FIGARO

(As he exits) Not as stupid as he looks, that one. Not as stupid as he looks.

END OF ACT ONE

ACT TWO

SCENE ONE

A sumptuous bedroom. A large bed recessed into an alcove, a dais down-stage of it. The main door upstage right, the door to a dressing room downstage left. Another door in the upstage wall, leading to the women's quarters. On the other side, a window.

Suzanne and the Countess enter through the main door on the right.

COUNTESS   *(Throwing herself into an easy chair)* Close the door, Suzanne, and tell me the whole story in every detail.

SUZANNE   I have kept nothing back, Madame.

COUNTESS   So truly, Suzon, he wanted to seduce you?

SUZANNE   Oh, not that! The Count stands on no such ceremony with his servant. He wanted to buy me.

COUNTESS   And the little page was present?

SUZANNE   In a manner of speaking. He was hiding behind the big armchair. He had come to see if I would persuade you to speak to the Count on his behalf.

COUNTESS   But why not ask me directly? Would I have refused, Suzon?

SUZANNE   That's what I told him. But the way he was feeling about having to leave the castle, and especially Madame!... "Oh, Suzon, she is so noble and so beautiful. But so awe-inspiring!"

COUNTESS   Is that how I seem, Suzon? But I have always protected him.

SUZANNE   Then he saw the ribbon from your nightcap that I was holding. He threw himself at it...

COUNTESS	*(Smiling)* My ribbon?... How childish!
SUZANNE	I tried to get it away from him. Madame, he was a lion! His eyes glittered... "You'll have to kill me first," he said, making his frail little voice go all shrill.
COUNTESS	*(Dreamily)* And then, Suzon?
SUZANNE	Well, Madame, how do you stop a little demon like that? One moment "She's my godmother", the next "I'd like to..." And because he doesn't dare even kiss the hem of Madame's dress, it's me he wants to embrace instead!
COUNTESS	*(Dreamily)* We mustn't... we mustn't carry on with this silliness... So, in the end, poor Suzon, how did my husband finish the conversation?
SUZANNE	By saying if I didn't do as he wanted he would give his support to Marceline's cause.
COUNTESS	*(Rising and walking up and down, fanning herself vigorously)* He doesn't love me at all any more.
SUZANNE	Then why is he so jealous?
COUNTESS	Pure self-regard, my dear. All husbands are the same. Oh! I have loved him too much! He's grown tired of my caresses, I have wearied him with my love. That is my only fault. But I don't wish you to suffer for your honesty, and you shall marry Figaro. He alone can help us. Will he be here?
SUZANNE	As soon as he's seen the hunting party off.
COUNTESS	*(Fanning herself)* Open the garden window a little. It's so hot in here!...
SUZANNE	Madame is allowing herself to be too much upset.

Suzanne goes to open the window upstage.

COUNTESS   *(Sunk in her reflections)* If only he didn't spend so
                  much time avoiding me... Why do men always do
                  that?

SUZANNE   *(Calling from the window)* Ah! There goes the
                  Count, passing the kitchen garden on his horse.
                  Pedrillo is with him, and two, three, four grey-
                  hounds.

COUNTESS   We have a little time. *(She sits.)* Is someone
                  knocking, Suzon?

SUZANNE   *(Singing out as she runs to the door)* Ah! It's my
                  Figaro, my Figaro!

SCENE TWO

Figaro, Suzanne, the Countess (seated)

SUZANNE   My dearest! Come on in! Madame is so impa-
                  tient to see you!...

FIGARO   And how about you, little Suzanne? Madame has
                  nothing to be concerned about. After all, what's
                  the problem? Next to nothing! The Count finds
                  our young bride attractive; he wants to make her
                  his mistress. It's perfectly natural.

SUZANNE   Natural?

FIGARO   So he appoints me his despatch runner, and Suzon
                  his ambassadorial assistant. That wasn't too stu-
                  pid, was it?

SUZANNE   Have you finished?

FIGARO   And because Suzanne, my fiancée, refuses the
                  post, he is going to support Marceline. What
                  could be more simple? Get your own back on
                  people who ruin your plans by ruining theirs,
                  everyone does it. It's what we're going to do our-
                  selves. But that's all there is to it.

COUNTESS	Figaro, how can you speak so lightly of a scheme which is going to cost all of us our happiness?
FIGARO	Who says that, Madame?
SUZANNE	You don't seem to be concerned about our troubles...
FIGARO	Because I'm taking them in hand: isn't that what you want? Now, to set about it methodically, like the Count, the first thing to do is cool his ardour for what belongs to us by giving him something to worry about on his own account.
COUNTESS	Well said. But how?
FIGARO	It is already done, Madame. A piece of false information concerning you...
COUNTESS	Concerning me! You must be mad!
FIGARO	Oh, no. He's the one who'll think he's mad.
COUNTESS	But he's so jealous!...
FIGARO	All the better. To turn people of his character to your own advantage, all you need is to whip them up a bit. It's a thing women understand very well! Then, once you've got them hopping with rage, you can lead them with only the merest bit of intrigue wherever you fancy, straight into the Guadalquivir river if you want. Bazile has received an anonymous letter warning the Count that an admirer will be trying to see you during the ball tonight.
COUNTESS	And you are prepared to distort the truth about a woman of honour?..
FIGARO	There are few other women I would have dared mention, Madame, for fear it might be no distor

tion.

COUNTESS	Then I suppose I must thank you for it!

FIGARO   But tell me, don't you think it's a clever idea to arrange his day's enjoyments for him so that he spends the time set aside for canoodling with my wife rushing about cursing his own? He's thoroughly confused already: should he gallop off after this one, or keep a close eye on that one? His mind is in turmoil. Look, look, there he goes, charging round the countryside hunting down a hare that isn't even running. The hour of the wedding is on him before he knows it. He'll have made no preparations against it, and he'll never dare stop it with Madame there.

SUZANNE   No, but Marceline of the famous mind and wit, *she* will.

FIGARO   Hah! Am I supposed to be put off by that? You will send a message to the Count agreeing to meet him in the garden at nightfall.

SUZANNE   Are you still working on that idea?

FIGARO   Give me strength! Listen: people who risk nothing get nothing and are good for nothing. That's what I say.

SUZANNE   Nothing like a saying!

COUNTESS   And do you say it? Would you really let her go?

FIGARO   Certainly not. I'm going to dress someone up in Suzanne's clothes. When we catch the Count at his assignation, how is he going to talk his way out of that?

SUZANNE   Who is going to wear my clothes?

FIGARO   Cherubin.

COUNTESS	He has left the castle.
FIGARO	Not as far as I'm concerned. So can I go ahead?
SUZANNE	We can rely on him when it comes to successful scheming.
FIGARO	Two, three, four, all at the same time, all entangled and interweaving. I'm a born politician.
SUZANNE	They say it's a terribly difficult trade.
FIGARO	Getting what you want, taking it, demanding it, there's the secret in three words.
COUNTESS	He's so confident he makes me feel it too.
FIGARO	That's my intention.
SUZANNE	What were you going to say, then?
FIGARO	While the Count is away, I'll send Cherubin in to you. Change his hair, find him some clothes, then I'll shut him away and teach him his lines. And later tonight, dance, my gallant Count, dance!

Exit Figaro

SCENE THREE

Suzanne, the Countess (seated)

COUNTESS	*(Reaching for her make-up box)* My God, Suzon, look at the state I'm in! ... And that young man coming in any minute!...
SUZANNE	Is Madame keen that he shouldn't get out again?
COUNTESS	*(Staring dreamily into her mirror)* Who, me? ... I'll give him a good telling-off, just you see.

SUZANNE	Let's make him sing the song he's been composing.

She puts it in the Countess's lap..

COUNTESS	But truly, my hair is coming to pieces!...
SUZANNE	*(Laughing)* I only have to pin back these two curls, and Madame will be able to tell him off much better.
COUNTESS	*(Emerging from her reverie)* What's that you say, my girl?

SCENE FOUR

Cherubin (looking shame-faced), Suzanne, the Countess (seated).

SUZANNE	Come in, bold officer. We are ready to receive visitors.
CHERUBIN	*(Coming forward trembling)* You don't know how the title wounds me, Madame! It means I must leave this place... leave a godmother who is so... good to me!...
SUZANNE	And so beautiful!
CHERUBIN	*(Sighing)* Oh! Yes!
SUZANNE	*(Mimicking)* Oh! Yes! Such a nice young man, with his humble hypocrite's downcast gaze. Come on, my fine bluebird, Madame wants to hear you sing your song.
COUNTESS	*(Unfolding the song)* Who is it written for ...does anyone know?
SUZANNE	See the culprit blush! He's got beetroot on his cheeks!
CHERUBIN	Is it forbidden to ... to value someone?...

SUZANNE	*(Waving a fist under his nose)* I'll give the whole game away, you good-for-nothing!
COUNTESS	Now then ... Can he sing?
CHERUBIN	Oh, Madame! I'm so nervous!...
SUZANNE	*(Laughing)* Neeah-neeah-neeah-neeah-neeah! As soon as Madame asks, the author goes all modest! I shall accompany him.
COUNTESS	Take my guitar.

The Countess, seated, holds the sheet of paper to follow the song. Suzanne stands behind her chair and practises a few notes, looking at the music over her mistress's shoulder. Cherubin stands before her, eyes downcast. The tableau is exactly as in the print called "Conversation espagnole", after Vanloo.

CHERUBIN   *(Sings, to the tune "Malbroug s'en va-t-en guerre" [Malbroug goes off to war])*
> My horse breathing shallow and sharp,
> (Oh, the pain, the pain, inside my heart!)
> I roamed, a man lost, without charts,
> My mount left to choose his own way.
>
> My mount left to choose his own way,
> With no servant or squire or valet:
> And there, where the fountain starts,
> (Oh, the pain, the pain, inside my heart!)
> My godmother, loved without art,
> Brought tears that my eyes could not stay.
>
> Brought tears that my eyes could not stay,
> And lost in a wave of dismay,
> I carved in an old ash tree's bark,
> (Oh, the pain, the pain, inside my heart!)
> Her name, but of mine made no mark.
> The King chanced to pass by that way.
>
> The King chanced to pass by that way,

With his clerics and barons so gay.
Pretty pageboy, the Queen made remark,
(Oh, the pain, the pain, inside my heart!)
What causes this grieving so stark?
What causes such weeping, I pray?

What causes such weeping, I pray?
I command you the reason to say.
- Your Majesty, Queen that thou art,
(Oh, the pain, the pain, inside my heart!)
I loved with my every part
A godmother, taken away.

A godmother, taken away;
Only death for me now can hold sway.
- Pretty pageboy, the Queen made remark,
(Oh, the pain, the pain, inside my heart!)
Small reason for looking so dark;
Your godmother I will now play.

Your godmother I will now play;
With me as my page you shall stay.
And Helen, as bright as a lark,
(Oh, the pain, the pain, inside my heart!)
A bold Captain's daughter, I mark,
To her you'll be married one day.

To her you'll be married one day.
- No, no, I won't hear what you say;
My love is my tumbril, my cart,
(Oh, the pain, the pain, inside my heart!)
I want no reprieve, let it smart,
Let me die from it, Madam, I pray.

COUNTESS   It has a certain simplicity ... some feeling, even.

SUZANNE   *(Going over to lay the guitar on a chair)* Oh! If you want feeling, this is a young man who ... Yes, well now, bold officer, did Figaro tell you about this evening's plans? We're going to liven the celebrations up, and first we need to know whether you can get into one of my dresses.

COUNTESS	I fear not.

SUZANNE	*(Measuring herself against him)* He's about my height. Let's get your coat off to begin with.

> *She removes his coat.*

COUNTESS	What if someone were to come in?

SUZANNE	Are we doing anything wrong, then? I'll go and lock the door. *(She runs over and does so.)* But I want to see what we can do with his hair.

COUNTESS	On my dressing table, there's a bonnet of mine.

> *Suzanne goes into the dressing room by the door down left.*

SCENE FIVE

Cherubin, the Countess (seated)

COUNTESS	Until the ball begins, the Count will not know you are in the castle. We shall tell him afterwards that the delay while waiting for your commission to be drawn up gave us the idea...

CHERUBIN	*(Showing her the document)* Sadly, Madame, I have it here. Bazile handed it to me on his behalf.

COUNTESS	So soon? They're frightened to lose a minute. *(She reads.)* They were in such a hurry, they have forgotten to attach his seal.

SCENE SIX

Cherubin, the Countess, Suzanne.

SUZANNE	*(Enters, carrying a large bonnet.)* A seal? What for?

COUNTESS	To confirm his commission.

SUZANNE	Already?
COUNTESS	Just what I was saying. Is that my bonnet?
SUZANNE	*(Sits beside the Countess.)* And the prettiest one of all. *(She sings, with pins in her mouth.)* "Turn and face me, handsome boy, John the Bold, my pride and joy." *(Cherubin kneels. She arranges his hair under the bonnet.)* Madame, doesn't he look charming!
COUNTESS	Arrange it at the neck to look more feminine.
SUZANNE	*(Arranging it)* There... But look at the youth, doesn't he make a pretty girl! I feel quite jealous of him! *(She takes his chin.)* Do you mind not looking as pretty as that?
COUNTESS	Foolish girl! He'll need his sleeves rolled up to get the dress on... *(She rolls back a shirt-sleeve.)* What's this on his arm? A ribbon?
SUZANNE	And a ribbon of yours. I am very pleased Madame has seen it. I told him I'd tell on him, so there! Ah, but if the Count hadn't come in, I promise I'd have got the ribbon back, I'm nearly as strong as he is.
COUNTESS	There's blood on it!
	She unties the ribbon.
CHERUBIN	*(Shame-faced)* I was arranging the horse's curb chain this morning, thinking I was about to leave. He tossed his head and the bit-pin grazed my arm.
COUNTESS	But no one ever uses a ribbon to ...
SUZANNE	And especially a stolen ribbon. Let's see the damage this horse's curb chain,... curvet,... cornet,... whatever these silly names mean... Oh! Isn't his arm white! It's like a woman's arm! Whiter than mine! Look, Madame!

> *She holds her arm next to Cherubin's for compari-*
> *son.*

COUNTESS   *(Icily)* You would be more usefully occupied find-
                ing some sticking plaster in my dressing room.

> *Suzanne laughs and pushes Cherubin's head*
> *away. He falls on his hands and knees. She goes*
> *into the dressing room down left.*

SCENE SEVEN

Cherubin (on his knees), the Countess (seated)

COUNTESS   *(Staring at the ribbon for a moment, without speak-*
                ing. Cherubin feasts his eyes on her.) On the sub-
                ject of my ribbon, Sir..., since it is the one whose
                colour suits me particularly well..., I was very
                angry to have lost it.

SCENE EIGHT

Cherubin (kneeling), the Countess (seated), Suzanne.

SUZANNE   *(Coming back)* And what shall we do for a ban-
                dage?

COUNTESS   When you are bringing him some clothes of yours,
                take the ribbon from another bonnet.

> *Suzanne exits by the upstage door, taking*
> *Cherubin's coat.*

SCENE NINE

Cherubin (kneeling), the Countess (seated).

CHERUBIN   *(Eyes lowered)* The one you have taken away
                would have healed me in no time.

COUNTESS	How could it do that? *(Showing him the plaster)* This works much better.
CHERUBIN	*(Hesitantly)* When a ribbon ... has been tied round the head... or touched the skin of a person ...
COUNTESS	*(Cutting him off)* ... you don't know at all well, it becomes ideal for treating wounds? It has properties I was unaware of. To try it out, I shall keep the one which bound your arm. The first time I get a scratch ... one of my women does, I shall put it to the test.
CHERUBIN	*(Stricken)* You are keeping it, and I am going away.
COUNTESS	Not for ever.
CHERUBIN	I am so unhappy!
COUNTESS	*(Moved)* Now look, he's crying! It's that dreadful Figaro with his terrible predictions!
CHERUBIN	*(In a state of exaltation)* Ah! All I want is to meet the fate he prophesied! On the point of death, perhaps then my lips would dare ...
COUNTESS	*(Interrupting him and drying his eyes with a handkerchief)* Quiet, child, quiet! There's not a scrap of sense in anything you say. *(A knock at the main door. She calls out.)* Who is knocking at my room like that?

SCENE TEN

Cherubin, the Countess, the Count (outside)

COUNT	*(Outside)* Why is your door locked?
COUNTESS	*(Alarmed, getting to her feet)* It's my husband! My God!... *(To Cherubin, also on his feet)* You here,

with no coat on, your shoulders and arms bare!
Alone with me! All this disarray, and that note
he's had, and his jealousy!...

COUNT   *(Outside)* Aren't you going to unlock the door?

COUNTESS   I locked it because ... I was by myself.

COUNT   *(Outside)* By yourself! ... Who are you talking to,
then?

COUNTESS   *(Desperate)*   ... To you, of course.

CHERUBIN   *(Aside)*   After what happened yesterday and this
morning, he'll kill me on the spot!

> *He runs into the dressing room and pulls the door
> shut behind him.*

SCENE ELEVEN

Countess (alone)

COUNTESS   *(Removes the dressing room key and runs to let the
Count in)* Oh! What a terrible mistake!

SCENE TWELVE

The Count, the Countess.

COUNT   *(Rather sharply)* You are not in the habit of lock-
ing yourself in!

COUNTESS   *(Confused)*   I ... I was sewing... Yes, I was
sewing with Suzanne.   She slipped out to her own
room for a moment.

COUNT   *(Looking at her closely)* You look different, and
your voice is odd!

COUNTESS   That is not surprising ... not surprising at all ... I assure you ... We were talking about you ... She's just slipped out, as I say ...

COUNT Talking about me!... I came back because I was anxious. While I was out riding, I was sent a note - I don't give it any credit - but nevertheless ... it disturbed me.

COUNTESS What's that, Sir? ... What note?

COUNT It has to be admitted, Madame, that either you or I are surrounded by creatures of ... of considerable ill-will! I am informed that during the day someone I believe to be absent will make an attempt to see you.

COUNTESS Whoever the foolhardy man is, he will have to break into my bedroom, for I intend not to leave it all day.

COUNT And Suzanne's wedding, this evening?

COUNTESS Not even for that. I am not at all well.

COUNT It's fortunate the Doctor is here. *(Cherubin knocks a chair over in the dressing room.)* What's that noise?

COUNTESS *(Even more troubled)* Noise?

COUNT Somebody knocked a piece of furniture over.

COUNTESS I ... *I* didn't hear anything.

COUNT Then you must be extremely distracted.

COUNTESS Distracted? What by?

COUNT There is someone in your dressing room, Madame.

COUNTESS What? ... Who do you imagine could be in there, Sir?

COUNT	That's why I'm asking. I have only just arrived.
COUNTESS	Ah, but ... Well, obviously it's Suzanne doing some tidying.
COUNT	You said she had slipped out to her own room!
COUNTESS	Slipped out ... or perhaps slipped in there. I don't remember where she went.
COUNT	If it's Suzanne, why are you looking so concerned?
COUNTESS	Concerned, for my chambermaid?
COUNT	For your chambermaid, I can't tell. But you're concerned about something, that's very plain.
COUNTESS	It is very plain to me, Sir, this girl troubles you far more than than she troubles me.
COUNT	*(Angry)* She troubles me sufficiently, Madame, to wish to see her immediately.
COUNTESS	Indeed, I believe that is your wish all too often. But these suspicions are quite without foundation...

SCENE THIRTEEN

The Count, the Countess; Suzanne (entering upstage with some clothes).

COUNT	Then they will be all the more easy to dismantle. *(He shouts in the direction of the dressing room.)* Come out, Suzon, I order you out here.

Suzanne stops beside the alcove upstage.

COUNTESS	She has virtually nothing on, Sir. Is it right to come and disturb women's privacy in this way? She was trying on the clothes I am giving her for her wedding. She fled when she heard you at the door.

COUNT   If she's too frightened to show herself, at least she can speak. *(He crosses to the dressing room door.)* Answer me, Suzanne; are you in that dressing room?

        Suzanne, still upstage, darts into the alcove and hides.

COUNTESS   *(Sharply, turning to the dressing room)* Suzon, I forbid you to answer. *(To the Count)* This is taking bullying too far!

COUNT   *(Striding up to the dressing room)* Very well! Since she won't speak, I will see her, dressed or not!

COUNTESS   *(Barring his way)* Anywhere else, I can't prevent you. But I hope that in my own room ...

COUNT   And I hope that in a moment I shall discover who this mysterious Suzanne is. I can see it would be futile to ask you for the key. But it's a simple matter to break down this flimsy door. A servant there!

COUNTESS   Do you want to summon the servants and make a public scandal? The very suspicion itself would be the talk of the castle!

COUNT   So be it, Madame. I can do the job myself. I shall go and fetch the tools I require straight away ... *(He moves towards the door, then comes back.)* But just to make sure everything here remains as it is, perhaps you would care to come with me, without scandal or fuss, of course, since you hate them so much?... Clearly, you won't refuse me something as simple as that!

COUNTESS   *(Confused)* Ah! Sir, who would want to go against your wishes?

COUNT   Oh! I was forgetting the door to your women's quarters. I must lock that one as well so you can be proved entirely right.

>*He goes and locks the upstage door, removing the key.*

COUNTESS   *(Aside)* My God, he's obsessive!

COUNT   *(Coming back to her)* Now this bedroom is sealed off, give me your arm, please. *(He raises his voice.)* And as for the Suzanne in the dressing room, she must be kind enough to wait for me. And if the slightest harm comes to her before my return ...

COUNTESS   Really, Sir, this is the most horrible situation ...

>*The Count leads her out and locks the door behind them.*

SCENE FOURTEEN

Suzanne, Cherubin.

SUZANNE   *(Leaving the alcove, running to the dressing room and calling through the keyhole)* Open up, Cherubin, open up, quick! It's Suzanne! Open the door and come out!

CHERUBIN   *(Emerging)* Ah! Suzon, what a terrible scene!

SUZANNE   Come on out, you haven't a second to lose.

CHERUBIN   *(Frightened)* How am I going to get away?

SUZANNE   I've no idea, but you can't stay in there.

CHERUBIN   What if there's no escape?

SUZANNE   After that little encounter, he'll rip you to pieces. And the Countess and I would be done for. - You must run and tell Figaro ...

CHERUBIN   Perhaps the window to the garden isn't too high.

He runs over to look.

SUZANNE   *(Horrified)* A whole storey up! Impossible! Oh, my poor mistress! And my marriage, oh my God!

CHERUBIN   *(Coming back)* It looks out over the kitchen garden. I may have to crush a bed or two.

SUZANNE   *(Holding him back and crying out)* He'll get himself killed!

CHERUBIN   *(In a state of exaltation)* If it were a blazing pit, Suzon, I would jump into it! Yes, I would, sooner than bring her any harm! ... And this kiss will bring me luck.

> *He embraces her and takes a running leap out of the window.*

SCENE FIFTEEN

Suzanne (alone).

SUZANNE   Ah! ... *(She gives a cry of horror and collapses in a chair. After a moment she goes stiffly to look out of the window and comes back.)* He's miles away already. Ah, the little imp, he's as agile as he's pretty. If that one ever goes short of women ... Let's take his place without delay. *(Entering the dressing room)* Now you may smash down the door if you like, my lord Count; I'm damned if I'll utter a word even if you do!

> *She locks herself in.*

SCENE SIXTEEN

The Count and Countess, (coming back into the bedroom).

COUNT   *(Carrying a crowbar, which he throws on to a chair)* It is all just as I left it. Madame, in forcing me to break down the door, consider the consequences.

I'll ask you once more: will you unlock it?

COUNTESS   Ah, Sir! What is this dreadful state of mind which lets you shatter the mutual respect betwen husband and wife? If it was love driving you to these acts of folly, I could forgive them in spite of their wildness. Given that motive, I could even forget how offensive they are to me. But is it possible that sheer vanity can drive a man of honour to such excesses?

COUNT   Vanity or love, I demand that you open the door, or in two seconds, I'll ...

COUNTESS   *(Barring his way)* Please, Sir, stop. Can you really believe me capable of failing in my duty to myself?

COUNT   I'll believe anything you like, Madame. But I intend to see who is in that dressing room.

COUNTESS   *(Frightened)* All right, Sir, you shall see. Listen to me ... calmly.

COUNT   So it's not Suzanne.

COUNTESS   *(Timidly)* In any case, it's not a person ... you have nothing to fear from anyway ... We were preparing a little practical joke ... perfectly innocent, believe me, for this evening... and I swear to you ...

COUNT   You swear to me...?

COUNTESS   That neither he nor I had the slightest intention of giving you any offence.

COUNT   *(Pouncing)* Neither he nor I? So it's a man.

COUNTESS   A child, Sir.

COUNT   Well, who then?

COUNTESS   I hardly dare say his name!

COUNT   *(Furious)* I'll kill him!

COUNTESS   Oh, my God!

COUNT   Tell me!

COUNTESS   It was young ... Cherubin ...

COUNT   Cherubin! The impudent...! That proves both
               my suspicions and the contents of the note.

COUNTESS   *(Clasping her hands)* Ah! Sir! You mustn't think
               ...

COUNT   *(Aside, stamping his foot)* I find that damned page
               wherever I go! *(Aloud)* All right, Madame, open
               the door. Now I know the whole story. You
               wouldn't have been so affected when he said good-
               bye this morning; what's more, he would have left
               when I ordered, and you wouldn't have concocted
               such a lying tale about Suzanne, and he wouldn't
               have hidden himself with such care, if there had
               been nothing criminal behind it all.

COUNTESS   He was scared to anger you by showing himself.

COUNT   *(Beside himself, yelling in the direction of the dressing
               room)* Come out, then, you little wretch!

COUNTESS   *(Seizing him round the waist and pulling him away)*
               Ah! Sir! Sir, your anger makes me frightened for
               him. I beg you, don't give way to unjust suspi-
               cions, and however disarrayed you find him now
               ...

COUNT   Disarrayed!

COUNTESS   I fear so, yes. In readiness for dressing up as a
               woman. He is wearing one of my bonnets, and he
               has no coat on, and his shirt is open and his arms
               bare. He was just going to try on ...

COUNT   And you were intending to stay in your bedroom

all day! And you call yourself my wife! Oh, you'll
be staying in your room all right, I'll see to that!
But first I'm going to throw that insolent wretch
out of it, and throw him so far I'll never set eyes
on him again.

COUNTESS   *(Throwing herself on her knees, arms raised in
entreaty)* My Lord, spare a mere child. I could
never forgive myself for being the cause ...

COUNT   Your alarm only worsens his crime.

COUNTESS   He is guilty of no crime, he was leaving. I was the
one who made him come back.

COUNT   *(Furious)* Stand up! Get out of here ...   You
have the nerve to plead with me for another man!

COUNTESS   Very well! I shall go, Sir, I shall get to my feet and
leave. You may even have the dressing room key.
But in the name of your love ...

COUNT   My love! Treacherous woman!

COUNTESS   *(Rising, and holding out the key)* Promise me you
will let that child go without any harm, and after
wards save all your rage for me, if I fail to convince
you ...

COUNT   *(Taking the key)* I don't hear a word you say.

COUNTESS   *(Throwing herself on a divan, a handkerchief over her
eyes)* Oh, my God! He's going to be killed!

COUNT   *(Opening the door and jumping back)* It's Suzanne!

SCENE SEVENTEEN

The Countess, the Count, Suzanne.

SUZANNE   *(Laughing as she emerges)* "I'll kill him! I'll kill
him!" Kill him, then, the wicked page!

COUNT	*(Aside)* Ah! What a trick! *(Looking at the Countess, who is stunned)* And you too, are you pretending to be astonished? ... But perhaps she's not the only one in there.

He goes into the dressing room.

SCENE EIGHTEEN

The Countess (seated), Suzanne.

SUZANNE	*(Rushing across to her mistress)* Collect yourself, madame, it's all right. He's miles away. He jumped ...
COUNTESS	Oh! Suzon, I'm half dead.

SCENE NINETEEN

The Countess (seated), Suzanne, the Count.

COUNT	*(Emerges from the dressing room looking confused. A short silence)* There's no one there. I'm wrong about this one. - Madame, it's a pretty game you're playing here.
SUZANNE	*(Cheerfully)* What about my part, Sir?

The Countess, recovering her wits behind her handkerchief, says nothing.

COUNT	*(Approaching the Countess)* Madame, you mean you were joking?
COUNTESS	*(Recovering a little)* And why not, Sir?
COUNT	What an appalling sense of humour! And what was the idea behind it, am I allowed to ask?

COUNTESS	Did you think your wild behaviour deserved pity?
COUNT	You call it wild when it's a question of my honour!
COUNTESS	*(Sounding steadily more confident)* Did I marry you to become a permanent victim of neglect and jealousy? Of which you dare to set yourself up as the sole arbiter?
COUNT	Ah! Madame, that is not my intention.
SUZANNE	Madame had only to let you go ahead and call in your servants.
COUNT	You are quite right, and I should be humbly grateful... Forgive me, I am so confused!...
SUZANNE	Admit it, Sir, you did deserve it a bit.
COUNT	But why didn't you come out when I called you? You're a wicked girl!
SUZANNE	I was getting my clothes back on, as best I could, there were a great many pins; and Madame who told me not to was perfectly justified in that.
COUNT	Instead of reminding me I was in the wrong, why don't you help me make it up to her?
COUNTESS	No, Sir. I can't pretend to ignore an outrage as deep as that. I intend to retire to the Ursuline convent, and I can see it is not before time.
COUNT	You couldn't do that, surely, not without some regrets at least?
SUZANNE	For my part, I know for certain there'd be tears here the day after you'd left.
COUNTESS	Ah, if that were only true, Suzon. I would rather weep for him than be base enough to forgive him. He has offended me too deeply for that.

COUNT	Rosine!...
COUNTESS	I'm not that girl any more, the Rosine you pursued so fiercely! I am poor Countess Almaviva, the sad, deserted wife you no longer love.
SUZANNE	Madame ...
COUNT	*(Begging)* For pity's sake!...
COUNTESS	You had none for me.
COUNT	But there was that note ... It made me see red!
COUNTESS	It was not written with my agreement.
COUNT	You knew about it?
COUNTESS	It was that irresponsible Figaro...
COUNT	*He* was in on it?
COUNTESS	... who gave it to Bazile.
COUNT	Who told me he had it from a peasant. You treacherous music man! You double-edged sword! You shall pay for everybody's misfortunes!
COUNTESS	You ask pardon for yourself when you refuse it to others. That's typical of a man. If I ever agreed to forgive your offence because of the letter that drove you to it, I would require the forgiveness to be on all sides.
COUNT	With all my heart, Countess. But how can I redeem so humiliating an error?
COUNTESS	*(Rising)* Humiliating for both of us.
COUNT	Oh, say it was all on my side! - But I have yet to understand how women can suit their words and looks to the situation so aptly and so quickly. You were red in the face, you were crying, your compo

sure had gone... To tell the truth, you look the same now.

COUNTESS *(Forcing a smile)* I was red ... with anger at your suspicions. But are men subtle enough to distinguish between the indignation of an honest soul outraged, and the embarrassment of a genuine culprit justly accused?

COUNT *(Smiling)* And this pageboy in disarray, no coat and almost naked ...

COUNTESS *(Indicating Suzanne)* He stands before you. Aren't you glad to have found this one and not the other? Generally speaking, you are not averse to meeting this one.

COUNT *(Laughing louder)* And all that pleading, those fake tears ...

COUNTESS You make me laugh, though I scarcely feel like it.

COUNT Men think they have a talent for political life, but they're mere children. You women, Madame, you're the ones the King should be sending out to London as his ambassadors! Your sex must have made a deep study of the art of appearances, to succeed so brilliantly!

COUNTESS It's always men who force us to it.

SUZANNE You'd only have to let us out into the world, like prisoners on parole, and you'd soon see whether we could be trusted.

COUNTESS Let's say no more, Sir. Perhaps I went too far. But if you want my indulgence over such a grave situation, you at least owe me yours.

COUNT But you will confirm that you forgive me.

COUNTESS Did I say that, Suzon?

SUZANNE	I didn't hear it, Madame.
COUNT	Well, say the word now!
COUNTESS	Do you deserve it, then, ungrateful man?
COUNT	Yes, because I repent.
SUZANNE	Suspecting Madame of having a man in her dressing room!
COUNT	She has punished me for it harshly enough!
SUZANNE	Doubting her word when she tells you it is her chambermaid!
COUNT	Rosine, are you not to be moved?
COUNTESS	Oh! Suzon, I am weak! What an example to set you! *(Giving the Count her hand)* A woman's anger will never be feared again.
SUZANNE	Ah, well! In the end, Madame, isn't this what we always have to come down to, with men?

The Count kisses the hand of his wife fervently.

SCENE TWENTY

Suzanne, Figaro, the Countess, the Count.

FIGARO	*(Arriving out of breath)* They said that Madame was unwell. I came as fast as I could ... I'm delighted to see it was a false alarm.
COUNT	*(Drily)* You are most attentive.
FIGARO	It is no more than my duty. But seeing that it *is* a false alarm, Sir, all your young subjects, men and women, are downstairs with their violins and bagpipes, waiting to form an escort as soon as you give the signal for me to lead my bride ...

COUNT   And who will stay to attend the Countess in the
             castle?

FIGARO   Attend her! She isn't ill.

COUNT   No. But what about that man who isn't here who
             is going to make an attempt to see her?

FIGARO   What man who isn't here?

COUNT   The man in the note you wrote for Bazile.

FIGARO   Who says that?

COUNT   Listen, villain, if I didn't know it anyway, the
             expression on your face gives you away and proves
             you're lying.

FIGARO   If that's the case, I'm not the liar, the expression
             on my face is.

SUZANNE   Give up, my poor Figaro. Don't waste your elo-
             quence in defeat. We have told the whole story.

FIGARO   Told what story? You're treating me like another
             Bazile!

SUZANNE   How you wrote that letter to make the Count
             believe that when he got here he'd find the little
             page in this dressing room where I had shut myself
             in.

COUNT   What have you to say to that?

COUNTESS   There's nothing left to hide, Figaro. Our little
             joke has run its course.

FIGARO   *(Trying to guess what she means)* The little joke ...
             has run its course?

COUNT   Run its course, yes. What do you say to that?

FIGARO   Me? I say ... I wish the same could be said for my marriage ceremony, and if you give the word ...

COUNT   So you admit the story of the letter?

FIGARO   Since Madame wishes it, since Suzanne wishes it, and since you wish it yourself, then I have no choice but to wish it as well. But to tell you the truth, Sir, if I were in your place, I wouldn't believe a word of what we're telling you.

COUNT   Against all the evidence, you're still prepared to lie! You'll end up making me angry!

COUNTESS   *(Laughing)* Ah, the poor fellow! Why do you want him to tell the truth for once, Sir?

FIGARO   *(Aside, to Suzanne)* I warn him of the danger he's in; what more can an honest man do?

SUZANNE   *(Aside)* Have you seen Cherubin?

FIGARO   *(Aside)* Still pretty shaken.

SUZANNE   *(Aside)* Ah! The poor boy!

COUNTESS   Come, Sir. They're dying to be married. It's only natural they're impatient. Let us go down for the ceremony.

COUNT   *(Aside)* And Marceline, Marceline ... *(Aloud)* I need at least ... to dress suitably for the occasion.

COUNTESS   For our own servants? Have *I* done so?

SCENE TWENTY-ONE

Figaro, Suzanne, the Countess, the Count, Antonio.

ANTONIO   *(Half drunk, carrying a pot of flattened wallflowers)* My Lord! My Lord!

COUNT	What do you want with me, Antonio?
ANTONIO	Once and for all, I insist you put bars on the windows overlooking my flower-beds. They chuck all kinds of things out of those windows, and just now they chucked out a man.
COUNT	From this window?
ANTONIO	Look what they've done to my wallflowers!
SUZANNE	*(Aside, to Figaro)* Watch out, Figaro! Keep your wits about you!
FIGARO	Sir, the man's been drunk since this morning.
ANTONIO	That's a lie. It's left over from yesterday. See how people jump to false conclusions!
COUNT	*(Fiercely)* That man! It's that man! Where is he?
ANTONIO	You're asking me where he is?
COUNT	Yes.
ANTONIO	That's what I say. I've been after him already. I am your servant; there's only me to look after all your gardens. A man goes and drops on them, and, well, you can see ... there's my reputation gone to pot.
SUZANNE	*(Aside, to Figaro)* Side-track him, quick!
FIGARO	And you intend to go on drinking in spite of it?
ANTONIO	Ah! If I didn't drink, I'd go out of my mind.
COUNTESS	But you take much more than you need ...
ANTONIO	Ah, but you see, Madame, drinking when we're not thirsty and making love when we feel like it, that's all that tells us apart from the animals.

COUNT	*(Sharply)* Answer my question, if you want to keep your job.
ANTONIO	Oh, I wouldn't go.
COUNT	I beg your pardon!
ANTONIO	*(Tapping his forehead)* Maybe you haven't got enough up here to know when to keep a good servant, but I'm not daft enough to sack a good master.
COUNT	*(In a rage, shaking him)* You're telling me they threw a man out of this window?
ANTONIO	Yes, Your Excellency, just now, wearing a white shirt, and he ran off, God's my witness, running ..
COUNT	*(Impatient)* And then?
ANTONIO	Well, I wanted to run after, but I caught myself such a crack against the gate with my hand, I can't move hide or hair of this finger.

Holds the finger up.

COUNT	At any rate, would you recognise the man?
ANTONIO	Oh! No mistake about that! ... If I'd had a chance to see who it was!
SUZANNE	*(Aside, to Figaro)* He didn't see him.
FIGARO	What a lot of fuss over a potted plant! How much do you want for your wallflower, you whining old fool? Sir, don't bother searching: it was me who jumped out.
COUNT	What do you mean, it was you?
ANTONIO	"How much do you want, whining old fool?" You've grown a lot bigger since then, because when I saw you, you were a lot littler and thinner!

FIGARO   Of course. When you jump, you bunch yourself
                        up...

ANTONIO   Looked to me as if was more like ... well, that
                        skinny little page.

COUNT   You mean Cherubin?

FIGARO   Oh, yes, very likely: came back especially, with his
                        horse, all the way from Seville; where doubtless
                        you'll find him at this moment.

ANTONIO   Oh, no! I'm not saying that, I'm not saying that.
                        I didn't see any horse jump out; I would have
                        mentioned it.

COUNT   God give me patience!

FIGARO   I was in the women's room, in my white shirt: my,
                        isn't it hot! I was waiting there for my Suzanne
                        when suddenly I heard the Count's voice and the
                        shouting going on. I don't know, I must have
                        taken fright because of that letter. Anyway, if I'm
                        forced to admit my stupidity, I jumped out with-
                        out thinking and landed on the flower-bed. I even
                        sprained my right ankle a bit.

                                He rubs his foot.

ANTONIO   Well, if it was you, it's only right to give you back
                        this bit of paper which came out of your jacket
                        when you fell.

COUNT   *(Seizing it)* Give it to me.

                        He looks at the paper and folds it up again.

FIGARO   *(Aside)* Now I've had it.

COUNT   *(To Figaro)* You didn't take fright so far as to for-
                        get what this paper is, or how it came to be in your
                        pocket?

FIGARO   *(Embarrassed, searches his pockets and pulls out vari-*
                ous papers) No, of course not ... But I have so
                many. There's so much to attend to ... *(He looks*
                at one of them.) What's this one? Ah! A letter
                from Marceline, four pages long; lovely ... And
                isn't this the petition from that poor poacher
                who's in prison? ... No, here it is ... I had the
                inventory of the castle furniture in the other pock-
                et ...

                The Count unfolds his paper again.

COUNTESS   *(Aside, to Suzanne)* Oh, my God, Suzon! It's the
                commissioning order!

SUZANNE   *(Aside, to Figaro)* We're done for, it's Cherubin's
                commission.

COUNT   *(Refolding the paper)* Well, quick-thinker, can't
                you hazard a guess?

ANTONIO   *(Approaching Figaro)* His Lordship wants to know
                if you can't guess!

FIGARO   *(Pushing him away)* Stand back! Old idiot, slob-
                bering over me!

COUNT   You don't recall what it might be?

FIGARO   A-a-a aha! What a fool! It'll be that young lad's
                commissioning order; he gave it to me and I forgot
                to hand it back. Tch-tch-tch! Aren't I half-wit-
                ted? What'll he do without his commission? I'll
                have to run ...

COUNT   Why would he have given it to you?

FIGARO   *(Embarrassed)* He ... he wanted me to do some-
                thing to it.

COUNT   *(Looking at the paper)* There's nothing wrong with
                it.

COUNTESS	*(Aside, to Suzanne)* The seal.
SUZANNE	*(Aside, to Figaro)* The seal's missing.
COUNT	*(To Figaro)* No answer, then?
FIGARO	It's just that ... well, actually there is something missing. He said it was normal to ...
COUNT	Normal! Normal! What's normal?
FIGARO	To attach your coat-of-arms as a seal. But then perhaps it wasn't worth the trouble.
COUNT	*(Re-examines the paper and screws it up in rage.)* Damn it, I'm fated to be kept in the dark. *(Aside)* Figaro is behind all this, does he think I won't get my revenge.

He is about to storm out. Figaro stops him.

FIGARO	Are you going, without giving the word for my marriage to proceed?

SCENE TWENTY-TWO

Bazile, Bartholo, Marceline, Figaro, the Count, Gripe-Soleil, the Countess, Suzanne, Antonio, servants and subjects of the Count.

MARCELINE	*(To the Count)* Don't give it, Sir. Before doing him that favour, you must do justice between us. He has obligations to me.
COUNT	*(Aside)* Here's my revenge, right on cue.
FIGARO	Obligations? What obligations? Explain youself.
MARCELINE	Oh, I'll explain myself, you cheat!...

The Countess sits on a divan. Suzanne stands behind her.

COUNT	What is this about, Marceline?
MARCELINE	A promise of marriage.
FIGARO	An IOU, that's all, for some money she lent.
MARCELINE	*(To the Count)* With a clause promising marriage. You are a great Lord, the leading justice of the province ...
COUNT	Present yourself at the Court Sessions; that's where I will judge everybody's dues.
BAZILE	*(Indicating Marceline)* In that case, will Your Excellency allow me to put forward my own claims on Marceline?
COUNT	*(Aside)* Ah! It's my letter-carrying scoundrel!
FIGARO	Another madman of the same sort!
COUNT	*(Angrily, to Bazile)* Your claims! Your claims! You dare speak out before me, you prize oaf!
ANTONIO	*(Punching his hand with his fist)* My word, got him in one! That's him, all right!
COUNT	Marceline, everything is postponed until your claims can be examined, which will take place publicly in the Great Hall. Honest Bazile, my sure and faithful agent, make your way to town to summon the lawyers for the Sessions.
BAZILE	To plead her case?
COUNT	And you will bring me the peasant who passed on the letter.
BAZILE	Am I supposed to know who he is?
COUNT	You refuse?
BAZILE	I didn't come to the castle to run its errands!

COUNT   What *are* you here for, then?

BAZILE   As a man of specialised gifts, I am the local organ-
               ist; I give harpsichord lessons to the Countess, I
               teach singing to her ladies, I instruct the pages on
               the mandolin, and my principal role is to brighten
               your day with my guitar whenever it is your plea-
               sure to hear me play.

GRIPE-SOLEIL   *(Stepping forward)* I'll go, Your Lordship, Sir, if it
               please you to ask.

COUNT   Who are you, and what do you do here?

GRIPE-SOLEIL   I'm Gripe-Soleil, Your kind Lordship, Sir, the lit-
               tle goat-herd, sent here for the fireworks. It's a
               holiday for the goats today; and I know where to
               find all that parcel of lawyer men.

COUNT   I am impressed by your keenness. Go. But you
               (To Bazile), go with the gentleman for company.
               Take a guitar and sing to entertain him on the
               way. He is one of my party.

GRIPE-SOLEIL   *(Excitedly)* I am? Me? I'm one of his...!

               Suzanne shuts him up with a wave of the hand,
               indicating the Countess.

BAZILE   *(Surprised)* You want me to go with Gripe-Soleil
               and *play* to him?

COUNT   That's what you're here for. On your way, or
               you're sacked.

               Exit Count.

SCENE TWENTY-THREEE

As before, minus the Count.

BAZILE   *(To himself)* Ah! There's no point in arguing with the high and mighty; what am I but a poor ...

FIGARO   Fiddler.

BAZILE   *(Aside)* I'm not sharing in their wedding celebra-
                tions. I'll go off and see about mine with
                Marceline instead. *(To Figaro)* Don't finalise any-
                thing, mind you, until I get back.

                *He goes over to collect the guitar from the chair
                upstage.*

FIGARO   *(Following him)* Finalise! Go on, get on your way,
                don't trouble yourself! You needn't bother com-
                ing back at all... You don't appear to be singing
                yet; do you want me to start for you?... Look live-
                ly, now! A nice tra-la for my bride.

                *He sets off, dancing backwards, leading Bazile,
                playing the guitar, and the whole company, who
                dance off in procession.*

FIGARO   *(Leading the seguidilla as they go off)*
                You can keep your rich pesetas,
                For no one is as great as
                My Suzon!
                Zon, zon, zon,
                Zon, zon, zon,
                Zon, zon, zon,
                Zon, zon, zon,

                No sweeter girl or wiser,
                No wonder that my eyes are
                On Suzon!
                Zon, zon, zon,
                Zon, zon, zon,
                Zon, zon, zon,
                Zon, zon, zon.

                The sound grows fainter and the rest is lost.

SCENE TWENTY-FOUR

Suzanne, the Countess.

COUNTESS   *(In her easy-chair)*   You see the fine scene your
                idiotic Figaro dragged me into with his letter.

SUZANNE   Oh, Madame! If you could have seen your face
                when I came out of the dressing room! It sudden-
                ly drained of all its colour. But it was only a pass-
                ing shadow, and gradually you began to go red,
                red as red!

COUNTESS   Did he really leap out of the window?

SUZANNE   He never hesitated, the sweet boy! Light as a but-
                terfly.

COUNTESS   Oh, that dreadful gardener! I was so shaken, I
                couldn't put two ideas together.

SUZANNE   Oh, Madame! On the contrary! It made me mar-
                vel at the way high born ladies can use their
                knowledge of society to lie without a trace of it
                showing.

COUNTESS   Do you think the Count was fooled? What if he
                finds the child in the castle?

SUZANNE   I'll make sure he's hidden so well ...

COUNTESS   He must go. After what's just happened, you'll
                understand that I can't send him to take your
                place in the garden.

SUZANNE   And I'm not going, that's for certain. So there
                goes my marriage again...

COUNTESS   *(Rising)* Wait ... instead of sending someone else
                or letting you go, what if I went myself?

SUZANNE   You, Madame?

COUNTESS   Then no one would be in any danger... And the Count couldn't deny any of it ... To punish him for his jealousy, and then give him proof of his infidelity, that would be ... Come on, the luck is on our side. We got away with it the first time: I don't see why we shouldn't get away with it again. We need to let him know quickly you'll meet him in the garden. But above all, don't let anybody ...

SUZANNE   Oh! Figaro...

COUNTESS   No, no. He'll only want to embroider the plan ... Fetch me my velvet mask and my cane, and I'll go out on the terrace and think about it.

Suzanne goes into the dressing room.

SCENE TWENTY-FIVE

The Countess (alone).

COUNTESS   My little plan, it's terribly impudent! *(She turns round.)* Ah, the ribbon! My pretty ribbon! I'd forgotten you! *(She picks it up off the easy-chair and rolls it up.)* I won't let you out of my sight again... You'll always remind me of the scene when that unhappy child ... Ah! My lord Count, what have you done? And me, the Countess, whatever am I doing now?

SCENE TWENTY-SIX

The Countess, Suzanne.
The Countess slips the ribbon into her dress.

SUZANNE   Here are your cane and your mask.

COUNTESS   Don't forget, I forbid you to say a word to Figaro.

SUZANNE   *(Happily)* Madame, I think your plan is wonderful. I've been thinking about it. It draws all the

strands together, ties them up, and settles everything. And whatever happens, my marriage is now
assured.

She kisses her mistress's hand. They both go out.

*During the interval, servants arrange the Great
Hall for the Court Sessions. Two high-backed
benches for the barristers, one down each side of the
room, with space to pass behind. A dais in the
middle, slightly upstage, with two steps leading up
to it. On the dais, the Count's presidential chair.
The clerk's table and chair downstage, to one side,
and seats for Brid'oison and other judges on either
side of the Count's dais.*

END OF ACT TWO

ACT THREE

SCENE ONE

The throne room of the castle, acting as Great Hall for the Court Sessions; on one side a portrait of the King, under a canopy.

The Count, Pedrillo (in riding coat and boots, holding a sealed package).

COUNT   *(Speaking rapidly)* Have you got that quite clear?

PEDRILLO   Yes, Your Excellency.

          He goes out.

SCENE TWO

The Count (alone, calling out).

COUNT   Pedrillo!

SCENE THREE

The Count, Pedrillo (returning).

PEDRILLO   Excellency?

COUNT   Has anyone seen you?

PEDRILLO   Not a soul.

COUNT   Take the fastest horse.

PEDRILLO   It's at the kitchen garden gate, saddled and ready.

COUNT   Ride hard, don't stop until you get to Seville.

PEDRILLO   It's only three leagues, and a good road.

COUNT	As soon as you get there, find out if the page has arrived.
PEDRILLO	At the house?
COUNT	Yes, and above all, how long he's been there.
PEDRILLO	Understood.
COUNT	Deliver his commission, then come back quickly.
PEDRILLO	What if he isn't there?
COUNT	Come back even quicker, and tell me. On your way.

SCENE FOUR

The Count (alone, striding up and down as he reflects).

COUNT   It was a mistake to send Bazile away! ... Anger serves no good purpose. - That letter he passed on, warning me of some attempt on the Countess ... The chambermaid locked in when I arrive ... My wife overcome by a terror which could be false or real ... One man jumps out of the window and later another man confesses... or pretends it was him ... I can't make the connection. There are some dark deeds in all this!... My subjects taking liberties, well, that's no matter with people like that. But the Countess! If some insolent man were to attempt to... Where's my mind going? The truth is, once you start to get worked up, even the best controlled imagination takes off wildly, like a bad dream! - She was just having a joke: that stifled laughter, the ill-concealed amusement! - She has too much respect for her position; and what about my honour ... where the devil does that stand now? On the other hand, where do I stand? Has that impudent Suzanne given away my secret? Figaro hasn't got her yet!... Why am I prisoner of this ridiculous fantasy? I've tried to give it up a dozen times ... Strange how uncertainty makes matters worse! If it wasn't such a struggle, I wouldn't desire her half as much! - That Figaro can be relied on to keep a man waiting! I must sound him out carefully ... *(Figaro appears upstage; he stops.)* ... and try to find out in the course of conversation whether he knows about my feelings for Suzanne.

SCENE FIVE

The Count, Figaro.

FIGARO	*(Aside)* Now we know where we are.
COUNT	... If she's breathed a single word of it ...
FIGARO	*(Aside)* I thought as much.
COUNT	... I'll see he marries that old woman.
FIGARO	*(Aside)* Bazile's love-bird, eh?
COUNT	... And then let's see what can be done with the girl.
FIGARO	*(Aside)* Ha! My wife, if you don't mind.
COUNT	*(Turning round)* Eh! What? What's that?
FIGARO	*(Stepping forward)* Just me, coming to see you, as ordered.
COUNT	And why did you say that, just then?
FIGARO	I didn't say anything.
COUNT	*(Repeating his words)* "My wife, if you don't mind"?
FIGARO	Er ... that was just the end of something I was saying to someone: "Could you go and tell my wife,

if you don't mind."

COUNT   *(Pacing up and down)* "His wife"! ... I would be glad to hear what business has kept my servant so long when I ordered him to meet me here.

FIGARO   *(Pretending to smooth down his clothes)* I made myself dirty falling in the flower-bed. I was getting changed.

COUNT   Does it take an hour?

FIGARO   It takes time.

COUNT   The servants here ... they take as long to get dressed as the masters!

FIGARO   That's because they don't have any servants to help them.

COUNT   ... I'm still not altogether clear what made you do such a risky thing just now as to jump through an open window ...

FIGARO   Risky? Anyone would think I'd been buried alive!...

COUNT   Don't try to put me off by deliberately getting hold of the wrong end of the stick, you insidious servant! You know perfectly well it's not the risk I'm concerned with: I want to know the reason for it.

FIGARO   You arrive in a fury, on a false piece of information, knocking everything out of your path like the torrent coming down from the Sierra Morena; and you're looking for a man, you're determined to find a man, or else you'll smash all the locks and break down the doors! And there, by chance, am I: who knows what you might do in your rage ...

COUNT   *(Interrupting)* You could have used the stairs.

FIGARO   And be caught by you in the corridor.

COUNT   *(Angry)* In the corridor? *(Aside)* I'm getting car-
                 ried away. I won't find out what I want to know.

FIGARO   *(Aside)* Let's see what's coming, and play it tight.

COUNT   *(Softening his tone)* That wasn't what I wanted to
                 talk about, let's drop the subject. I had an idea ...
                 yes, I had an idea I might take you to London with
                 me as my messenger,... but thinking about it
                 again, ...

FIGARO   The Count has changed his mind?

COUNT   In the first place, you don't know any English.

FIGARO   I know "God damn it".

COUNT   I don't follow you.

FIGARO   I say, I know "God damn it".

COUNT   What of it?

FIGARO   Well, heavens! I mean, English is a wonderful lan-
                 guage. You can go a long way with very little. In
                 England, if you can manage "God damn it", you'll
                 never go short wherever you are. - You fancy a
                 mouthful of plump, tasty chicken? Just enter a
                 tavern and go like this to the waiter... *(He turns a
                 spit.)*: "God damn it!" - and they bring you a
                 knuckle of beef and no bread. Marvellous! Or
                 you think you'd like a nice bottle of good bur-
                 gundy or claret? You simply go ... *(He pulls a
                 cork.)*: "God damn it!" - they serve you up a
                 pewter pot of beer with froth running all down the
                 sides. Wonderful! You meet one of those pretty
                 young women who trip along with their elbows
                 jutting and waggling their hips? Put your fingers
                 daintily to your lips, ah! "God damn it!": she
                 fetches you such a clout your head's ringing.
                 Which proves she has understood. It's true, the
                 English drop a few extra words into the general
                 conversation here and there, but it's easy to tell

that "God damn it" is the basis of the language. And if that's the only reason why the Count is intending to leave me behind in Spain, ...

COUNT   *(Aside)* He wants to come to London. She can't have said anything.

FIGARO   *(Aside)* He thinks I don't know. Let's play his game a bit more.

COUNT   Tell me why the Countess decided to play a trick like that on me.

FIGARO   Heavens, Sir, you must know better than I do.

COUNT   I think of everything she might want, I give her presents all the time.

FIGARO   You give her things, but you don't remain faithful to her. Women can't take any pleasure in luxuries when they're deprived of necessities.

COUNT   ... There was a time when you told me everything.

FIGARO   And now I conceal nothing from you.

COUNT   How much has the Countess given you to take sides with her in this charming manner?

FIGARO   How much did you give me for prising her from the Doctor's clutches once? So, Sir, let's not humiliate the man who supports his master loyally, for fear of turning him into a bad servant.

COUNT   Why does there always have to be something shifty about what you do?

FIGARO   Just that you see shiftiness all around you when you're looking for the wrong in people.

COUNT   It's an appalling reputation to have!

FIGARO   Who says I'm not a better man than people think?

Are there many noblemen who can claim as much?

COUNT   Dozens of times I've seen you heading towards your fortune, but never once in a straight line.

FIGARO   What do you expect? Everyone's on the same road, and everyone's in a hurry. They jostle, they push, they elbow each other aside, they knock each other down: you make it any way you can. The rest get flattened. That's how it is. For my part, I've given it all up.

COUNT   Finding your fortune? *(Aside)* There's something new.

FIGARO   *(Aside)* Now it's my turn. *(Aloud)* Your Excellency has graciously appointed me steward of the castle, and I'm very happy with my lot. True, I shan't be your roving agent who's first with the exciting news; but in recompense, here I'll be, living happily with my wife in the heart of Andalusia …

COUNT   Why shouldn't you bring her to London with you?

FIGARO   I'd have to leave her on her own so often, I'd soon be thoroughly fed up with marriage.

COUNT   With sufficient wit and strength of character, you could make your way up into administration eventually.

FIGARO   Make my way by wit? Your Lordship laughs at mine. No, be mediocre and crawling, and you'll get everywhere you want.

COUNT   … You need only take a few lessons from me in politics.

FIGARO   I know all about politics.

COUNT   Like English, is it? The basis of the language!

FIGARO   Yes, not that there's anything in it to boast about.
                  Pretending not to know when you do know, and
                  to know when in fact you don't; pretending to
                  understand when you don't understand, and not
                  to hear when you do; and in particular, pretending
                  you can do things it's not in your capacity to do.
                  Then there's making a big secret out of concealing
                  the fact that there is no secret; hiding yourself out
                  of the way, twiddling your thumbs, and making
                  out you're profound when in fact you're an empty
                  vessel; putting on an act, good or bad; sending out
                  spies and giving hand-outs to traitors; tampering
                  with seals and intercepting letters; and trying to
                  elevate the shoddiness of your methods by the
                  loftiness of your goals - That's all politics is, and
                  you can hang me if I'm wrong!

COUNT   Ah, no! What you've just defined is called
                  intrigue!

FIGARO   Politics, intrigue, call it what you like. But since
                  they seem pretty similar to me, anyone interested
                  can just get on with it. "My true love hath my
                  heart and I have hers", as the old master has it.

COUNT   *(Aside)* He wants to stay. I know what that
                  means: Suzanne has given me away.

FIGARO   *(Aside)* I'm stringing him along and paying him
                  back in his own coin.

COUNT   So, you hope to win your case against Marceline?

FIGARO   Would you make me a criminal for rejecting an
                  old spinster when Your Excellency permits himself
                  the liberty of grabbing all our young ones?

COUNT   *(Teasing)* In Court, the magistrate forgets his own
                  interests and sees nothing but the law.

FIGARO   Which indulges the strong and punishes the
                  weak...

COUNT	Do you think I am joking, then?
FIGARO	Ah, who knows, Sir? "Tempo è galant' uomo", as the Italians say. Time will tell. And they always speak the truth: time will reveal who is for me or against me.
COUNT	*(Aside)* She has clearly told him everything. He shall marry the old duenna.
FIGARO	*(Aside)* He's played a clever game with me. What has he found out?

SCENE SIX

The Count, a Lackey, Figaro.

LACKEY	*(Announcing an arrival)* Don Guzman Brid'oison.
COUNT	Brid'oison?
FIGARO	Oh! Yes, of course. He's the local judge and chairman of the bench, your fellow justice.
COUNT	Ask him to wait.

The lackey goes out.

SCENE SEVEN

The Count, Figaro.

FIGARO	*(Eyeing the Count, who is lost in his thoughts.)* ...Was there anything else, Sir?
COUNT	*(Collecting himself)* What? ... I wanted you to have the room arranged for the Court Sessions.

FIGARO   But what else do we need? The presidential chair
                for you, some other chairs for the justices, the
                clerk's stool, two benches for the lawyers, the front
                part of the floor for the gentry, and the rabble
                behind. I must go and send the cleaners away.

                He goes out.

SCENE EIGHT

The Count (alone).

COUNT   The villain had me embarrassed! You try to argue
                with him, and he turns it to his own advantage, he
                ties you down, wraps you up ... Ah, scoundrels,
                the pair of them! Get your heads together to trick
                me, would you? Go ahead and be friends, be
                lovers, be anything you like, I don't care. But, my
                God, if you think you're getting married ...

SCENE NINE

Suzanne, the Count.

SUZANNE   *(Out of breath)* Sir, ... forgive me, Sir.

COUNT   *(Ill-humoured)*   What's the matter, young lady?

SUZANNE   Are you angry?

COUNT   I take it you want something?

SUZANNE   *(Timidly)* The Countess is having one of her little
                turns. I ran to ask if you would lend us your
                smelling salts. I'll bring them back straight away.

COUNT   *(Giving her his little bottle)* No, no, keep them for
                yourself. I'm sure you'll find them useful before
                long.

SUZANNE	Do women in my position have little turns, then? That's a sickness reserved for people of quality, you only have attacks in your boudoir.
COUNT	Here's a bride truly in love, and about to lose her husband ...
SUZANNE	Not if I pay off Marceline with the dowry you promised me...
COUNT	*I* promised you?
SUZANNE	*(Lowering her eyes)* Sir, that's what I thought I understood.
COUNT	Yes, if you yourself consented to understand me.
SUZANNE	*(Looking down)* And is it not my duty to listen to His Excellency?
COUNT	In that case, cruel girl, why couldn't you have told me earlier?
SUZANNE	Is it ever too late to tell the truth?
COUNT	You are prepared to go down to the garden when it gets dark?
SUZANNE	Don't I take a walk there every evening?
COUNT	You treated me so severely this morning!
SUZANNE	This morning?... The page was behind the chair!
COUNT	She is right, I was forgetting. But why the stubborn refusal when Bazile came to speak on my behalf?
SUZANNE	Why do we have to have a Bazile...?
COUNT	She's right again. However, there is a certain Figaro, and I fear you may have told him everything!

SUZANNE	Heavens! Yes, I tell him everything, except the things he oughtn't to hear.
COUNT	*(Laughing)* What a clever girl! And is it a promise? If you went back on your word, my sweetheart, let's be clear we understand each other: no meeting, no dowry, no marriage.
SUZANNE	*(Curtseying)* But also, no marriage, no droit du seigneur, Your Lordship.
COUNT	Where does she get it from? I tell you, she'll have me crazy about her! But the Countess is waiting for the smelling salts …
SUZANNE	*(Giving the bottle back with a laugh)* How could I have come and talked to you without a pretext?
COUNT	*(Trying to kiss her)* You delicious creature!
SUZANNE	*(Dodging)* People are coming.
COUNT	*(Aside)* She's mine!

He slips out.

SUZANNE	I must run quickly and tell the Countess.

SCENE TEN

Suzanne, Figaro.

FIGARO	Suzanne! Suzanne! You've just been with the Count - where are you rushing off to?
SUZANNE	Go ahead and plead your case if you like: you've just won it.

She runs off.

FIGARO	*(Following her)* What's that? Hey, tell me …

SCENE ELEVEN

The Count (alone).

COUNT   *(Coming back)*   "You've just won it"! - I was
                 walking right into a trap! Oh, you'll be punished
                 for that all right, my impertinent friends! I'll see
                 your case is judged fittingly... But what if he actu-
                 ally paid the old duenna her money?... What with?
                 But if he did pay ... Ah!   Haven't I got the proud
                 Antonio, whose family dignity sneers at having an
                 unknown like Figaro for his niece? If I massage his
                 ridiculous snobbery ... Why not? In the broad
                 pastures of intrigue a man must be able to harvest
                 any crop, even the vanity of a half-wit. *(He calls.)*
                 Anto...

                      He sees Marceline etc arrriving.
                      Exit Count.

SCENE TWELVE

Bartholo, Marceline, Brid'oison.

MARCELINE   *(To Brid'oison)* Sir, let me explain my case.

BRID'OISON   *(In his gown, and with a slight stammer)* Very well,
                 let's ta-alk about it verbally.

BARTHOLO   It is a promise of marriage.

MARCELINE   Along with a loan of money.

BRID'OISON   Et caetera, I u-understand the rest.

MARCELIN   No, Sir, there's no et caetera.

BRID'OISON   I u-understand: you have the money ready.

MARCELINE   No, Sir. I'm the one who lent it.

BRID'OISON	I u-understand now: you-ou are demanding the money back.
MARCELINE	No, Sir. I'm demanding that he marry me.
BRID'OISON	Ah, well, I u-understand perfectly. And the man, does he wa-ant to marry you?
MARCELINE	No, Sir. That's the whole point of the hearing!
BRID'OISON	Do you think I don't u-understand the point?
MARCELINE	No, Sir. *(To Bartholo)* What are we doing here! *(To Brid'oison)* Do you mean to say you'll be judging the case?
BRID'OISON	Would I have pur-urchased my office otherwise?
MARCELINE	*(Sighing)* It's a terrible abuse to sell them in the first place!
BRID'OISON	Yes, much be-etter to let us have them for noth-ing. Who is the defe-endant?

SCENE THIRTEEN

Bartholo, Marceline, Brid'oison, Figaro (coming back, rubbing his hands)

MARCELINE	*(Pointing to Figaro)* This cheating man here, Sir.
FIGARO	*(Cheerfully, to Marceline)* Am I in the way, per-haps? - His Lordship will be here in a moment, Sir.
BRID'OISON	I've seen that fe-ellow before somewhere.
FIGARO	With your good lady wife, Sir, in Seville: I was in her service.
BRID'OISON	Whe-en was that?

FIGARO	A little less than a year before your youngest son was born, and a fine lad he is, if I say so myself.
BRID'OISON	Yes, the fi-inest of them all. They say you're still u-up to your old tricks here.
FIGARO	Sir is too kind. It's really nothing at all.
BRID'OISON	A promise of marriage. O-oh, the poor simpleton!
FIGARO	Sir, ...
BRID'OISON	Has this good fellow see-een my secretary any-where?
FIGARO	You mean Clawfingers, the clerk of the court?
BRID'OISON	Yes, he ra-akes in the cash.
FIGARO	Rakes it in! Believe me, he positively swallows it! Oh, yes! I've seen him: clerk's special expenses, supplement to the clerk's special expenses - all standard legal practice, needless to say.
BRID'OISON	One must kee-eep to the forms.
FIGARO	Absolutely, Sir. If the legal substance of a case belongs to the litigants, then it's well known that the forms provide the living for the courts.
BRID'OISON	That fe-ellow isn't as simple as I thought. Well now, my friend, since you u-understand all about it, we-ee'll see your case is looked after for you.
FIGARO	Sir, I rely on your probity, even though you repre-sent what they call justice.
BRID'OISON	What? ... Yes, I re-epresent justice. But if you do owe money, a-and you don't pay it back ...
FIGARO	Then Sir can see it's just as if I never owed any.
BRID'OISON	A-absolutely. - Eh, what's he saying?

SCENE FOURTEEN

Bartholo, Marceline, the Count, Brid'oison, Figaro, an Usher.

USHER   *(Preceding the Count in)* Gentlemen, His Lordship!

COUNT   Fully robed to come here, Justice Brid'oison? It's only a domestic matter. Ordinary dress would have been more than good enough.

BRID'OISON   It is yo-ou who are more than good, my Lord Count. But I never go out withou-out it. A question of the forms, you see, the forms! A man who would laugh at a full judge in a short coat tre-embles at the mere sight of a prosecutor in a gown. The forms, the fo-orms!

COUNT   *(To the Usher)* Have the public admitted.

USHER   *(Opens the door, shouting)* Assemble in Court!

SCENE FIFTEEN

As before, plus Antonio, the castle servants, the peasants in their festival clothes. (The Count takes the presidential chair; Brid'oison a chair to one side; the clerk sits on the stool behind his table; the judges and lawyers on the benches. Marceline sits next to Bartholo, and Figaro on the other bench. The peasants and servants stand at the back.)

BRID'OISON   *(To Clawfingers)* Clawfingers, ca-all the cases.

CLAWFINGERS   *(Reading from a paper)* "The noble, very noble, infinitely noble Don Pedro George, Spanish nobleman, Baron of the Heights, Baron of the Wild Mountains, and Baron of other Mountains; against Alonzo Calderon, playwright." It's to do with a play that failed. Each man disclaims it and attributes it to the other.

COUNT   They are both right. Case dismissed. To give

their next play a better chance in society, if they ever work together on one again order the noble-man to contribute his name and the poet his talent.

CLAWFINGERS   (*Reading from another paper*) "Andre Petrutchio, farm labourer; against the Provincial Collector of Taxes." It concerns a sequestration order.

COUNT   The case is outside my competence. I can better serve my subjects as their patron in matters affecting the crown. Next.

CLAWFINGERS   (*Taking a third paper. Bartholo and Figaro rise.*) "Barbe-Agar-Raab-Madeleine-Nicole-Marceline de Verte-Allure, spinster (*Marceline rises and curtseys.*); against Figaro ..." Patron saint's given name left blank.

FIGARO   Anonymous.

BRID'OISON   A-anonymous? What kind of pa-atron saint is that?

FIGARO   It's mine.

CLAWFINGERS   (*Writing*) "Against Anonymous Figaro." Titles?

FIGARO   Gentleman.

COUNT   You, a gentleman?

                The clerk is still writing.

FIGARO   If God had wished it, I'd be the son of a prince.

COUNT   Get on with it.

USHER   (*Bawling*) Silence, gentlemen!

CLAWFINGERS   (*Reading*) "... The case before the court being the opposition of the marriage of the said Figaro by the said De Verte Allure. Doctor Bartholo appearing for the plaintiff, and the said Figaro for himself, if the Court permits, it being contrary to the stated practice and precedent of the bench."

FIGARO   The practice, master Clawfingers, is often a plain abuse. Any client with a little knowledge is invariably better informed about his case than certain lawyers, who weep crocodile tears, trumpet at the tops of their voices, and because they know everything but the facts, are as unconcerned at ruining the client as they are at boring the public and sending the gentlemen of the bench into a deep sleep. And who then sit down more swollen with pride than if they'd composed Cicero's speech in defence of Murena. I, on the other hand, will state my case in a few words. Gentlemen, ...

CLAWFINGERS   You've just wasted a whole string of them, because you're not putting the case, you're only answering it. Step forward, Doctor, and read out the promise of marriage.

FIGARO   Ha! Promise!

BARTHOLO   *(Putting on his spectacles)* It is extremely precise.

BRID'OISON   We nee-eed to have it before the Court.

CLAWFINGERS   Silence, then, gentlemen!

USHER   *(Bawling)* Silence!

BARTHOLO   *(Reading)* "I, the undersigned, acknowledge receipt from Miss ...etc. Marceline de Verte Allure, in the castle of Aguas Frescas, the sum of two thousand milled-edged piastres; which sum I will return on demand, in this castle, and in default of which, I will marry her, ... etc., etc. Signed: Figaro, other name blank." My request is for the settling of the debt and the fulfilment of the promise, with costs. *(He launches into his speech.)* Gentlemen, ... never was a more fascinating case set before the judgement of the Court! Not since

Alexander the Great promised marriage to the fair
Thalestris ...

COUNT   *(Interrupting)* Before counsel for the plaintiff pro-
                  ceeds any further, are we agreed on the validity of
                  the document?

BRID'OISON   *(To Figaro)* Is there a-anything in the reading of
                  the do-ocument that you challenge?

FIGARO   I challenge, gentlemen, the malice, the inaccuracy,
                  or the carelessness with which the document was
                  read. For the words set down are not: "which sum
                  I will return, AND I will marry her"; but: "which
                  sum I will return, OR I will marry her"; which is
                  entirely different.

COUNT   Does the document say AND, or OR?

BARTHOLO   It says AND.

BRID'OISON   Claw-awfingers, read it yourself.

CLAWFINGERS   *(Taking the document)* And far safer, too.
                  Interested parties are often inexact when they
                  read. *(He reads.)* "Da, da, da, da, Miss da, da, da,
                  De Verte Allure, da, da, da. Ah! Which sum I will
                  return on demand, in this castle ... AND ... OR ...
                  AND ... OR ... " The word is so poorly written ...
                  there's a blot.

BRID'OISON   A blo-ot? I know about those.

BARTHOLO   *(Pleading his case)* I submit, for my part, that it is
                  the copulative conjunction AND which links the
                  coordinate clauses: I will pay the lady, AND I will
                  marry her.

FIGARO   *(Pleading his case)* I submit, for my part, that it is
                  the alternating conjunction OR which separates
                  the said clauses: I will pay the hussy, OR I will
                  marry her. If the man wants to play at pedants,
                  he's out-pedanted. A word of Latin from him and

I'll floor him with Greek. I'll exterminate him.

COUNT   How do you expect me to decide a question of this sort?

BARTHOLO   To cut matters short, gentlemen, and save haggling over just one word, we accept that it says OR.

FIGARO   I want that in writing.

BARTHOLO   And we agree. The guilty man will find no refuge in such pettiness. Let us consider the document as follows: *(He reads.)* "Which sum I will return, in this castle, or in the vault of which I will marry her." It's as if you were to say, gentlemen: "I will bleed you here and now, or you may have a second opinion." In other words, either - or. "He shall take two grains of rhubarb, or you will mix him a pinch of tamarind." One thing or the other, as preferred. It's the same with: "Which sum I will return, in this castle, or in the vault of which I will marry her." The money, or a wedding in the castle crypt. My client has a choice.

FIGARO   Not at all. The expression should read : "In default of which." "The disease will probably kill you, in default of which the doctor certainly will." If the disease doesn't; the meaning is undeniable. Another example: "You shall write nothing but rubbish, in default of which stupid critics will pan you." If you fail to write rubbish, you will be criticised. "In default of" introduces the subordinate clauses, and "stupid", or "wicked" people govern the subordinates. Does Master Bartholo think I've forgotten my syntax? So what it says is: "Which sum I will return, in this castle, or IN DEFAULT of which, I will marry her."

BARTHOLO   *(Rapidly)* IN THE VAULT of which.

FIGARO   *(Rapidly)* IN DEFAULT of which. It's DEFAULT, gentlemen, or else I will marry her.

BARTHOLO	*(Looking at the paper, rapidly)* THE VAULT, gentlemen.

FIGARO	*(Rapidly)* DEFAULT is what it said when I saw it, gentlemen. If I married her, would I still be expected to pay her as well?

BARTHOLO	*(Rapidly)* Yes, we marry but count our property as separate.

FIGARO	*(Rapidly)* We'll keep our bodies separate as well, if I'm forced to do both.

The judges rise and have a whispered discussion.

BARTHOLO	A fine way to wriggle out of it!

CLAWFINGERS	Silence, gentlemen.

USHER	*(Bawling)* Silence!

BARTHOLO	It takes a villain like you to call that paying his debts!

FIGARO	It takes a lawyer like you to call that pleading his case.

BARTHOLO	I am defending this lady.

FIGARO	Then stick to your rotten arguments, but cut out the insults. It was because they feared the litigants might get carried away that the Courts allowed third parties to be called in. But it was not their intention that these more restrained advocates should assume the privilege of being insolent with impunity. It degrades a most noble institution.

The judges continue to confer in whispers.

ANTONIO	*(To Marceline, pointing to the judges)* What's all the muttering about?

MARCELINE	Someone has got at the presiding judge, and he is corrupting the other one, and I am losing my case.
BARTHOLO	*(In an undertone, gloomily)* I fear so.
FIGARO	*(Cheerfully)* Put a brave face on it, Marceline!
CLAWFINGERS	*(Rising; to Marceline)* Ah! Now you've gone too far! Before judgement is given, I demand a ruling on this clear case of contempt!
COUNT	*(Resuming his seat)* No, clerk, I will give no ruling on any personal insult. A Spanish judge has no need to take umbrage at behaviour worthy at best of Asiatic Courts. There are plenty of other abuses as it is! And I shall correct one of them now by explaining the reasoning behind my judgement. Any judge who declines to do so is an enemy of the law! What is it that the plaintiff can justifiably be demanding? Marriage, failing payment of the debt. The two together would imply a contradiction.
CLAWFINGERS	Silence, gentlemen!
USHER	*(Bawling)* Silence!
COUNT	What is the defendant's response? Does he wish to retain his right to his own person? Then it is granted.
FIGARO	*(Delighted)* I've won!
COUNT	But since the agreement states: "Which sum I will return on demand, or in default of which I will marry her, and so on," the Court rules that the defendant shall pay two thousand piastres to the plaintiff, or else marry her, and marry her today.

He rises.

FIGARO	*(Stunned)* I've lost!

ANTONIO	*(Delighted)* That's a superb ruling!

FIGARO — What's so superb about it?

ANTONIO — You're not going to be my nephew any more. Thank you very much, my Lord.

USHER — *(Bawling)* Gentlemen, clear the Court!

The public disperse.

ANTONIO — I'm going straight off to tell my niece all about it.

SCENE SIXTEEN

The Count (moving through the remaining people), Marceline, Bartholo, Figaro, Brid'oison.

MARCELINE — *(Sitting down)* Ah! I can breathe again.

FIGARO — And I'm choked.

COUNT — *(Aside)* There's my revenge, at least. That's something.

FIGARO — *(Aside)* And that Bazile, supposed to be fighting Marceline's marriage - he came back quickly, didn't he? *(To the Count)* - Sir, are you leaving us?

COUNT — My rulings are all made.

FIGARO — *(To Brid'oison)* It's this great puffed-up balloon of a Justice...

BRID'OISON — Puffed-up balloo-oon, me!

FIGARO — Exactly. And I shan't marry her. I'll show how a gentleman behaves for once.

The Count stops.

BARTHOLO   You'll marry her.

FIGARO   Without the consent of my noble parents?

BARTHOLO   Name them. Show us them.

FIGARO   Just give me a little time. I'm very close to seeing
                them again now: I've spent fifteen years searching
                for them.

BARTHOLO   He's giving himself airs, the clown! He's just
                some foundling!

FIGARO   Lost, doctor: a lost child. Or perhaps a stolen
                one.

COUNT   *(Coming back)* Stolen, lost? Show us your evi-
                dence! And I bet he'd claim that as an insult too!

FIGARO   Sir, when I was found by bandits, I was wearing
                gold ornaments, lace baby clothes and embroi-
                dered wrappings. And if that isn't enough to prove
                my birth, consider the care they took to demon-
                strate I was someone's precious son by giving me
                these distinguishing marks. Here, this design on
                my arm ...

                He prepares to roll up his right sleeve.

MARCELINE   *(Springing to her feet)* On your right arm, in the
                shape of a spatula?

FIGARO   How do you know that's what it is?

MARCELINE   My God! It's him!

BARTHOLO   *(To Marceline)* Who? Who's him?

MARCELINE   *(Excitedly)* It's Emmanuel!

BARTHOLO   *(To Figaro)* You were stolen by gypsies?

FIGARO   *(In a state of exaltation)* Just near a castle. My
dear Doctor, if you know how to return me to my
noble family, name your price for that service.
Mountains of gold will be no bar to my illustrious
parents.

BARTHOLO   *(Pointing to Marceline)* Your mother is there.

FIGARO   ... My nurse?

BARTHOLO   Your own mother.

COUNT   His mother!

FIGARO   Explain yourself.

MARCELINE   *(Pointing to Bartholo)*   There is your father.

FIGARO   *(Stricken)* Oh, oh, oh! Help me!

MARCELINE   Did nature not tell you so a thousand times?

FIGARO   Not once.

COUNT   *(Aside)* His mother!

BRID'OISON   He-e won't be marrying her, that's obvious.

BARTHOLO   Neither will I.

MARCELINE   Neither will you! And what about your son? You
swore to me ...

BARTHOLO   I was not in my right mind. If old incidents like
that counted as promises, we'd be obliged to
marry just about everyone.

BRID'OISON   A-and if we looked at things that closely, nobody
would marry anybody.

BARTHOLO   And the woman's failings so well-known! She had
a deplorable youth!

MARCELINE   *(Steadily growing more heated)* Yes, it was
               deplorable, and more than you think! I do not
               intend to deny my faults: today has proved them
               only too plainly! But it's hard to be forced to expi-
               ate them after thirty years of living the life of a
               decent woman. I was born to be virtuous, it was
               in my nature, and virtuous I became, as soon as I
               was allowed to exercise my own mind. But at an
               age when we are prey to illusions, inexperience
               and necessity, besieged by would-be seducers and
               impaled on our own poverty, what resistance can a
               mere child put up against such an army of ene-
               mies? Any man who passes harsh judgements on
               us today has very likely been the ruination of ten
               such luckless women in his own lifetime!

FIGARO   It is the guiltiest men who pass the harshest judge-
               ments, that's how life works.

MARCELINE   *(Sharply)* Men of no compunction, you brand us
               with contempt as the playthings of your passions,
               your victims! You are the ones who should be
               punished for the errors of our youth! You and
               your magistrates, so smug about your right to pass
               judgement on us - you are the ones who allow us
               to be deprived of any honest means of earning our
               keep. Through your criminal negligence! Is there
               a single decent livelihood open to these unfortu-
               nate girls? Wasn't it their natural right to be
               employed in anything to do with what women
               need, sewing, dress-making, all these things?
               Instead they thrust those jobs on thousands of the
               opposite sex!

FIGARO   *(Angry)* They even set soldiers to doing embroi-
               dery!

MARCELINE   *(In a state of exaltation)* And even in the higher
               ranks of society, women only receive your derisory
               consideration. Fobbed off with superficial marks
               of respect, but in reality kept subservient: treated
               as minors so far as our possessions go, but pun-
               ished as adults when it comes to our failings! Ah,

every way you look at it, your behaviour towards
us can only inspire pity, if it doesn't inspire horror.

FIGARO   She is right!

COUNT   *(Aside)* Only too right!

BRID'OISON   My-y God, she *is* right!

MARCELINE   An unjust man refuses to meet his obligations, but
                what does that matter to us, my son? Don't look
                back at where you came from: look ahead to where
                you are going. That's the only thing that matters
                to any of us. In a few months' time, your fiancée
                will depend on no one but herself. She will say yes
                to you, I'll answer for that. So live side by side
                with your wife and your mother, and each of us
                will vie happily to prove who loves you best. Be
                indulgent towards them both, and happy in your
                own good fortune, my son: be cheerful, open-
                hearted and good to all around you. Your mother
                will lack nothing she desires.

FIGARO   Your words are like gold, mother, and I take your
                advice to heart. And really, how stupid we are!
                The world has been turning for thousands and
                thousands of years, and in this vast ocean of time
                from which I have scooped maybe some thirty pal-
                try years, I was going to torture myself with won-
                dering who I owed them to! Well, hard luck to
                anyone who worries himself about that! Spending
                your life on such petty squabbles is like being one
                of those horses that pull barges up-river: the
                weight is always on their collars; even when they
                stop walking they never get a rest, for they're
                pulling against the current even when they're
                standing still. No, we shall simply wait.

COUNT   My plans all ruined by a ridiculous accident!

BRID'OISON   *(To Figaro)* What about your noble birth, your
                castle? You-ou are trying to force your will on
                justice.

FIGARO   Justice? Justice was about to force me into com-
mitting a gross imbecility! Think of it, on account
of that blasted hundred crowns, I've twenty times
come close to assaulting this gentleman, who
today turns out to be my father! But since providence has rescued me from the danger of ruining
my good name: father, accept my apologies ...
And you, my mother, embrace me... in as moth-
erly fashion as you can. (Marceline flings her arms
round him)

SCENE SEVENTEEN

Bartholo, Figaro, Marceline, Brid'oison, Suzanne, Antonio, the Count.

SUZANNE   *(Rushing in with a purse)* Sir, stop! Don't let them
marry! I've come to pay Madame what she is
owed with the dowry the Countess is giving me.

COUNT   *(Aside)* Damn the Countess! There seems to be
a whole conspiracy against me!

                  He goes out.

SCENE EIGHTEEN

Bartholo, Antonio, Suzanne, Figaro, Marceline, Brid'oison.

ANTONIO   *(Seeing Figaro embracing Marceline; to Suzanne)*
It's not paying she wants! Look, look!

SUZANNE   *(Turning away)* I can see all I need. Come on,
uncle, let's go.

FIGARO   *(Stopping her)* No, if you don't mind. So what
can you see, then?

SUZANNE   My own stupidity, and your cowardice.

FIGARO	No more of one than of the other.
SUZANNE	*(Angry)* If you fancy her, marry her, since you've got your paws all over her!
FIGARO	*(Cheerfully)* My arms are round her, but I'm not marrying her!

Suzanne tries to walk out; Figaro holds her back.

SUZANNE	*(Slapping his face)* How dare you grab at me!
FIGARO	*(To the assembled company)* Is that a loving way to behave? Before you leave us, I beg you to take a proper look at this dear woman.
SUZANNE	I'm looking.
FIGARO	And what do you think of her...?
SUZANNE	Repulsive.
FIGARO	Three cheers for jealousy, it never does things by halves!
MARCELINE	*(Opening her arms)* Come and embrace your mother, pretty Suzanette. That wicked man tormenting you is my son.
SUZANNE	*(Running to her)* You, his mother?

They embrace.

ANTONIO	She's just become his mother? Just now?
FIGARO	I've just found out now.
MARCELINE	*(In a state of exaltation)* No. My heart was always drawn to him. The feeling behind it was misdirected, that's all. It was his blood calling to me.
FIGARO	And it was native good sense calling on my instinct, mother, which made me refuse you. For

I never disliked you at all: witness the money I borrowed ...

MARCELINE   *(Handing him a paper)* It's yours to keep. Have your agreement back. Consider it as your wedding gift.

SUZANNE   *(Tossing him the purse)* Take this one as well.

FIGARO   Why, thank you very much.

MARCELINE   *(In a state of exaltation)* Miserable enough as a girl, I was about to become the most wretched of wives; and now I am the luckiest of mothers. Embrace me, both my children: all my tenderness is united in you. I am as happy as I can ever be, and, ah! my children, how I am going to love you!

FIGARO   *(Touched, and stepping in quickly)* There now, mother, stop, stop! Do you want to see my eyes drown in the first tears they've ever shed? At least they're tears of joy. But this is silly: I was about to be ashamed of them! I could feel them running between my fingers. Look. *(He holds his fingers splayed.)* And I was stupidly holding them back! To hell with shame! I want to laugh and cry at the same time. What I feel is only felt once in a lifetime.

                 He embraces his mother on one side, Suzanne on the other.

MARCELINE   Oh, my darling boy!

SUZANNE   My darling man!

BRID'OISON   *(Wiping his eyes with a handkerchief)* Well, look at me! Am I just si-illy too?

FIGARO   *(In a state of exaltation)* All the griefs of the world, I can defy you now! Come for me, if you dare, with these two beloved women at my side!

ANTONIO	*(To Figaro)* Less of the hugging, if you don't mind. In cases of marriage within families, the parents' one comes first. Hadn't you heard? So what about your two, are they going to give each other their hand?
BARTHOLO	Give her my hand? May it wither and drop off if I ever give it to the mother of a clown like him!
ANTONIO	*(To Bartholo)* You mean you only count as a step-father? *(To Figaro)* In that case, my fancy lad, I've nothing more to say to you.
SUZANNE	Oh! Uncle!...
ANTONIO	Am I going to go and give our sister's little girl to this fellow, who isn't the child of anybody at all?
BRID'OISON	How can tha-at be possible, fool? E-everybody's the child of somebody.
ANTONIO	Well, suck on that, then! ... He'll never have her!

He goes out.

SCENE NINETEEN

Bartholo, Suzanne, Figaro, Marceline, Brid'oison.

BARTHOLO	*(To Figaro)* And now go and see if you can find someone to adopt you.

He begins to walk off.

MARCELINE	*(Running after Bartholo and grabbing him round the waist; drags him back)* Stop, Doctor, you can't leave!
FIGARO	*(Aside)* This is ridiculous. Every imbecile in Andalusia seems to be out to prevent my marriage!

SUZANNE	*(To Bartholo)* Nice little Daddy, he's your son.
MARCELINE	*(To Bartholo)* The wit, the talents, the looks.
FIGARO	*(To Bartholo)* And he hasn't cost you a farthing.
BARTHOLO	And the hundred crowns he robbed me of?
MARCELINE	*(Stroking him)* We'll take such care of you, Daddy!
SUZANNE	*(Stroking him)* We'll love you so much, little Daddy!
BARTHOLO	*(Touched)* Daddy! Nice Daddy! Little Daddy! Look at me, I'm even more soft-headed than the Justice here. *(Indicating Brid'oison)* I'm letting myself be swayed like a child. (Marceline and Suzanne kiss him) Ah, no! I haven't said yes. *(He turns round.)* Where has the Count got to?
FIGARO	Let's go and find him quickly. We need to get him to give his final word. If he were to come up with some new trick, we'd have to start all over again.
ALL	Come along! Hurry! Hurry!

They drag Bartholo out with them.

SCENE TWENTY

Brid'oison (alone)

BRID'OISON	Even more so-oft-headed than the Justice! It's all right to say tha-at sort of thing to yourself, but, ... They a-are not at all polite, the people in thi-is place.

He exits.

END OF ACT THREE

ACT FOUR

SCENE ONE

A gallery with candelabra and chandeliers burning, flowers, garlands, everything for a festive ceremony. Down left, a table with a writing desk, and an armchair behind.
Figaro, Suzanne.

FIGARO
(His arms round Suzanne's waist) Well, my love, are you happy? The gilded tongue of my clever mother has won the Doctor over! In spite of his repugnance, he's going to marry her, and that surly uncle of yours is muzzled. That only leaves the Count out of sorts, since our marriage has now become the price of theirs. Don't you have to laugh at such a happy ending?

SUZANNE
Did you ever see anything so strange?

FIGARO
Or rather so funny. All we ever wanted to do was extract a dowry from His Excellency. And now two have fallen into our hands, neither of them given by him. You were being hounded by a desperate rival; I was being tormented by a fury: now all that has changed and we have the most loving of mothers. Yesterday I was so to speak alone in the world; and today I have a whole family. Not quite as magnificent as I had pictured them, admittedly, but good enough for people like us who don't suffer from the vanity of the rich.

SUZANNE
All the same, my dear, none of the plans you made, and that we were depending on, has come to anything.

FIGARO
Chance has arranged things better than any of us could, my love. That's life for you. You work, you plan, you fix things as far as you can; and meanwhile chance settles the matter in its own way. From the ravenous conqueror who wants to

gobble up the earth to the blind man who peace-
ably follows where his dog leads him, everyone is
the plaything of the whims of chance. In fact, the
blind man is often better led, less deceived in what
he sees, than that other blind man with all his
advisers. - As for that other, delightful blind
chance they call Love, ...

He takes her tenderly in his arms again.

SUZANNE   Ah! He's the only one I'm interested in!

FIGARO   Then let me improve on the conceit, and permit
            me to be the faithful dog who leads Love to your
            sweet little door, and there finds lodging for the
            rest of our lives.

SUZANNE   *(Laughing)* You and Love?

FIGARO   Me and Love.

SUZANNE   And you won't ever look for any other home?

FIGARO   If you catch me doing that, then let a thousand
            million dashing lovers ...

SUZANNE   You're going to say something completely silly.
            Just tell me your real truth.

FIGARO   The truthfullest of all my truths?

SUZANNE   Why, you villain! How many have you got?

FIGARO   Oh, several! Ever since people began to notice
            that with time, old follies became received wis-
            dom, and what were once ill-sown little lies have
            produced vast and magnificent truths, there have
            been thousands of different varieties. Those you
            know but don't dare divulge, because not every
            truth is fit to be told; and those you parade but
            give little credit to, because not every truth is fit
            to be believed. And then there are passionate
            oaths, a mother's threats, a drunkard's protesta

tions, the promises of people with power, a dealer's final word: it never ends. The only genuine, trustworthy truth is my love for Suzon.

SUZANNE   I love to hear you in full spate: it tells me you're happy. But we have to talk about this rendez-vous of mine with the Count.

FIGARO   I'd prefer never to mention it again. It nearly cost me Suzanne.

SUZANNE   Don't you want it to take place after all, then?

FIGARO   If you love me, Suzon, promise me this: just let him turn up and fret there all by himself, and that can be punishment enough.

SUZANNE   It cost me a lot more to agree to the rendez-vous than it does to break it off.   Consider it cancelled.

FIGARO   I want your truthfullest of truths!

SUZANNE   I'm not like you educated men: I only have the one.

FIGARO   And will you love me a little?

SUZANNE   A lot.

FIGARO   That's scarcely at all.

SUZANNE   And how is that?

FIGARO   In matters of love, you see, even too much isn't enough.

SUZANNE   I don't understand all these subtleties; but I know that I shall love only my husband.

FIGARO   Keep your word, and you'll make a beautiful exception to the normal rule.

He tries to kiss her.

SCENE TWO

Figaro, Suzanne, the Countess.

COUNTESS   Ah! I was right when I said it: wherever they are, you may be sure they'll be together. Now then, Figaro, stealing a private meeting like this. You're robbing the future, the marriage, and even yourself. Everyone is waiting for you. They are getting impatient.

FIGARO   That is true, Madame, I'm forgetting myself. I'll show them my excuse.

He tries to lead Suzanne off with him.

COUNTESS   *(Holding Suzanne back)* She'll follow you in a moment.

SCENE THREE

Suzanne, the Countess.

COUNTESS   Have you arranged what we need for swapping clothes?

SUZANNE   We don't need anything, Madame. The rendezvous has been cancelled.

COUNTESS   Ah! You've changed your mind!

SUZANNE   Figaro has.

COUNTESS   You've betrayed me!

SUZANNE   No! God's my witness!

COUNTESS   Figaro is not the man to let a dowry get away.

SUZANNE   Madame! Oh! What are you thinking?

COUNTESS   You've agreed to do as the Count wishes, and
            now, here you are angry with yourself for having
            told me his plans. I know you inside out. Leave
            me!

            She tries to walk out.

SUZANNE   *(Throwing herself on her knees)* In the name of
            God, in whom we hope! Madame, you don't
            know how you wrong Suzanne! When you've
            always been so good to me; and the dowry you've
            given me!...

COUNTESS   *(Lifting her to her feet)* Oh! What's come over me?
            ... I don't know what I'm saying! My dear girl,
            you're changing places with me in the garden, so
            of course you're not going there yourself. You're
            keeping your word with your husband, and help-
            ing me bring back mine.

SUZANNE   But you said such a hurtful thing!

COUNTESS   I was being stupid because I was confused. *(She
            kisses Suzanne on the forehead.)* Where have you
            arranged to meet?

SUZANNE   *(Kissing her hand)* All he said was the garden.

COUNTESS   *(Pointing to the table)* Take that pen, and we'll fix
            a place.

SUZANNE   Write to him?

COUNTESS   We must.

SUZANNE   Madame! But surely, you're the one ...

COUNTESS   I take full responsibility. *(Suzanne sits down, the
            Countess dictates.)* "A new song, to this tune ...
            How fine it will be tonight, beneath the tall chest-
            nut trees... How fine ... it will be tonight ..."

SUZANNE   *(Writing)* "Beneath the tall ... chestnut trees ... "

	What next?
COUNTESS	Are you afraid he won't understand?
SUZANNE	*(Reading it over)* No, that's just right. *(She folds the note.)* How shall we seal it?
COUNTESS	With a pin. Quick. He can use it to reply. Write on the other side: "Send the seal back to me."
SUZANNE	*(Laughing as she writes)* Ah! "The seal!"... This one is much nicer than the one on that commission, Madame!
COUNTESS	*(With a sorrowful sigh)* Ah!
SUZANNE	*(Searching)* I haven't got a pin on me.
COUNTESS	*(Unpinning the top of her dress)* Take this one. *(Cherubin's ribbon flutters to the ground.)* Oh! My ribbon!
SUZANNE	*(Picking it up)* It's the one that little thief stole! How could you be so cruel...?
COUNTESS	Should I have let him keep it on his arm? That would have been a fine thing! Give it to me!
SUZANNE	Madame can't wear it any more, with that young man's blood-stains on it.
COUNTESS	*(Taking it back)* It'll do perfectly for Fanchette... The first bunch of flowers she brings me, ...

SCENE FOUR

A young shepherdess (Cherubin dressed up as a girl), Fanchette, several young girls similarly dressed and carrying bouquets; the Countess, Suzanne.

FANCHETTE	Madame, these are the girls from the village; they

have come to offer you flowers.

COUNTESS   *(Hastily putting her ribbon away)*   They look
                    delightful! You must forgive me, pretty girls, if I
                    do not know all your names. *(Pointing to
                    Cherubin)*   Who is that charming child with such a
                    modest look?

ONE OF THE
SHEPHERDESSES   She's one of my cousins, Madame, come especial-
                    ly for the wedding.

COUNTESS   She's very pretty. Since I can't carry all twenty
                    bouquets, the visitor shall have the honour. *(She
                    takes Cherubin's flowers, and kisses him on the* fore-
                    head.)   Look, I've made her blush! *(To Suzanne)*
                    Suzon, don't you think she looks like ... someone
                    we know?

SUZANNE   Oh, yes. You could easily be deceived.

CHERUBIN   *(Aside, clutching his heart)* Ah! That kiss missed
                    its true home!

SCENE FIVE

*The village girls, Cherubin amongst them, Fanchette, Antonio, The
Count, the Countess, Suzanne.*

ANTONIO   I tell you, my Lord, he's there with them. They
                    dressed him up in my daughter's room. His own
                    clothes are still there, and here's his uniform cap, I
                    picked it up.   *(He steps forward, looks at all the
                    girls, and picking out Cherubin, removes his woman's
                    bonnet, causing the tresses of his long hair to fall down.
                    He puts the soldier's hat on his head, and announces:)*
                    Look, dammit, there's our officer for you!

COUNTESS   *(Starting back)* Oh, my God!

SUZANNE   The little rascal!

ANTONIO	And I was telling you back there it was him!...
COUNT	*(Angry)* Well, Madame?
COUNTESS	Well, Sir! You find me even more astonished than you are, and, not the least of it, just as angry.
COUNT	Yes. But earlier on today, this morning? What about that?
COUNTESS	Indeed, it would be doing you wrong if I were to dissemble further. He had come to my apartments. We were beginning to plan the little joke which these children have just acted out. You caught us trying out his costume. Your instant reaction was so violent! He jumped to safety, I was covered in confusion, and our general fright did the rest.
COUNT	*(Vexed, to Cherubin)* Why did you not leave?
CHERUBIN	*(Snatching his hat off)* My Lord, ...
COUNT	I shall punish you for your disobedience.
FANCHETTE	*(Rashly)* Ah, my Lord, listen to me. You know how each time you come to give me kisses you always say: "If you will love me, little Fanchette, I'll give you anything you want"?
COUNT	*(Reddening)* I said that? Me?
FANCHETTE	Yes, my Lord. Well, instead of punishing Cherubin, let me marry him, and I'll love you to distraction.
COUNT	*(Aside)* I've a curse put on me, and by a pageboy!
COUNTESS	Well, Sir, now it's your turn! This child's admission, as candid as my own, proves once and for all two truths: I never knowingly give you occasion for the distress I apparently cause you; whereas you explore every avenue that might increase and

justify mine.

ANTONIO   You as well, my Lord? Damn me, I'm going to have to knock her into shape as I did her late mother, who is dead now. Not that anything is going to happen, of course. But as Her Ladyship well knows, little girls, once they become big girls ...

COUNT   *(Aside, disconcerted)* There's an evil spirit around here, turning everything against me!

SCENE SIX

The village girls, Cherubin, Antonio, Figaro, the Count, the Countess, Suzanne.

FIGARO   Sir, if you keep our girls any longer, we shan't be able to start the ceremony, or the dancing.

COUNT   Dancing? You? After your fall this morning and the sprained right ankle!

FIGARO   *(Flexing his leg)* It still hurts a bit, but it's nothing. *(To the girls)* Come along, pretty things, come along!

COUNT   *(Swinging him round)* You were extremely fortunate my flower-beds only contained good soft earth!

FIGARO   Very fortunate, I agree, otherwise ...

ANTONIO   *(Swinging him round)* Since he fell right down to the bottom curled up in a ball.

FIGARO   A more agile man would have floated in mid-air, would he? *(To the girls)* Are you coming, ladies?

ANTONIO   *(Swinging him round)* And in the meantime the little page was galloping off to Seville on his horse?

FIGARO	Galloping; or trotting, for all I know!...
COUNT	*(Swinging him round)* And you had his commission in your pocket?
FIGARO	*(A little surprised)* Certainly. But why all the questions? *(To the girls)* Come along now, girls!
ANTONIO	*(Catching Cherubin by the arm)* Here's one of them who says my future nephew is nothing but a liar.
FIGARO	*(Caught unawares)* Cherubin!... *(Aside)* Damn the little idiot!
ANTONIO	Have you got it, now?
FIGARO	*(Casting around for ideas)* I've got it ... I've got it ... So! What line is he spinning this time?
COUNT	*(Drily)* No line at all. He says it was him who jumped out on to the wallflowers.
FIGARO	*(Thinking)* Ah! Well, if he says so ... it's very possible. I don't quarrel with what I don't know.
COUNT	You mean to say, you and he both ... ?
FIGARO	Why not? It's the sort of craze that catches on, jumping. Look at Panurge's sheep. And when you're in a rage, there isn't anyone who would prefer the risk ...
COUNT	What, two at the same time!...
FIGARO	Two dozen of us, easily, all jumping at once. And what does it matter, Sir, since there's nobody hurt? *(To the girls)* Now look, are you coming, yes or no?
COUNT	*(Furious)* Are we acting in some play?

A fanfare sounds offstage.

FIGARO   There's the signal for the procession.   Places, everybody, places! Suzanne, come on. Give me your arm.

> *They all rush off. Cherubin alone remains, hanging his head.*

SCENE SEVEN

Cherubin, the Count, the Countess.

COUNT   *(Watching Figaro go)*   Did you ever see anyone so brazen? *(To the page)* As for you, sly young man, shaming yourself like this, go and put your proper clothes on, fast; and don't let me catch you anywhere about tonight.

COUNTESS   He's going to get very lonely.

CHERUBIN   *(Rashly)* Lonely! I've got enough happiness planted on my forehead to last a hundred years in prison!

> *He puts on his hat and flees.*

SCENE EIGHT

The Count, the Countess (fanning herself rapidly but saying nothing).

COUNT   What's this happiness he's got planted on his forehead?

COUNTESS   *(Embarrassed)* It's ... his first soldier's cap, I expect. You know children, everything's a toy to them.

> *She is about to go.*

COUNT   Are you not staying with us, Countess?

COUNTESS   You know I'm not feeling well.

COUNT   The girl is your protégée: surely you'll spare her a
               few moments? Otherwise I'll think you're still
               angry.

COUNTESS   Here come the two wedding parties. We had bet-
               ter sit down and receive them.

COUNT   *(Aside)* The wedding!   What I can't prevent, I
               suppose I'll have to endure.

               *The Count and Countess take seats at one side of
               the gallery.*

SCENE NINE

*The Count and Countess (seated); the procession (comes in, to the tune of
"Les Folies d'Espagne").*

*Bridal Procession. Huntsmen, with guns on shoulders. Policeman, The
Magistrates, Brid'oison. The Village Men and Women in their best
clothes. Two Young Girls, bearing the bridal crown with its white feathers. Two other girls with the white veil. Two others with the gloves and bouquet. Antonio offering his arm to Suzanne as the man who is giving her
away. Other young girls, bearing a second crown, a second veil, a second
white bouquet, like the first, for Marceline. Figaro offering his arm to
Marceline, as the man giving her away to: Doctor Bartholo who brings up
the rear, with a large bouquet.*

*As the young girls pass before the Count, they hand over to his valets all
the items of dress intended for Suzanne and Marceline.*

*When the Villagers have formed two lines down each side of the gallery,
the fandango is danced again, with castagnettes. Then, while the refrain
for the duet is being played, Antonio leads Suzanne towards the Count;
she kneels before him.*

*While the Count sets the veil and crown over her head and gives her the
bouquet, two young girls sing the following duet:*

Young bride, sing the glory of the greatest treasure:
His right now renounced by a master who could bed you,
Preferring nobler victory to mere passing pleasure,
He gives you chaste and pure to the husband who would
wed you.

*Suzanne is still kneeling, and during the last line of the duet, she
tugs the Count's coat and shows him the note in her hand.
Then she brings this hand, which only the audience can see, up
to her head, where the Count pretends to adjust her crown. She
gives him the note.*

*The Count slips it furtively inside his coat. The duet ends. The
bride rises and makes him a deep curtsey.*

*Figaro comes to receive her from the Count's hands, and with-
draws to the other side of the room with her, taking up his position near Marceline.*

In the meantime the fandango is danced again.

*The Count, anxious to read the note he has received, comes
down to the edge of the stage and pulls the paper from his inside
pocket. But in pulling it out, he makes the movements of a man
who has pricked his finger painfully: he shakes it, squeezes it,
sucks it; and as he stares at the paper with its pin for a seal,
says:*

COUNT   *(While he and Figaro are speaking, the orchestra plays pianissimo.)* Damn these women, sticking pins everywhere!

          *He flings the pin to the floor; then reads the letter, and kisses
          it.*

FIGARO   *(Who has seen everything, to his mother and Suzanne)* It's a
love-letter some girl must have slipped into his hand during the procession. It was fastened with a pin, and it's just
given him a good jabbing.

          *The dance resumes. The Count, who has read the note,
          turns it over. He sees the instruction to return the seal as an
          answer. He searches the floor and eventually finds the pin,
          which he fixes in the sleeve of his coat.*

FIGARO   *(To Suzanne and Marceline)* When you love some-
              one, everything belonging to them is precious.
              He's picking up the pin, look. Ah! He's a mad
              fellow!

              Meanwhile, Suzanne has been exchanging signals
              with the Countess. The dance ends. The refrain
              from the duet starts again.

              Figaro leads Marceline over to the Count, copying
              the ceremony for Suzanne. Just as the Count
              takes the bridal crown and the duet is about to be
              sung, they are interrupted by a series of shouts.

USHER   *(At the door, shouting)* Stop there, gentlemen!
              You can't all come in ... Guards, guards! Over
              here!

.COUNT   *(Rising)* What's the matter?

USHER   My Lord, it's Don Bazile, surrounded by the
              entire village. He's been singing all the way here.

COUNT   Send him in by himself.

COUNTESS   Give me permission to withdraw.

COUNT   I'm grateful for your tolerance in staying so long.

COUNTESS   Suzanne? ... She'll be back shortly. *(Aside, to*
              Suzanne) We must go and change our clothes.

              She goes out with Suzanne.

MARCELINE   He only ever turns up to spoil things.

FIGARO   Oh, I'll soon take him down a tone or two!

SCENE TEN

As for the previous scene, except for the Countess and Suzanne; plus

Bazile, holding his guitar, and Gripe-Soleil.

BAZILE
(Enters, singing)
Hearts that are tender, hearts that are true,
You always condemn any love that is light;
Away with your sharp-tongued, carping crew:
It's no crime to want a new love every night.
If Cupid has wings, then what's a man to do,
But fly from heart to heart: it's every lover's right.
But fly from heart to heart: it's every lover's right.
But fly from heart to heart: it's every lover's right.

FIGARO
(Going over to him) Yes, that's what the wings on his back are for, all right. But tell me, friend, what's all this music for?

BAZILE
(Pointing to Gripe-Soleil) It's proof of my obedience to His Lordship. I've been entertaining this gentleman, who is one of his party; and in turn I shall be able to demand justice of him.

GRIPE-SOLEIL
Hah! I don't call that entertainment, my Lord, tatty bits of tunes like that ...

COUNT
So, Bazile, what is it you demand?

BAZILE
What belongs to me by right, my Lord: the hand of Marceline. And I've come to object ...

FIGARO
(Stepping up to him) Sir, how long is it since you saw what a fool looked like?

BAZILE
Sir, I'm looking at one now.

FIGARO
Since my eyes make such a good mirror for you, study the effect of this prediction in them. If you so much as move a muscle in the lady's direction ...

BARTHOLO
Llaughing) Why not? Let him have his say.

BRID'OISON
(Stepping between them) Is it ne-ecessary for two friends ...?

FIGARO	Friends! Us!
BAZILE	The man's joking!
FIGARO	*(Rapidly)* Just because he churns out dirges in chapel?
BAZILE	*(Rapidly)* And he churns out verses like babble?
FIGARO	*(Rapidly)* A coffee-house tinkler!
BAZILE	*(Rapidly)* A tabloid scribbler!
FIGARO	*(Rapidly)* An operatic prig!
BAZILE	*(Rapidly)* A diplomatic hick!
COUNT	*(Seated in his chair)* And insolent, the pair of them!
BAZILE	He never shows me the slightest respect.
FIGARO	True. What is there to show?
BAZILE	Goes around saying I'm nothing but a fool.
FIGARO	Now he thinks I'm an echo.
BAZILE	When in fact there isn't a singer who doesn't owe his success to me. Without my talent they wouldn't matter at all.
FIGARO	Caterwaul.
BAZILE	There he goes again!
FIGARO	And why not, if it's true? Are you some royalty that we have to fawn on? Listen to the truth and lump it, fat-head! It's not as if there was anything to get out of you by telling you lies. Or if you're frightened to hear me tell the truth, why come and disturb our wedding celebrations?

BAZILE   *(To Marceline)* Did you make me a promise, yes or no, that if you weren't provided for within four years, I'd be the man you'd have?

MARCELINE   And on what condition did I make the promise?

BAZILE   If you found the son you lost, I'd adopt him out of kindness.

EVERYONE
TOGETHER   He's been found!

BAZILE   What's that to me?

EVERYONE
TOGETHER   *(Pointing at Figaro)* And there he is!

BAZILE   *(Recoiling in horror)* The Devil stands before me!

BRID'OISON   *(To Bazile)* You-ou mean you are renouncing your claim to his dear mother?

BAZILE   Can you imagine anything worse than being taken for the father of a feckless oaf?

FIGARO   Being taken for the son of one. Are you kidding?

BAZILE   *(Pointing to Figaro)* If that man is going to be considered a somebody round here, then let me tell you this: I want to be a nobody.

He goes out.

SCENE ELEVEN

As before, except for Bazile.

BARTHOLO   *(Laughing)* Ha, ha, ha, ha!

FIGARO   *(Jumping for joy)* So in the end I shall have my wife!

COUNT	*(Aside)* And I'll have my mistress.

He rises.

BRID'OISON	*(To Marceline)* And e-everybody is satisfied.
COUNT	Have the two contracts drawn up, and I shall sign them.
EVERYONE TOGETHER	Long live His Lordship!
COUNT	I need to retire for a while.

He makes as if to leave with the others.

SCENE TWELVE

Gripe-Soleil, Figaro, Marceline, the Count.

GRIPE-SOLEIL	*(To Figaro)* I'm off now to help set up the fireworks under the big chestnut trees, as we arranged.
COUNT	*(Comes running back)* What idiot ordered you to do that?
FIGARO	What's wrong with that?
COUNT	*(Sharply)* Have you forgotten the Countess is unwell? How will she be able to see the fireworks from there? They need to be out on the terrace, opposite her apartment.
FIGARO	Got that, Gripe-Soleil? On the terrace.
COUNT	Under the chestnut trees, indeed! What kind of place is that! *(Aside, as he goes out)* They were going to incinerate my rendez-vous!

SCENE THIRTEEN

Figaro, Marceline.

FIGARO   How amazingly considerate towards his wife!

          He makes as if to go.

MARCELINE   *(Stopping him)* A quick word, my son. There's
                something I need to straighten out with you. A
                misguided notion had made me behave unjustly
                towards your charming wife. I presumed she had
                come to an agreement with the Count, even
                though Bazile told me she had consistently put
                him off.

FIGARO   You don't know your son very well if you thought
                any woman's impulses could rattle me. I defy the
                most cunning of them to make a fool out of me.

MARCELINE   That's always a good way to think, my son.
                Because jealousy ...

FIGARO   ... is merely one of pride's more foolish children;
                or else it's the disease of a madman. Ah, mother, I
                have a philosophy on that subject which is ... quite
                unflappable. And if Suzanne is to deceive me one
                day, I forgive her in advance: she'll have exhaust-
                ed herself just finding the chance ...

          *He turns round and sees Fanchette, who is peering
          from side to side.*

SCENE FOURTEEN

Figaro, Fanchette, Marceline.

FIGARO   He-ey! My little cousin, spying on us!

FANCHETTE   Oh! Not that, no! People say it's not right.

FIGARO	True. But as it's also very useful, people often get confused between the two.
FANCHETTE	I was looking to see if someone was here.
FIGARO	Up to pretences already, you bad girl! You know perfectly well he can't be here.
FANCHETTE	Who can't?
FIGARO	Cherubin.
FANCHETTE	I'm not looking for him; I know where he is. I'm looking for my cousin Suzanne.
FIGARO	And what does my little cousin want with her?
FANCHETTE	Well, little cousin, I don't mind telling you. - It's... it's just a pin which I have to give back to her.
FIGARO	*(Sharply)* A pin! A pin! Where did you get it from, you wicked girl? Only half-grown, and already acting the go-between... *(He recovers his self-control, and continues more gently.)* Already acting very responsibly in every way, Fanchette. And my little cousin is always so helpful ...
FANCHETTE	Then what's there to get so cross about? I'm going.
FIGARO	*(Stopping her)* No, no. I'm only joking. I know, your little pin is the one the Count told you to give back to Suzanne; it had been used to fasten up a little piece of paper he had. See? I knew all along.
FANCHETTE	Then why do you need to ask, if you're so clever?
FIGARO	*(Casting round)* Because it's fun trying to guess what His Lordship must have said to get you to run his errand.

FANCHETTE	*(Naively)* Well, it was no different from what you said: "Here, little Fanchette, take this pin back to your pretty cousin, and just tell her it's the seal for the big chestnut trees."
FIGARO	For the big ... ?
FANCHETTE	"Chestnut trees." It's true that he did also say: "Take care no one sees you."
FIGARO	You must do as he says, my cousin. Fortunately no one has seen us. So run your errand like a good girl, and don't say to Suzanne any more than His Lordship ordered.
FANCHETTE	Why should I say any more? My cousin Figaro takes me for a child!

She skips out.

SCENE FIFTEEN

Figaro, Marceline.

FIGARO	Well, mother, what about that?
MARCELINE	Well, my son, what about it?
FIGARO	*(As if choking)* Well, this is the last straw!... Really, there are some things...!
MARCELINE	Some things! What things?
FIGARO	*(Clutching his chest)* What I've just heard, mother. It's like a lump of lead in my heart.
MARCELINE	*(Laughing)* So that heart swelling with confidence was just a puffed-up balloon? A single pin has burst everything!
FIGARO	*(Furious)* Not any old pin, mother. That's the pin

he picked up off the floor...!

MARCELINE   *(Reminding him of his recent words)* Jealousy! Ah,
              I have a philosophy on that subject which is ...
              quite unflappable. And if Suzanne ever catches me
              out, I forgive her ...

FIGARO   *(Impassioned)* Oh, mother! A man speaks as he
              feels. Take the iciest of judges and make him
              plead his own case, and just watch him talk his
              way round the law! - No wonder he was so
              annoyed about the fireworks! - As for my sweet
              darling with her sly little pins, she's sorely mistak-
              en if she thinks she's given me the slip, her and
              her chestnut trees! If we're near enough married
              for my anger to be justified, it's still not so final I
              can't marry someone else, and just abandon her
              altogether ...

MARCELINE   Now there's an intelligent solution! Let's smash
              everything to pieces on a mere suspicion! Listen,
              who says you're the one she's cheating on, and not
              the Count? Has her character suddenly changed,
              to make you condemn her without trial? How do
              you know she'll actually turn up at the rendez-
              vous? Or what her plan is if she does; what she'll
              say there; what she'll do? I thought you had better
              judgement!

FIGARO   *(Kissing her hand with relief)* She's right! My
              mother is right, always, always right! But allow
              human nature its rushes of blood, mother: we're
              better for it afterwards. Yes, we must see what's
              going on, before leaping into accusation or action.
              And I know where they are to meet. Goodbye,
              mother!

              He goes out.

SCENE SIXTEEN

Marceline (alone).

MARCELINE   Goodbye. And I know too. Now he's acting more sensibly, let's go and see what Suzanne is up to; or rather, warn her. She's such a pretty creature! Ah! When personal interest doesn't set us against each other, all women want to help their poor oppressed sex against that proud, fearsome ... *(Laughing)* and yet a touch simple-minded tribe of men!

END OF ACT FOUR

ACT FIVE

SCENE ONE

A grove of chestnut trees, in a park. Two pavilions, summer houses or temples are to right and left. Upstage is a landscaped glade. Downstage a garden seat. It is dark.

Fanchette, alone, holding in one hand two biscuits and an orange, and in the other a paper lantern, lighted.

FANCHETTE   In the pavilion on the left, he said. That's this one. - What if he didn't come, though? My little errand would be ... ! Those horrible people in the kitchen didn't even want to give me an orange and two biscuits! - "Who is it for, Miss?" - "Well, sir, I need them for someone." - "Oh, we know who ... " - Well, what if they do know? Just because the Count won't have him in his sight, does he have to starve to death? - And all these things cost me a great big kiss on the cheek!... But who knows: perhaps he'll pay me it back! *(She sees Figaro, who comes up and peers at her. She gives a cry.)* Ah!...

> *She turns and flees, running into the pavilion on her left.*

SCENE TWO

Figaro, a long cloak over his shoulders, and wearing a hat with its broad rim turned down; Bazile, Antonio, Bartholo, Brid'oison, Gripe-Soleil, and a band of servants and workmen.

FIGARO   *(Initially alone)* That was Fanchette! *(He scans the others as they arrive, and says fiercely.)* Gather round, gentlemen, good evening. Are you all here?

BAZILE   Everyone you insisted should come.

FIGARO   So what's the time, about?

ANTONIO   *(Looking up into the sky)* The moon should have been up by now.

BARTHOLO   Well! What murky scheme are you up to now? He looks like some conspirator!

FIGARO   *(Getting agitated)*   Look, what have you all assembled at the castle for? Wasn't it for a wedding?

BRID'OISON   It cer-ertainly was.

ANTONIO   We were going down to the park to wait for the signal for the celebrations to begin.

FIGARO   This is as far as you'll need to go, gentlemen. Here, under these chestnut trees, is where we are all to celebrate together the faithful bride I am marrying and the loyal Lord who has marked her down for himself.

BAZILE   *(Remembering the day's events)* Ah! Now I know what this is all about. Take my word for it, we're better off keeping our distance: there's a rendezvous due to happen here. I'll tell you all about it if you go off a little way.

BRID'OISON   *(To Figaro)* We'll co-ome back later.

FIGARO   When you hear me call, get here as fast as you can. Don't let me down. And if you don't witness a remarkable sight, you can call Figaro any sort of liar you like.

BARTHOLO   Remember that a wise man doesn't stir up trouble with his betters.

FIGARO   I'll remember.

BARTHOLO   You can't win against the nobility: it's game, set and match to them every time, because of who they are.

FIGARO

Not to mention their busy little intrigues, which you're forgetting. But remember also that a man who's known to be easily frightened is at the mercy of every kind of villain.

BARTHOLO

Very true.

FIGARO

And that I bear the name of De Verte Allure on my honoured mother's side.

BARTHOLO

He's got the very Devil in him tonight.

BRID'OISON

Ha-asn't he just!

BAZILE

(Aside) The Count and Suzanne have arranged this without using me at all! There's a hell of a row brewing, and that suits me fine!

FIGARO

(To the servants) As for you scoundrels, you've got my orders. Give me some light here, or, by the Grim Reaper I'd like to sink my teeth into, just let me catch one of you by the arm ...

He seizes Gripe-Soleil's arm.

GRIPE-SOLEIL

(Runs off howling) Ah, ah! Ow! Ow! Damned brute!

BAZILE

(Going out) May God give you joy, Figaro-the-Married-Man!

They all go out.

SCENE THREE

Figaro, alone.

FIGARO

(Sombrely, pacing up and down in the dark) Oh, woman! Woman! Woman! Weak and faithless creature! ... There isn't an animal in creation which doesn't follow its instinct; and is yours then

to betray? ... After stubbornly refusing when I
urged her to it in the Countess's presence; even at
the instant she gives me her word; in the middle
of the ceremony itself... He was laughing as he
read it, the traitor! And me, like a poor fool ...!
No, my Lord Count, you shall not have her ... you
shall not have her ... Because you are a great
Lord, you think your talents are infinite! ...
Nobility, fortune, rank, influence: they all make a
man so proud! What have you ever done to earn
such wealth? You took the trouble to be born,
and that's the sum total of your efforts. For the
rest, a pretty ordinary man! Whereas me, my
God! Lost in the obscurity of the herd, I needed
more skill and know-how even to exist than it's
taken to govern the Spanish empire for the last
hundred years - and you want to cross swords
with me! ... Someone's coming ... it's her ... it's
nobody. - The night's as black as hell, and here I
am acting out the moronic role of husband, even
though I'm only half way there yet! *(He sits on a
garden seat.)* Did anyone ever tread a crazier
path through life! Stolen by a band of brigands,
I've no idea who my father is. I'm brought up to
these bandit ways, but they disgust me and I want
to pursue an honest career. And everywhere I go,
I'm rejected! I study chemistry, pharmacy,
surgery - and with all the weight of a great nobleman's recommendation to back me up, it's as
much as I can do to get my hands on a miserable
vet's lancet! - Weary of making sick beasts even
sadder, I decide to go to the opposite extreme and
plunge body and soul into the theatre. I wish I'd
tied a stone round my neck and jumped off a
bridge! I dash off one of those plays with a fash-
ionable harem setting: you'd think I could poke a
bit of fun at Mohammed without too many worries. Before I can blink an eye, an ambassador
from heaven knows where complains that my piece
is offensive to the government of Turkey, to
Persia, to parts of the the East Indies, to the whole
of Egypt, to the kingdoms of Cyrenaica, Tripoli,
Tunis, Algiers and Morocco. And there goes my

play, up in smoke, just to please a few Muslim
princes, not one of whom can read, or so I understand, and who spend all their energy beating us
over the head and calling us "Christian dogs!" -
Since a man's spirit can't be crushed, they set
about abusing it instead. - My cheeks started to
turn hollow; I owed a whole quarter's rent; I could
see the dreaded bailiff on the way, pen stuck in his
wig. With a shudder of fear, I try anything I can.
A debate blows up on the nature of richness, and
since you don't actually need first-hand experience
of things in order to argue about them, and since I
didn't have a penny to my name, I write a piece
about the value of money and its net product. I
immediately find myself in the back of a prison
waggon, watching the drawbridge of a fortress
being lowered to allow me in, abandoning at its
entrance all hope and all freedom. *(He stands up.)*
The carefree way they wreck people's lives! My
God, I'd like to get my hands on one of those
jumped-up officials when he'd had his pride
cooled down by a disgrace of his own. I'd tell
him a thing or two ... The idiocies that appear in
print don't matter a jot until someone tries to
block them. Without the freedom to criticise there
can be no such thing as praise. Only little men are
fearful of little scribblings. *(He sits down again.)*
Then they grow tired of feeding an obscure gaol-
bird and throw me out on the street. And since a
man has to eat even if he's no longer in prison, I
sharpen my pen again and ask around to see
what's new. And I'm told that since my little holi-
day on the State, Madrid has set up a system of
free trade on all products, even extending to the
press. Provided my writings avoid all mention of
authority, religion, politics, morals, people in high
places, influential institutions, the Opera, any
other public entertainment, or anyone who has
any interest in anything, I can freely print whatever I wish, subject to the inspection of two or three
censors. To take advantage of this sweet liberty, I
announce the forthcoming appearance of a new
periodical, and, imagining I'm poaching on no-

one's territory, I call it "The Daily Futile".   And,
wow! A thousand miserable hacks rise in chorus
against me. My paper is suppressed and there I
am out of a job yet again! - Despair is about to
overwhelm me. I get mentioned for a position
that comes up, but as bad luck would have it, it
suited me just right: they needed someone good at
figures, so a dancer got the job. The only thing
left was to turn to robbery, so I became a banker
for a card school. And, good people, listen! I dine
out on the town, and members of so-called polite
society invite me to their homes, retaining three
quarters of the profit for themselves. I could easily
have reconstructed my life. I was even beginning
to appreciate that if you want to acquire wealth,
know-how is worth far more than knowledge. But
with everyone around me lining his pockets while
insisting that I remain honest, I inevitably landed
up as before, down and out. This time I was really
going to leave the world, and a dozen strokes out
into the river would have settled it, when a benev-
olent God called me back to my first and original
trade. I take up my strop of English leather and
my case of instruments. Then leaving the fog of
dreams to the idiots who thrive on it, and dump-
ing shame at the side of the road as being too bur-
densome for a mere pedestrian, I barber my way
from town to town, shaving and travelling, and living at last without a care. A distinguished nobleman arrives in Seville. He recognises me, I con-
trive his marriage, and as he owes his wife entirely
to my intervention, he rewards me by trying to
intervene with mine! And so to intrigues and
storms. Ready to plunge into a terrible abyss, on
the verge of marrying my mother, my parents turn
up one after the other. *(He stands up, growing
heated.)*   There's a huge argument: it's you, it's
him, it's me, it's you; no, it isn't us. Well, who is
it, then? *(He falls back on the seat.)*   Such a bizarre
chain of events! How has all this happened to me?
Why these things, and not others? Who planted
them on my head? Forced to tread a path I've
been set on without knowing anything about it,

just as I shall one day have to step off it without
any choice in the matter, I have strewn it with as
many flowers as my good spirits have allowed.
Yet I say good spirits, without knowing whether
they are really mine any more than the rest of me,
or even what is this ME I'm wrapped up in.   A
shapeless collection of meaningless bits; then a
mindless, puny being, a playful little animal, a
pleasure-seeking youth, with a taste for every variety of enjoyment, undertaking every variety of
trade to earn a living. Here a master, there a servant, according to the whim of fortune! Ambitious
out of vanity, hard-working out of necessity, but
idle ... for the sheer delight of it! A spinner of
words if danger threatens, a poet by way of diver-
sion, a musician when the occasion demands, a
lover in fits of folly, I have seen everything, done
everything, worn out everything. Then the illusion
shattered, leaving me too disabused to ...
Disabused! ... Suzon, Suzon, Suzon! How can
you torture me like this! - I hear footsteps ...
someone's coming. Now we're at the moment of
crisis.

*He slips out of sight near the side of the stage, on
the right.*

SCENE FOUR

*Figaro, the Countess (wearing Suzanne's clothes), Suzanne (wearing the
Countess's clothes), Marceline.*

SUZANNE	*(In a low voice, to the Countess)* Yes, Marceline told me Figaro would be here.
MARCELINE	He is here, too. Keep your voice down.
SUZANNE	So one is listening to us, and the other is about to come and look for me. We're ready to begin.
MARCELINE	I'm going to hide in the pavilion: I don't want to miss a word.

She enters the pavilion Fanchette went into.

SCENE FIVE

Figaro, the Countess, Suzanne.

SUZANNE	*(Speaking out loud)* Madame is shivering! Are you cold?
COUNTESS	*(Loudly)* It's damp this evening. I'm going back indoors.
SUZANNE	*(Loudly)* If Madame doesn't need me, perhaps I could take the air under these trees for a while.
COUNTESS	*(Loudly)* It's the evening dew you'll be taking .
SUZANNE	*(Loudly)* Oh, I'm ready for that.
FIGARO	*(Aside)* Ready for the dew, oh yes!

Suzanne withdraws to the other side of the stage from Figaro.

SCENE SIX

Figaro, Cherubin, the Count, the Countess, Suzanne (Figaro and Suzanne concealed down right and down left).

CHERUBIN	*(Enters, in officer's uniform, happily singing the refrain from his song.)* La, la, la, etc. I loved with my every part A godmother, taken away.
COUNTESS	*(Aside)* The little page!
CHERUBIN	*(Stops)* There are people about. I must run for my hiding place, where little Fanchette ... There's a woman there!

COUNTESS   *(Listening)* Oh, my God!

CHERUBIN   *(Stooping and trying to peer into the darkness)* Am I mistaken in this twilight, or does that feathered hat I seem to make out over there mean it's Suzon?

COUNTESS   *(Aside)* If the Count were to arrive now!...

                The Count appears upstage.

CHERUBIN   *(Goes across and takes the hand of the Countess, who tries to protect herself.)* Yes, it's that charming girl they call Suzanne. Ah, how could I mistake the softness of this hand, the way it gives a little shiver; and the beating of my own heart, especially!

                He tries to press the back of the Countess's hand against his heart. She pulls it away.

COUNTESS   *(In a low voice)* Go away.

CHERUBIN   If it is compassion that has led you deliberately to this corner of the park where I have been hiding, ...

COUNTESS   Figaro will be here soon.

COUNT   *(Aside, stepping forward)* Isn't that Suzanne I can see?

CHERUBIN   *(To the Countess)* I'm not in the least scared of Figaro, because it's not him you're waiting for.

COUNTESS   Who, then?

COUNT   *(Aside)* She's with someone.

CHERUBIN   The Count, you wicked girl. He asked you for this rendez-vous this morning. I was there, behind the chair.

COUNT   *(Aside, furiously)* It's that damned little page again!

FIGARO   *(Aside)* And they say you should never listen!

SUZANNE   *(Aside)*   The little blabbermouth!

COUNTESS   *(To Cherubin)* Be good enough to withdraw.

CHERUBIN   Not until you've at least paid me the price of my
                obedience.

COUNTESS   *(Horrified)* Are you demanding ... ?

CHERUBIN   *(Hotly)* Twenty kisses on your own account to
                start with, and then a hundred for your beautiful
                mistress.

COUNTESS   You mean you'd dare to ... ?

CHERUBIN   Would I dare? Oh, yes! If you're taking her place
                beside the Count, I'm taking his beside you. The
                only loser is Figaro.

FIGARO   *(Aside)* That little bandit!

SUZANNE   *(Aside)* Only a pageboy would have the cheek.

                *Cherubin attempts to kiss the Countess. The
                Count steps between them, and receives the kiss.*

COUNTESS   *(Stepping back)* Oh, my God!

FIGARO   *(Aside, hearing the kiss)* A sweet little girl I was
                marrying!

                He listens.

CHERUBIN   *(Feeling the Count's clothes in the dark)* It's the
                Count!

                *He rushes into the pavilion Fanchette and
                Marceline entered.*

SCENE SEVEN

Figaro, the Count, the Countess, Suzanne.

FIGARO   *(Moving forward)* I'm going to ...

COUNT   *(Mistaking him for the page)* Since you're not
                offering me another kiss ... *(Strikes out.)*

FIGARO   *(Taking the blow)* Ah!

COUNT   ... Here's payment for the first one anyway.

FIGARO   *(Aside, moving away, rubbing his cheek)* Though
                mind you, listening isn't all profit.

SUZANNE   *(Laughing out loud from the other side)* Ha! Ha!
                Ha! Ha!

COUNT   *(To Countess, taking her for Suzanne)* That page is
                beyond me! He gets the full force of my fist and
                runs off laughing!

FIGARO   *(Aside)* Not if he'd got this one! ...

COUNT   It's ridiculous! I can't take a step without ... *(To
                the Countess)* But never mind these bizarre goings-
                on, it would sour my pleasure in finding you in
                this charming spot.

COUNTESS   *(Imitating Suzanne's voice)* What pleasure might
                you be hoping for?

COUNT   After your clever letter? *(He takes her hand.)*
                You're shaking!

COUNTESS   I was frightened.

COUNT   I got the kiss intended for you, but now I'm going
                to make up for your loss.

                He kisses her on the forehead.

COUNTESS   The liberties!

FIGARO   *(Aside)* The litle flirt!

SUZANNE   *(Aside)* Charming!

COUNT   *(Taking his wife's hand)* But what smooth, soft
              skin. If only the Countess could boast such beau-
              tiful hands!

COUNTESS   *(Aside)* Oh, the falseness of the man!

COUNT   Does she have such firm, round arms? These
              pretty fingers full of elegance and mischief?

COUNTESS   *(In Suzanne's voice)* And love?...

COUNT   Love ... is only the fiction of the heart. It's plea-
              sure that is its history. It has brought me to your
              knees.

COUNTESS   Do you not love her any more?

COUNT   I love her a great deal, but three years of marriage
              make wedded bliss so respectable!

COUNTESS   What were you looking for in her?

COUNT   *(Stroking her)* What I find in you, my beauty ...

COUNTESS   But tell me, though.

COUNT   ... I don't know. Less steadiness, perhaps.
              Something a little sharper in her ways. Those lit-
              tle things that give a woman charm, so hard to
              describe. An occasional refusal. How can I say?
              Our wives believe that loving us settles everything.
              Once that's been said, they just love us, love us!
              (When they do love us.) And they are so compli-
              ant and so constantly obliging, and for ever, and
              without respite, that the husband is surprised one
              fine evening to find repletion where he had been
              looking for happiness.

COUNTESS	*(Aside)* Oh! Is this the lesson?
COUNT	The truth is, Suzon, I've thought this a thousand times over: if we run elsewhere in search of the pleasure we can't find with them, the reason is that they don't take enough care to study the art of keeping our attention, of reawakening themselves to love, of spicing the charms of possession with the charms of variety.
COUNTESS	So they have to do everything?...
COUNT	*(Laughing)* And the man nothing? Shall we ever change the march of nature? The task assigned to us was to win them in the first place; their task ...
COUNTESS	Theirs...?
COUNT	Is to keep us. People too readily forget.
COUNTESS	I shan't forget it.
COUNT	Nor I.
FIGARO	*(Aside)* Nor I.
SUZANNE	*(Aside)* Nor I.
COUNT	*(Taking his wife's hand)* There's an echo here. Let's keep our voices down. You don't have to think about any of that, love has made you both too lively and too pretty! With a pinch of capriciousness, you'll make the most provocative of mistresses! *(He kisses her on the forehead.)* My Suzanne, a Castilian is nothing if not a man of his word: here is all the gold that was promised for the reinstatement of the right to this delicious moment you are granting me, and is a right no more. But since the graciousness with which you grant it is beyond price, let me add this diamond, which you shall wear for love of me.
COUNTESS	*(Curtseying)* Suzanne accepts everything.

FIGARO	*(Aside)* You can't get any more fickle than that.
SUZANNE	*(Aside)* There's a handy bit of extra coming our way.
COUNT	*(Aside)* She likes presents: all the better.
COUNTESS	*(Looking back upstage)* I can see torches.
COUNT	They're making the preparations to celebrate your wedding. Shall we slip into one of these pavilions for a moment, to let them pass?
COUNTESS	Without a light?
COUNT	*(Leading her gently off)* What for? We haven't brought anything to read.
FIGARO	*(Aside)* My God, she's going in! I knew it!

He steps forward.

COUNT	*(Raising his voice and turning round)* Who's that wandering about here?
FIGARO	*(Angry)* Wandering about! I'm here for a purpose!
COUNT	*(In a low voice, to the Countess)* It's Figaro!...

He runs off.

COUNTESS	I'm following right behind.

She runs into the pavilion on the right, while the Count loses himself in the woods upstage.

SCENE EIGHT

Figaro, Suzanne, (in the dark).

FIGARO   *(Trying to see where the Count and Countess are going, and still taking the Countess for Suzanne)* I can't hear anything now. They've gone inside. And there I am. *(In a new tone of voice)* You other husbands, the unskilled ones, who pay spies to do your work for you, and spend months on end at the mercy of a single suspicion, and still never pin it down: why don't you take example from me? I'm on my wife's tracks right from the first day, and I eavesdrop. Straight away, I know everything. It's wonderful: no lingering doubts, I know what I'm up against. *(Pacing rapidly about)* Fortunately, I hardly even care, and her treachery doesn't matter to me the slightest little bit. So I've got them at last!

SUZANNE   *(Aside, having crept up quietly in the dark)* You're going to pay for your noble suspicions. *(Putting on the Countess's voice)* Who goes there?

FIGARO   *(Wildly)* "Who goes there?" The man who wishes the plague had come along at birth and choked ...

SUZANNE   *(In the Countess's voice)* Oh! But it's Figaro!

FIGARO   *(Peering at her, startled)* The Countess! Madame!

SUZANNE   Keep your voice down.

FIGARO   *(Rapidly)* Ah, Madame! Providence has brought you just at the right moment! Where do you believe the Count to be?

SUZANNE   What does a hard-hearted monster matter to me? Tell me ...

FIGARO   *(Rapidly)* And my bride, Suzanne: where do you believe her to be?

SUZANNE   You must keep your voice down.

FIGARO   *(Very rapidly)* That Suzon everyone believed to be so virtuous, who acted so modestly! They've shut themselves in there! I'm going to call for help.

SUZANNE   *(Stopping his mouth with her hand, and forgetting to disguise her voice)* Don't call out!

FIGARO   *(Aside)* It's Suzon! God damn it!

SUZANNE   *(In the Countess's voice)* You seem upset.

FIGARO   *(Aside)* Traitress! Trying to catch me out!

SUZANNE   We must have our revenge, Figaro!

FIGARO   Are you certain you really want it?

SUZANNE   Am I not true to my sex? But men know a hundred ways of going about it.

FIGARO   *(Confidently)* Madame, you are far from being a mere by-stander. A woman's revenge beats anything a man can dream up.

SUZANNE   *(Aside)* He's going to get such a clout!

FIGARO   *(Aside)* Wouldn't it be fun if I could get her to ... before the marriage!

SUZANNE   But what is that sort of womanly revenge worth, if not seasoned with a pinch of love?

FIGARO   Ah, you may not see it, but it's always there, masked by the pretence of respect.

SUZANNE   *(Stung)* I don't know if you really believe that, but it's not a gracious thing to say.

FIGARO   *(With mock fervour, falling to his knees)* Oh, Madame! I adore you! Consider the place, the time, the circumstances, and if my pleading lacks grace, let your own anger be compensation.

SUZANNE   *(Aside)* My hand is itching!

FIGARO   *(Aside)* My heart's racing.

SUZANNE   But, Sir, have you thought...?

FIGARO   Yes, Madame. Yes, I have thought.

SUZANNE   ... That when it comes to love and anger ...

FIGARO   ... Those who hesitate lose their chance. Will you give me your hand, Madame?

SUZANNE   *(In her natural voice, slapping him)* Here it is.

FIGARO   Ow! *Demonio!* What a wallop!

SUZANNE   *(Giving him a second one)* What a wallop? How about this one?

FIGARO   What's all this, dammit? Is today beating day?

SUZANNE   *(Hitting him with each phrase)* Ah! "What's all this?" This is Suzanne. And that's for you suspicious mind; that's for your revenge and your treachery; that's for your tricks, for your insults, and for your evil intentions. Is this what you call love? You were singing a different tune this morning.

FIGARO   *(Getting to his feet)* Santa Barbara! Yes, this is what I call love. Oh, the happiness! Oh, the joy of it! Figaro is delirious with delight! Beat away, my darling beloved, don't stop. But when you've turned me black and blue with bruises, look with kindness, Suzon, on the happiest man that was ever walloped by woman.

SUZANNE   "The happiest man!" You villain, it didn't stop you trying to seduce the Countess. And such a torrent of lying patter, I tell you, it made me forget who I really was, it had me giving way on her behalf.

FIGARO   How could I possibly have been taken in once I heard the sound of your pretty voice?

SUZANNE   *(Laughing)* You mean you recognised me? Oh!
See if I don't get my revenge!

FIGARO   Beat a man half to death and still hold a grievance?
Typically female again. But tell me how I have the
good fortune to see you here, when I thought you
were with him? And why those clothes, which took
me in at first and now prove your innocence?

SUZANNE   Ha! You're the big innocent, getting yourself
caught in the trap prepared for someone else! Is
it our fault if we tried to muzzle one fox and ended
up catching two?

FIGARO   So who's caught the other one?

SUZANNE   His wife.

FIGARO   His wife?

SUZANNE   His wife.

FIGARO   *(Excitedly)* Ah, Figaro! You should go and hang
yourself! Couldn't you guess that one? - His
wife! Ah, how can we compete with the wit of
women! - That means his kisses a moment ago ?

SUZANNE   Were given to the Countess.

FIGARO   And the page's kiss?

SUZANNE   *(Laughing)* To the Count.

FIGARO   And the one this morning, behind the chair?

SUZANNE   To nobody.

FIGARO   Are you sure?

SUZANNE   *(Laughing)* I've got plenty of smacks left, Figaro.

FIGARO	*(Kissing her hands)* Your smacks are jewels. But the Count's fist meant business.
SUZANNE	Enough of that pride! Humble yourself in the dust!
FIGARO	*(Fitting the actions to his words)* You are right. It is only justice. On my knees, bowing before you, prostrate, eating the dirt.
SUZANNE	*(Laughing)* Ah! That poor Count! Going to all that trouble ...
FIGARO	*(Clambering to his knees)* ... to seduce his wife!

SCENE NINE

The Count (entering from upstage and going straight to the pavilion on his right), Figaro, Suzanne.

COUNT	*(To himself)* I've looked for her everywhere in the woods. Perhaps she went in here.
SUZANNE	*(In a low voice, to Figaro)* It's him.
COUNT	*(Opening the door to the pavilion)* Suzon, are you in there?
FIGARO	*(In a low voice)* He's looking for her. And I thought he was already ...
SUZANNE	*(In a low voice)* He hasn't recognised her.
FIGARO	Let's finish him off. Shall we?
	He kisses her hand.
COUNT	*(Turning round)* A man on his knees to the Countess...! Ah! I've no sword with me.
	He steps forward.

FIGARO   *(Gets to his feet, disguising his voice)* Forgive me,
                Madame. I did not appreciate that our usual meet-
                ing place had been chosen for the wedding cele-
                brations.

COUNT   *(Aside)*   It's the man in the dressing room this
                morning.

                He claps a hand to his forehead.

FIGARO   *(Continuing)* But we shall certainly not allow so
                trivial an obstacle to hold back our pleasures.

COUNT   *(Aside)*   Massacre, death, hell!

FIGARO   *(Leading her towards the pavilion on the left; in a low
                voice)* He's swearing.   *(Out loud)* So let's not
                delay, Madame. We'll make up for this morning's
                disturbance, when I jumped from the window.

COUNT   *(Aside)*   Ah! All is revealed at last!

SUZANNE   *(Near the pavilion on the left)*   Before you come in,
                check that no one has followed us.

                He kisses her on the forehead.

COUNT   *(Crying out)*   Vengeance!

                *Suzanne runs into the pavilion where Fanchette,
                Marceline and Cherubin are.*

SCENE TEN

The Count, Figaro.
The Count seizes Figaro's arm.

FIGARO   *(Feigning extreme fright)*   It's my master.

COUNT   *(Recognising him)* Ha! It's you, you villain! Help,
                there! Servants, guards!

SCENE ELEVEN

Pedrillo, the Count, Figaro.

PEDRILLO   *(In his riding boots)*   My Lord, I've found you at last.

COUNT   It's Pedrillo. Good. Are you all by yourself?

PEDRILLO   Just arrived back post haste from Seville.

COUNT   Come over here. Yell at the top of your voice.

PEDRILLO   *(Yelling as loud as he can)*   No sign of the page anywhere. I've brought back the package.

COUNT   *(Pushing him away)*   Hey, you numbskull!

PEDRILLO   My Lord told me to yell.

COUNT   *(Still clutching Figaro)*   For help. - Servants, guards! Anyone there? If you can hear me, over here, quick, all of you!

PEDRILLO   You've got Figaro and me, that's two of us with you. What's the danger?

SCENE TWELVE

As before, plus Brid'oison, Bartholo, Bazile, Antonio, Gripe-Soleil, and the whole of the wedding party, running up with torches.

BARTHOLO   *(To Figaro)*   Here we are, you see, as soon as you gave the signal ...

COUNT   *(Pointing to the pavilion on his left)*   Pedrillo, guard that door.

Pedrillo goes over to it.

BAZILE	*(To Figaro, in a low voice)* Did you catch him with Suzanne?
COUNT	*(Pointing at Figaro)* And all of you, my subjects, surround this man. And answer for him with your lives.
BAZILE	Ha! Ha!
COUNT	*(Furious)* Will you be quiet! *(To Figaro, in icy tones)* Now, my fine gentleman, are you going to answer my questions?
FIGARO	*(Coldly)* How could I possibly decline, Sir? You control everything here, apart from yourself.
COUNT	*(Restraining himself)* Apart from myself!
ANTONIO	That's telling him.
COUNT	*(His anger bursting through)* This is too much. If one thing could make me any more furious, it's his affecting coolness.
FIGARO	Are we just rank and file soldiers who kill and get killed without anyone telling us whose interests we're serving? That's not good enough for me: I want to know why I'm supposed to be angry.
COUNT	*(Beside himself)* I'll show you anger! *(Controlling himself)* You're no simpleton, don't pretend you don't know! Will you at least condescend to inform us who is the lady escorted by yourself a moment ago into that pavilion?
FIGARO	*(Maliciously pointing to the other one)* Into that one?
COUNT	*(Rapidly)* Into this one.
FIGARO	*(Coldly)* That's a different matter. A young lady who has honoured me with her special favours.

BAZILE	*(Surprised)* Ha! Ha!
COUNT	*(Rapidly)* Do you hear him, gentlemen?
BARTHOLO	*(Surprised)* We hear him.
COUNT	*(To Figaro)* And does this young lady have any other attachments that you know of?
FIGARO	*(Coldly)* I am aware that a distinguished nobleman paid her some attention at one time. But either because he has neglected her, or because I please her more than some more suitable man, she now prefers me.
COUNT	*(Sharply)* Prefers ... *(Controlling himself)* Well, the man's ingenuousness is something. What he himself openly admits, gentlemen, I have heard, I give you my word, from the very mouth of his accomplice.
BRID'OISON	*(Amazed)* His a-accomplice!
COUNT	*(In a fury)* And so, when dishonour is made public, vengeance must be public too.

He goes into the pavilion.

SCENE THIRTEEN

As before, minus the Count.

ANTONIO	Quite right, it's only proper.
BRID'OISON	*(To Figaro)* So who-o has taken whose wife?
FIGARO	*(Laughing)* No one has enjoyed that particular pleasure.

SCENE FOURTEEN

As before, plus the Count, Cherubin.

COUNT   *(Speaking inside the pavilion, and pulling out someone as yet unseen)* It's no use, there's nothing you can do. You are found out, Madame, and your hour has come! *(He emerges without looking behind him.)* And what a sincere pleasure to know that no other ties bind me to a union I detest ...

FIGARO   *(Crying out)* Cherubin!

COUNT   My page?

BAZILE   Ha! Ha!

COUNT   *(Aside, furious)* It's the bloody page yet again! *(To Cherubin)* What were you doing in that room?

CHERUBIN   *(Timidly)* I was keeping out of sight, as you ordered.

PEDRILLO   And I drove my horse into the ground for this!

COUNT   Antonio, you go in. Bring out before her judge the infamous woman who has dishonoured me.

BRID'OISON   Is it the Cou-ountess you're looking for in there?

ANTONIO   Damn me if Providence isn't getting its own back: you've done so much of it in these parts yourself!...

COUNT   *(Furious)* Just get inside!

         Antonio goes in.

SCENE FIFTEEN

As before, minus Antonio.

COUNT   You will soon see, gentlemen, that the page was
                not alone.

CHERUBIN   *(Timidly)*   My fate would have been too cruel
                altogether, if one particular caring soul hadn't
                sweetened the bitterness.

SCENE SIXTEEN

As before, plus Antonio, Fanchette.

ANTONIO   *(Pulling out by the arm someone as yet unseen)*
                Come along, Your Ladyship, can't wait until we
                beg you to come out, seeing as we know you went
                in there.

FIGARO   *(Crying out)*   My little cousin!

BAZILE   Ha! Ha!

COUNT   Fanchette!

ANTONIO   *(Turning round and crying out)*   Ah! Well, damn
                my eyes! My Lord, that's a harsh joke, choosing
                me to show all and sundry it's my own daughter
                causing all this upset.

COUNT   *(Outraged)*   Who knew she was in there?

                He makes as if to enter the pavilion himself.

BARTHOLO   *(Intercepting him)*   Allow me, Your Excellency.
                Things are far from clear. At least I have a cool
                head.

                He goes in.

BRID'OISON   Here's a business that's getting a-all too tangled.

SCENE SEVENTEEN

As before, plus Marceline.

BARTHOLO   *(Speaking inside, then coming out)* Have no fear,
                  Madame, you will come to no harm. I guarantee
                  it. *(He turns round and cries out.)*   Marceline!...

BAZILE   Ha! Ha!

FIGARO   *(Laughing)* What a mad carry-on! Is my mother
                  in it as well?

ANTONIO   It's getting worse.

COUNT   *(Enraged)* What do I care! The Countess ...

SCENE EIGHTEEN

As before, plus Suzanne, shielding her face with her fan.

COUNT   ... Ah! She's coming out! *(He grabs her roughly
                  by the arm.)* - What punishement, gentlemen,
                  do you judge should be meted out to a hateful ...

                  Suzanne falls to her knees, head lowered.

COUNT   No! No!

                  Figaro falls to his knees, on the other side.

COUNT   *(Louder)* No! No!

                  Marceline falls to her knees in front of him.

COUNT   *(Louder)* No! No!

All fall to their knees, except Brid'oison.

COUNT   *(Beside himself)* Not if there were a hundred of
               you!

SCENE NINETEEN

As before, plus the Countess, who walks out from the other pavilion.

COUNTESS   *(Falling to her knees)* Let me at least swell the
               numbers.

COUNT   *(Staring at the Countess and Suzanne)* Ah! What
               am I seeing!

BRID'OISON   *(Laughing)* Bless me, i-it's the Countess.

COUNT   *(Trying to urge the Countess to her feet)* What! Do
               you mean that was you, Countess? *(In a tone of
               humble entreaty)* Only the most generous pardon ...

COUNTESS   *(Laughing)* If you were me, you would be saying
               "No, no!"; and I, for the third time in one day, I
               grant it unconditionally.

               She rises.

SUZANNE   *(Rising)* And so do I.

MARCELINE   *(Rising)* And so do I.

FIGARO   *(Rising)* And so do I. There's an echo here!

               All rise.

COUNT   An echo! - I tried to deceive them with cunning;
               they've treated me as if I were a little boy!

COUNTESS   *(Laughing)* Don't take it badly, my Lord Count!

FIGARO   *(Brushing his knees with his hat)* Today's little escapades make excellent training for an ambassador!

COUNT   *(To Suzanne)* That note sealed with a pin?...

SUZANNE   It was Madame who dictated it.

COUNT   Then her reply is overdue.

> *He kisses the Countess's hand.*

COUNTESS   Everyone shall have what belongs to him or her.

> *She gives the purse to Figaro, and the diamond to Suzanne.*

SUZANNE   *(To Figaro)* Another dowry.

FIGARO   *(Slapping the purse in his hand)* And that makes three. This was a tough one to win!

SUZANNE   Like our marriage.

GRIPE-SOLEIL   And the bride's garter? Who's to get that? Does I?

COUNTESS   *(Pulling out the ribbon she has made such a business over, and throwing it on the ground)* The garter? It was with her clothes. There it is.

> *The village boys from the wedding party scrabble to pick it up.*

CHERUBIN   *(Quicker than the rest, darts forward and grabs it)* Anyone who wants it will have to fight me for it!

COUNT   *(Laughing, to Cherubin)* For such a touchy gentleman, what was so funny about a certain crack on the head you got a little while ago?

CHERUBIN   *(Stepping back and half-drawing his sword)* Someone struck me, Colonel, Sir?

FIGARO   *(Pretending anger)* It was my cheek he was hit on:
                  see how great men hand out justice!

COUNT   *(Laughing)* His cheek?   Ha, ha, ha! What do
                  you say to that, my dear Countess?

COUNTESS   *(Preoccupied, startled, reacting with fervour)* Oh!
                  Yes, dear Count, for the whole of my life, and
                  never wavering, I promise you.

COUNT   *(Clapping Brid'oison the judge on the shoulder)* And
                  so to you, Brid'oison, let's hear your opinion now.

BRID'OISON   My opinion on e-everything I've seen, my Lord
                  Count? We-ell, speaking for myself, I-I don't
                  know what to say to you: that's my way of think-
                  ing.

EVERYONE
TOGETHER   Well said, judge!

FIGARO   I was poor, and they scorned me. I showed a bit
                  of wit, and they hated me.   Now, with a pretty
                  wife and a fine fortune ...

BARTHOLO   *(Laughing)* Good friends and good hearts will
                  swarm around you.

FIGARO   Is that possible?

BARTHOLO   I know them.

FIGARO   *(Doffing his hat to the audience)* My wife and my
                  fortune apart, they are all welcome, and will do me
                  honour and pleasure.

                       *The orchestra strikes up the introduction to the
                       vaudeville - as heard in Act Four, Scene Ten -
                       and all join in singing and dancing.*

<u>VAUDEVILLE</u>

BAZILE   Three-fold dowry and superb wife,
            Plenty of wealth for a husband to keep;
            Mad to be jealous - it isn't worth the strife -
            Of a Lord or a page with no hairs on his cheek.
            The clever man learns to rule his life
            On the old Latin proverb which we all should thank:

FIGARO   I know ... *(He sings)*
            "Gaudeant to men born of high rank."

BAZILE   No ...   *(He sings)*
            "Gaudeant if you've cash in the bank."

SUZANNE   It's all right for husbands to cheat their wives, Everyone
            laughs when they boast and brag;
            Just let the wife start making eyes,
            She's punished with the label of slut and slag.
            If it doesn't seem fair, don't faint with surprise, How can the
            weak hope for justice, when
            The power that makes the laws is the power of men?

FIGARO   Dicky Dickson is jealous, he's a figure of fun:
            Wants to keep his wife and live a life of peace;
            Buys himself a dog, thinks the battle is won,
            His garden patrolled by a terrible beast.
            Then one night, what a din, it's a racket that would stun,
            Everyone is bitten as the doggie rushes round,
            Except the crafty lover who sold poor Dick the hound.

COUNTESS   One wife is proud, and has her own way,
            She doesn't love her husband any more;
            Another is faithful, to her own dismay,
            But bravely she keeps to the husband's love she swore. The
            least mad's the wife, alas I have to say,
            Who settles for her husband, forgetting her own needs, And
            never passes judgement on that other person's deeds.

COUNT

Who wants a country wife, stuck out in the sticks,
Homely duties the height of her desires?
 Slim chance of joy, if a woman's got no tricks,
 So here's to the wife who can light a fellow's fires!
Like a coin in circulation, she's a better chance to mix,
 Stamped with her husband's name, her value cannot fall,
And freely passing round, she serves the good of all.

MARCELINE

Every man knows his own tender mother:
She is the one who gave him light of day;
All else is left for mystery to cover,
Love's a misty secret, and every truth is grey.

FIGARO

(Continuing her verse)
That misty secret perhaps explains another:
 How the son of a father whose ways are rough and cold
Turns out often to be worth his weight in gold.

FIGARO

Fate is the only thing that gives a chap his start:
One man is King, the other tends his sheep;
Chance is the distance keeping them apart,
But if you've got the wit, no mountain is too steep.
Anoint me twenty kings, each with his royal mark,
Death will pluck them down from their thrones, however high:
But talent is immortal: Voltaire will never die!

CHERUBIN

Sex whom we love, as fickle as you're fair,
Our finest days of manhood you torment;
Even though we curse till blue turns the air,
 We always return because we want what we resent.
You're like the paying audience sitting out there:
Although he makes a show of disdaining your applause,
A man does all he can to win you to his cause.

SUZANNE

If this gay and giddy piece of work
Encloses a moral or a lesson you should heed,

It's not about flirtation, which is but a quirk, So
give grace to reason, for that is what we need. For
nature has its wisdom where even follies lurk, It
draws us ever on by fanning our desires, And uses
simple pleasure to lead where it aspires.

BRID'OISON   Now, gentlemen, take note that this co-omic little
play,
 Which now we have to judge without fa-avour or
fear,
Portrays for us the life, co-orrect in every way,
Of all good people, or those with ears to hear.
 For if you oppress them, they only make affray,
And cry and curse; but i-if they're done no wrong,
Everything conclu-udes in dances and in song.

Everybody dances.

THE END

THE GUILTY MOTHER

CHARACTERS

COUNT ALMAVIVA (Grand nobleman of Spain, proud of his family, and yet without hauteur.)

COUNTESS ALMAVIVA (An unhappy lady, and angelic in her piety.)

THE CHEVALIER LEON (Their son, a young man in love with liberty, like all fresh and fiery souls.)

FLORESTINE (Ward and god-daughter of Count Almaviva, a young lady of high sensibility.)

MONSIEUR BEGEARSS (Irish, a major in a Spanish infantry regiment, former ambassadorial secretary to the Count. A man of depth, an intriguer, a skilled formenter of trouble.)

FIGARO (Apothecary, valet and confidant to the Count. A man moulded by experience of the world, of society, of its disturbances.)

SUZANNE (Principal chambermaid and companion to the Countess. Wife of Figaro. An excellent woman, devoted to her mistress, and no longer subject to the illusions of youth.)

MONSIEUR FAL (The Count's lawyer, a precise and upright man.)

GUILLAUME (M. Bégearss's German valet, too simple a man for his master.)

ACT ONE

SCENE ONE

The set represents a heavily decorated drawing room.

SUZANNE *(Alone, holding dark-coloured flowers which she is making into a bouquet)* Let my mistress wake now and ring for me; my sorry task is done. *(She drops into a chair.)* It's hardly nine o'clock and already I'm exhausted... Her last order, when I prepared her bed, has spoiled my whole night... "Tomorrow, Suzanne, as soon as it's light, have bunches of flowers brought, and decorate my room with them." She told the porter: "I'm at home to nobody all day." And to me: "Make a wreath of flowers for me, black and red, a single white carnation in their middle."... There it is. My poor mistress. There were tears in her eyes. All these preparations, who are they meant for? Ah! Ah! If we were in Spain, today would be the feast day of her son Léon... *(Mysteriously)* ... and of another man who is no more. *(She contemplates the flowers.)* The colours of blood and of mourning. *(Sighs)* There's no cure for the wound in that woman's heart. Let's tie this up with a black ribbon, to match her sad caprice.

Ties the bouquet.

SCENE TWO

Suzanne, Figaro, looking mystified. (This scene must move ahead heatedly)

SUZANNE	Figaro! Come in! Sneaking in to see your wife like some crafty lover!
FIGARO	Is it safe to talk?
SUZANNE	Yes, if you leave the door open.
FIGARO	Why the precautions?
SUZANNE	Just that You Know Who might suddenly walk in.
FIGARO	*(Pressing)* Honoré Tartuffe Bégearss?
SUZANNE	And I've agreed to meet him. So don't get into the habit of embellishing his name; it could get passed around and harm your plans.
FIGARO	Honoré IS his name!
SUZANNE	But not Tartuffe.
FIGARO:	Damn him!
SUZANNE	You sound upset.
FIGARO	I'm furious! *(She gets up.)* Is this what we agreed? Tell me straight, Suzanne, do I have your help in preventing a disaster? Are you still taken in by this vicious man?
SUZANNE	No, but I think he is suspicious of me. He doesn't tell me anything any more. In fact, I'm afraid he may believe we're back on speaking terms again.
FIGA	We must keep pretending we're not.

SUZANNE: But what have you found out to put you in such a
                mood?

FIGARO: First let's go back over the facts. Since we've
                been in Paris, and since Monsieur Almaviva ...
                there's no choice but to call him by his name now
                that he refuses to allow his title ...

SUZANNE   (*Vigorously*) A fine state of affairs. And madame
                going out without a footman. We look like any-
                one off the streeet!

FIGARO   And since, as I say, he lost his playboy of an elder
                son in some gambling duel, you know how every-
                thing has altered for us. Look how bleak and
                angry his moods have become.

SUZANN   You're not much sunnier yourself.

FIGARO: Look how he seems to hate the sight of his other
                son.

SUZANN   Too true.

FIGARO: Look how unhappy the mistress is.

SUZANNE   It's a crime, what he's doing.

FIGARO   Look how he's fawning over his ward Florestine.
                Especially look how he's doing everything he can
                to dispose of his fortune.

SUZANNE   My poor Figaro, you're starting to rave, can you
                hear yourself? If I can see all that, why bother to
                tell me?

FIGARO	It's still necessary to have things out in the open to make sure we understand each other. Has it not become clear to us that this clever Irishman, the scourge of this family, having played secretary to the Count in a few commissions, has learnt the secrets of every one of them? Don't we know that this deep intriguer managed to persuade them away from the easy delights of Spain to this country, turned upside down by revolution, and here hopes to take better advantage of the discord they live in to separate the husband from the wife, marry the ward, and clean up the spoils of a household in disarray?
SUZA	All right, but what can I do to stop him?
FIGARO:	Never let him out of your sight. Keep me informed of everything he does ...
SUZANNE:	But I already tell you everything he says.
FIGARO:	Ah, what he says ... merely the words he chooses to use. But if you can catch the words he doesn't say, when you're talking together, his slightest gesture, a flicker of reaction, that's where he keeps the secrets of his soul. Some horror is being sewn together here. He must be made to feel assured of success. Because there's something about him more false, more tricky than ever, and more smug. That feeling you get from the fools in this country, triumphing in anticipation of success. Can you be as tricky as he is? Lead him on, raise his hopes? Whatever he asks, let him have it?
SUZANNE	That's asking a lot!
FIGA	Everything is fine, and everything will go accord-

ingly to plan if I'm kept immediately informed.

SUZANNE: ... And if I inform my mistress.

FIGARO: It's not yet time: they're all under his spell. No
             one would believe you: You'd destroy us without
             saving them. Follow him everywhere, like his
             shadow ... while I watch his movements outside.

SUZANNE   My dear, I told you, he's suspicious of me. And if
             he were to surprise us together ... There he is,
             coming downstairs now. Quiet! Make it sound as
             if we're having a row. *(She puts the bouquet down
             on the table.)*

FIGA   *(Raising his voice)* And I say no! Just let me catch
             you once more!

SUZANNE: *(Raising her voice)* Oh yes, I'm scared of you!

FIGARO: *(Pretending to strike her)* Oh brave with it, are we!
             ... Take that for your insolence!

SUZANNE   *(Pretending to be struck)* Hit me, would you ... in
             my mistress's room!

SCENE THREE

Major Bégearss, Figaro, Suzanne.

BEGEARSS   *(In uniform, wearing a black armband)* What's all
             this? The noise! I could hear you rowing from
             my room for the last hour.

FIGARO   *(Aside)* For an hour!

BEGEARSS   I come down, I find a woman in tears ...

SUZANNE	*(Pretending to weep)* The beast lifted his fist to me!
BEGEARSS	Ah, the disgrace, Mr Figaro! Did a gentleman ever strike a person of the other sex?
FIGARO	*(Roughly)* For heaven's sake! Sir, leave us alone. I am not "a gentleman", and this woman is not "a person of the other sex". She is my wife, whose insolence leads her to meddle in intrigues, and who thinks she can challenge me to my face because she has people here who support her. Oh, I mean to take her to task for this!
BEGEARSS	Is a man to be therefore a mere brute?
FIGARO	Sir, if ever I seek an arbiter in my dealings with her, you will be the last man I shall look to. The reason why, you know all too well.
BEGEARSS	Sir, you are disrespectful. I shall make a complaint to your master.
FIGARO	*(Mocking)* Disrespectful, me? ... Impossible!

Exits.

SCENE FOUR

Bégearss, Suzanne.

BEGEARSS	My child, I am astonished. What has caused his rage?
SUZANNE	He came to pick a quarrel. He told me a hundred

horror stories about you. He was ordering me not
to see you, never to dare to speak to you. I
defended you. The argument grew heated. It
ended with his hitting me ... for the first time in
his life. But for me that's enough, I'm going to
leave him. You saw him ...

BEGEARSS Leave it there. Some slight cloud had made me
doubt you. But what I've just heard has blown it
away.

SUZAN And that's enough to make it all all right?

BEGEARSS You can leave your revenge in my hands. It's high
time I paid my debts to you, my poor Suzanne.
And to make a start, I'll let you into a secret... But
are we quite sure that door is shut? *(Suzanne goes
over to check. Bégearss continues, aside.)* Ah, just
leave me alone for two minutes with that jewel
case I had made for the Countess, all her important letters are in its false bottom...

SUZANNE *(Returning)* Well then, this great secret?

BEGEARSS Just serve your friend. Your dreams are about to
be fulfilled. I marry Florestine. The matter is
decided. Her father insists on it.

SUZANNE Her father? Who's that?

BEGEARSS Well where have you been hiding? It's a reliable
rule, my dear, when a particular orphan girl
arrives in someone's household as a ward or else
as a god-daughter, she is always the daughter of
the husband. *(Becoming serious again.)* In short, I
can marry her ... if you get to work on her on my
behalf.

SUZAN	Oh, but Léon is very much in love with her.
BEGEARS	Their son? *(Coldly)* I shall separate him from his love.
SUZANNE	*(Surprised)* Ha!... She is deeply in love.
BEGEARSS	With him?
SUZANNE	Yes.
BEGEARSS	*(Cold)* I will cure her of it.
SUZANNE	*(More suprised)* Ha! Ha! ... The mistress, who knows all about it, has given them her blessing.
BEGEARSS	*(Cold)* We will make her change her mind.
SUZANNE	*(Astonished)* As well? But Figaro, if my eyes don't deceive me, is in the young man's confidence.
BEGEARSS	That is the least of my concerns. Would you not be pleased to be rid of him?
SUZANNE	Only if he comes to no harm...
BEGEARSS	Come now! The mere idea stains my unimpeach-able integrity. When they understand what each other is up to, they'll change their minds of their own accord.
SUZANNE	*(Incredulous)* If you did that, monsieur, ...
BEGEARSS	I shall do it. You know that love hardly comes into arrangements of this kind. *(Caressingly)* You are the only one I have ever truly loved.

SUZANNE   *(Incredulous)* Ah? If my mistress had desired ...

BEGEARSS   I would certainly have been her consolation. But she spurned my approaches!... In accordance with the Count's plan, the Countess will be going to a nunnery.

SUZANNE   *(Vigorously)* I won't be party to any plan against her.

BEGEARSS   Devil take it, he's helping her fulfil her own wishes! I'm always hearing you say, "Oh, she's an angel on earth!"

SUZANNE   *(Angry)* Well then, do you have to make it into a cruel joke?

BEGEARSS   *(Laughing)* No, but at least we can bring her closer back to that heaven, that kingdom of angels from which she has momentarily fallen!... And since, amongst all these new and wonderful laws, divorce has been made possible...

SUZANNE   *(Vigorously)* The Count wants a separation?

BEGEARSS   If he can.

SUZANNE   *(Angry)* Ah, men are vile! They should be strangled, the lot of them!

BEGEARSS   I like to think you will make an exception in my case.

SUZANNE   Ha! Don't count on it.

BEGEARSS   Your anger is adorable. It shows the goodness of

your heart. As for the lovesick young knight, the
Count is sending him on a voyage, a long one.
Figaro, a man of experience, will be his discreet
guide. *(He takes her hand.)* And as for us, the
Count, Florestine and I will live in the same
house; and our dear Suzanne, with the gift of our
complete trust, will be our housekeeper, will have
charge of the household, will have the controlling
hand in every affair. No more husband, no more
blows, no more brutal tyranny. Days spun with
gold and silk, and the happiest of lives.

SUZANNE   From your winning words, I take it you'd like me
to tackle Florestine on your behalf.

BEGEARSS   *(Coaxing)* In truth, I have been counting on your
good offices. You were always an excellent
woman. All the rest is in my own hands; this
point alone lies within yours. *(With vigour)* For
instance, today you can do us a vital service...
(Suzanne stares at him. Bégearss restrains himself.)
I say "vital" because of the importance the Count
attaches to it. *(Coldly)* For, upon my word, it is
but a small thing. It would appear to be the
Count's fancy ... to give his daughter, when the
contract is signed a piece of jewellery identical to
the Countess's diamonds. He would like it to be
kept a secret.

SUZANNE   *(Surprised)* Ha! Ha!

BEGEARSS   It's a perfectly sound idea. Beautiful diamonds
round off many a transaction. He might ask you
to bring his wife's jewel case, to match the design
for his jeweller...

SUZANN   Why the same as the mistress's? That's a fairly strange idea.

BEGEARSS: He insists the new ones should be just as beautiful. As you know, it matters little as far as I'm
concerned. Look, here he comes.

SCENE FIVE

The Count, Suzanne, Bégearss.

COUNT   Mr Bégearss, I was looking for you.

BEGEARSS   Before coming to you, sir, I was calling on
Suzanne to warn her you would be asking for that
jewel case...

SUZANNE   Or anyway, My Lord, you know...

COUNT   Ah, none of your "My Lord". When we moved to
France, did I not order..?

SUZANNE   I find we are, My Lord, diminished by it.

COUNT   Because you appreciate vanity better than true
pride. When one desires to live in a certain country, one does not insult its customs.

SUZANNE   Well, sir, provided you mean what you say...

COUNT   *(Proud)* Since when have I been misunderstood?

SUZANNE   Then I will go and find it for you. *(Aside)* Oh,
goodness! Figaro told me to agree to everything.

<u>SCENE SIX</u>

The Count, Bégearss.

COUNT

This little matter that seemed to be worrying Suzanne, I've quite made up my mind on it.

BÉGEARSS

There is another, sir, which worries me much more. You seem to be afflicted by some great burden.

COUNT

Shall I tell you, my friend? The death of my son seemed to me to be the heaviest of all burdens. But now I am bruised by a harsher grief, one which is making my life unbearable.

BÉGEARSS

Had you not forbidden me thus to rouse your anger, I would say that your younger son...

COUNT

My younger son! I have none!

BÉGEARSS

Calm yourself, sir. Let us use our reason. The loss of a loved child can make a father unjust towards the one remaining, unjust towards his wife, towards himself. Ought one to judge these things on no better basis than conjecture?

COUNT

Conjecture! Ah, I'm all too certain. My great grief is to lack proof. Whilst my poor son was alive, it mattered little. As the heir to my name, my lands, my fortune ... what did that other fellow matter? My cold disdain, some minor title and an allowance would have been sufficient vengeance on his mother and him. But can you imagine my despair, on losing a son, to see a stranger inherit my rank and title; and to torture me in my anguish by coming to me each day and addressing me with the hated name of "father"?

BEGEARSS   Sir, I fear I may aggravate your anger in attempt-
ing to appease it, but the virtue of your wife...

COUNT   *(Angry)* Ah, that is but an additional crime. To
mask behind an exemplary life such an affront.
To command the respect and regard of the whole
of society, with all her excellent habits and rigid
piety, for twenty years, while raining down on me
alone through this affectation of blamelessness all
the wrongs my supposedly strange behaviour
brings in its wake... My hatred of them only
increases.

BEGEARSS   What else would you have her do? Even suppos-
ing her guilty, is there any error in the world that
twenty years of repentance must not eventually
erase? Were you yourself without reproach? And
that young Florestine, whom you call your ward,
and for whom you feel more closely than that...

COUNT   Let her be my revenge! I will disinherit my
wealth, and she shall have it all. Three million
francs in gold, sent from Vera Cruz, are already
destined for her dowry. And it is to you that I
entrust them. Only give me your help in casting
over this gift an impenetrable veil. When you
receive this sum, and when you present yourself as
her husband, explain that it is an inheritance, a
legacy from some far-off relative.

BEGEARSS   *(Showing his black arm band)* See how I have put
on mourning in readiness to obey you.

COUNT   When I have the King of Spain's authority for the
exchange of all my Spanish holdings for an equiv-

alent wealth here in France, I shall find a way to ensure that its possession falls to the two of you.

BEGEARSS (*Vigorously*) And I say I want none of it. Can you think that on a mere suspicion,... which may yet have little foundation, I will make myself an accomplice to the complete disinheriting of the rightful heir to your name, a young man full of merit. For you must allow he has merit...

COUNT (*Impatient*) More than my son, do you mean? Everyone thinks the same way as you. And that only sets me against him all the more resolutely...

BEGEARSS If your ward accepts me, and if, out of your great wealth, you extract for her dowry those three million francs in Mexican gold, I cannot permit the idea that I should become their owner, and I will not take them unless the marriage contract confirms them as a gift, matching the gift of loving duty I make to her.

COUNT (*Embracing him*) A loyal and frankly-spoken friend! What a husband my daughter shall have!

SCENE SEVEN

Suzanne, Count, Bégearss.

SUZANNE Sir, here is the case with the diamonds. Don't keep it too long: let me put it back before the mistress is up.

COUNT Suzanne, on your way out, say that we are to be left alone, unless I ring.

SUZANNE   *(Aside)* Figaro must hear of this.

                 Exits.

SCENE EIGHT

Count, Bégearss.

BEGEARS   What have you in mind with the jewel case?

COUNT   *(Takes from his pocket a diamond-studded bracelet.)*
                 I shall conceal from you no longer the details of
                 the injury I have suffered. A certain Leon of
                 Astorga, who was once my page, and whom they
                 used to call Cherubin ...

BEGEARSS   I knew him. We served in the same regiment,
                 where thanks to you I was a major. But he has
                 been dead now for more than twenty years.

COUNT   That is the basis of my suspicions. He had the
                 temerity to love my wife. I believed her in love
                 with him. I sent him away from Andalusia, on
                 some service with my legions. One year after the
                 birth of my son ... taken from me in that hated
                 duel *(He covers his eyes.)* ... when I was embarking
                 for Mexico as viceroy, my wife, instead of remain-
                 ing in Madrid, or in my palace in Seville, or of liv-
                 ing at Aguas Frescas, which is a superb country
                 seat, where do you think she chose to retire to, my
                 friend? The evil castle of Astorga, the local capital
                 of a poor patch of land I had purchased from the
                 relations of this page. That was where she wanted
                 to spend the three years that I was absent; that
                 was where she brought into the world (after nine
                 or ten months, how can I tell exactly?) this

wretched child who bears a traitor's features. It
was at that period that the painter who had made
a miniature of me for the Countess's bracelet,
found my page a handsome young fellow and
asked to make a sketch of him. It is now one of
those fine paintings which hang in my study.

BEGEARSS   Yes... *(He lowers his eyes.)* So much so that your
wife..

COUNT   *(Strongly)* Never wishes to set eyes on it? Well,
from that portrait I have had this miniature made,
here in this bracelet, which is identical in every
detail to hers, set by the same jeweller who
mounted all her diamonds. I am going to make a
substitution. If she remains silent, you will know
that I have my proof. And if she does speak out,
whatever she says, there will be some difficult
explaining to do, and my shame will soon find out
if it has cause.

BEGEARSS   If you were to seek my opinion, sir, I do not find
the plan altogether wise.

COUNT   Why not?

BEGEARSS   Such methods insult our honour. If some stroke
of chance, lucky or otherwise, had presented you
with certain facts, I would understand it if you
were to explore them further. But to set a trap!
To trick her! Ah, sir, what man of the slightest
delicacy would stoop to taking such advantage of
even his most despised enemy?

COUNT   It is too late to step back: the bracelet is made, the
page's likeness is inside

BEGEARS   *(Taking the jewel case)* Sir, in the name of all that
            is honourable...

COUNT   *(Who has snatched the bracelet from the case)* Ah,
            my own dear likeness! I have you now. Give me
            at least the joy of seeing you adorn my daughter's
            arm, a hundred times more worthy to bear it!

            > *(He replaces it with the other one. Bégearss pre-
            > tends to resist. Each pulls at the case from one
            > end. Bégearss neatly causes the double bottom to
            > fall open.)*

BEGEARSS   *(Angry)* Ah, look! Now the box is broken!

COUNT   *(Looking)* No. It's only one more secret our
            argument has revealed. This is a false bottom,
            and there are papers hidden inside!

BEGEARSS   *(Resisting)* Allow me to believe, sir, that you do
            not intend to abuse...

COUNT   *(Impatient)* If some lucky chance had presented
            you with certain facts, you were saying a moment
            ago, I would understand it if you were to explore
            them further. Chance has offered me some facts,
            and I shall now follow your advice. *(He tears out
            the papers.)*

BEGEARSS   *(Heatedly)* By all my life is worth, I cannot be
            party to such a crime! Return those papers, sir, or
            else allow me to withdraw.

            > *He moves away. The Count holds the papers and
            > reads. Bégearss watches him surreptitiously, and
            > secretly congratulates himself.*

COUNT	(*Enraged*) I don't wish to see any more. Shut all the others away. But this one I'll keep.
BEGEARSS	No, whatever the circumstances, you are too much a man of honour to commit a ...
COUNT	To commit a ...? Finish your sentence! Don't mince your words, I can hear what you have to say.
BEGEARSS	(*Bowing forward*) Sir, my benefactor, forgive me! If my reproach was indecent, impute it only to my strength of conviction.
COUNT	You do not offend me. On the contrary, I hold you in higher regard for saying it. (*He flings himself into an armchair.*) Ah, treacherous Rosine! For all that I was easy with my favours, she is the one woman for whom I ever felt... Other women I have bent to my will! Ah, I can tell from my rage how much this unworthy passion... I despise myself for loving her!
BEGEARSS	In God's name, sir, put that terrible letter back!

SCENE NINE

Figaro, Count, Bégearss.

COUNT	(*Rising*) What are you doing here? What do you want?
FIGARO	I came because you rang.
COUNT	(*Angry*) Rang? You interfering valet...!
FIGARO	Ask the jeweller. He heard the same as I did.

COUNT	My jeweller? What does he want?
BEGEARSS	He says he has an appointment with you about a bracelet he has been making.

Bégearss, noticing Figaro trying to get a look at the jewel case, does his best to screen it.

COUNT	Oh!... Tell him to come back another day.
FIGARO	*(Maliciously)* But while sir happens to have the mistress's jewel case open, perhaps it would be convenient...
COUNT	*(Angry)* Mister Inquisitor, leave us! And if you breathe a single word...
FIGARO	A single word? Not nearly enough. I'm not a man to do things by halves.

He examines the box, the paper in the Count's hands, stares proudly at Bégearss and exists.

SCENE TEN

Count, Bégearss.

COUNT	Put that wretched case back together. I have the proof I was looking for. I have it, and it freezes my heart. Why did I ever have to find it? Ah, God! Read it, Mr Bégearss, read it!
BEGEARSS	*(Pushing the letter away)* Be party to spying? God preserve me from any such accusation!
COUNT	What kind of arid friendship is this, refusing my confidences? Men obviously feel compassion only

for the injuries they suffer themselves.

BEGEARSS   What! Because I won't look at that letter! *(Urgently)* Put it away, here comes Suzanne.

> *He swiftly closes the secret compartment of the jewel case. The Count hides the letter inside his coat, against his breast.*

SCENE ELEVEN

Suzanne, Count, Bégearss. Count is overcome.

SUZANNE   *(Running in)* The box! The box! Madame is ringing for it!

BEGEARSS   *(Passing it over)* Suzanne, all in good order, as you see.

SUZANNE   What is the matter with sir, then? He looks upset.

BEGEARSS   Nothing more than a touch of anger with your indiscreet husband, who burst in here in spite of his orders.

SUZANNE   *(Slyly)* But I told him exactly what the situation was.

> *Exits.*

SCENE TWELVE

Leon, Count, Bégearss.
The Count is about to leave, but sees Léon *approaching.*

COUNT   Here comes that other one!

LEON   *(Timid, wishing to embrace the Count)* Father,
             respectful greetings. Did you have a good night?

COUNT   *(Repulsing him, acidly)* Where were you, sir, yes-
             terday evening.

LEON   Father, I was invited to a well-respected gather-
             ing...

COUNT   Where you delivered a lecture?

LEON   I was asked to read an article I had composed on
             the abuse of monastic vows and the right to be
             relieved of them.

COUNT   *(Bitterly)* As with the vows of a gentleman?

BEGEARSS   And which was, I hear, well received?

LEON   Sir, I was granted some indulgence for my tender
             years.

COUNT   So, instead of preparing yourself for your immi-
             nent travels, instead of preparing to fulfil the
             obligations of your rank, you spend your time
             making enemies? You go about composing arti-
             cles, falling in with the fashions of the day? Soon
             we won't be able to distinguish a gentleman from
             a teacher!

LEON   *(Timidly)* Father, there is a more important dis-
             tinction to be made: between an educated and an
             uneducated man; between a free man and a slave.

COUNT   He talks like one of those do-gooding busybodies.
             It's easy to see which path you're going to take.

He makes as if to leave.

LEON   Father!...

COUNT   *(Scornful)* Leave these trivial discussions to the
                tradespeople! Families of our quality speak a
                higher language. Who in court circles says
                "father", sir? Address me as "sir". You sound
                like a man from the common people! "His
                father!" *(He goes out. Leon follows him, glancing at
                Bégearss, who makes a sympathetic gesture.)* Come
                along, Mr Bégearss, come along!

                END OF ACT ONE

ACT TWO

SCENE ONE

The Count's library.
The Count.

COUNT   Now that I am at last alone, let me read this
          astonishing letter which chance has delivered into
          my almost disbelieving hands. *(Takes from his
          inside pocket the letter from the jewel case and reads it
          with heavy emphasis.)* "Unhappy man, we took
          leave of our senses and our fate is sealed. The
          night when you dared so to take me by surprise, in
          the castle where you were raised, whose secret
          passages you know so well; the wild scene which
          then ensued; finally, your crime..., and mine. *(He
          stops.)* Mine receives its just punishment. This
          day, feast day of Saint Léon, patron saint of this
          place and of your own name, this day I have
          brought into the world a son, my disgrace and my
          despair. Thanks to our sad precautions, our hon-
          our is safe; but virtue is for ever lost. Condemned
          henceforth to tears without end, I know they can
          never wash away a crime ... whose result lives on.
          You must never see me again. That is the irrevo-
          cable order of the wretched Rosine ... who dares
          no longer sign herself by any other name." *(He
          presses his hand, with the letter, to his forehead, and
          paces up and down.)* Who dares no longer sign
          herself by any other name!... Ah, Rosine! Rosine!
          Where has time fled to? You have debased your-
          self! ... *(He becomes troubled.)* But these are not
          the words of an evil woman! It was foul, corrupt-

ing man ... But look here is his reply, written on this same letter. *(Reads)* "Since I must see you no more, my life is only hateful, and I will lose it with the utmost joy in an immediate assault on an enemy fort which no orders command me to attack. I return to you all your reproaches, and the portrait I made for you, and the lock of hair I stole from you. You may trust the man who gives you these things after I am dead. He has seen the bottomless depths of my despair. If the death of a poor unfortunate were to inspire in you some remnant of pity, amongst the names with which the infant heir - heir to a happier man than I! - is christened, may I hope that the name of Léon will recall sometimes the memory of the wretched man... who adores you even as he expires, and who signs himself for the last time CHERUBIN-LEON D'ASTORGA?" Then, in a blood-smeared hand... "Mortally wounded, I open this letter once more and send, written in my own blood, this grieving, this eternal farewell. Remember..." The rest has been obliterated by tears... *(He becomes troubled.)* These are not the words of an evil man either. An unhappy aberration... *(He sits, lost in contemplation.)* And I am rent in two!

SCENE TWO

Bégearss, Count.
Bégearss, entering, stops, stares at Count, nibbling at his fingertips in his uncertainty.

COUNT   Ah, my dear friend, come in!... You have caught me in some distress...

BEGEARSS   It frightened me to see it, sir. I dared not
            interrrupt.

COUNT   I have just read this letter. No, these were not
            traitors or monsters, but unhappy wretches who
            lost their senses, as they themselves accuse each
            other.

BEGEARSS   I was of your opinion, sir, in presuming it thus
            myself.

COUNT   *(Rising and pacing the room)* When hapless women
            allow themselves to be seduced, they scarcely
            know the evils they are hatching. On they go, all
            serene... the injuries accumulate,... and an unjust
            world frivolously blames the father who keeps his
            silence, who gnaws his pain in secret! He is taxed
            with being excessively stern because he withholds
            natural affection from the fruits of a criminal adul-
            tery. Our own misdeeds inflict on them virtually
            no loss at all; or at least men's misdeeds cannot
            rob them of the certainty of being mothers, of
            having that priceless gift of motherhood! Whilst
            their merest whim, a passing taste, some small
            thoughtlessness, destroys in a man all happiness,...
            the happiness of his whole life, the knowledge of
            being a father. Ah, not lightly is so much impor-
            tance attached to the faithfulness of women! It is
            on their conduct that are hinged both the good
            and the evil of our society. Whether the family is
            to be a paradise or an inferno depends entirely on
            the opinion they hold of themselves.

BEGEARSS   You must remain calm. Here comes your daugh-
            ter.

<u>SCENE THREE</u>

Florestine, Count, Bégearss.

FLORESTINE   *(Carrying flowers)* They said you had so much on
                  your mind, sir, that I did not dare disturb you by
                  calling to pay my respects.

COUNT   It was you who were on my mind, my child, my
                  daughter! Ah, how it pleases me to call you that.
                  For I cared for you as a child. Your mother's hus-
                  band was a troubled man. When he died he left
                  you nothing. She herself, on departing this world,
                  entrusted you to my keeping. I gave her my word,
                  and I shall keep it, my daughter, by giving you a
                  worthy husband. I can speak to you freely before
                  this friend, who loves us both. Look around you:
                  choose! Do you not find one here worthy to pos-
                  sess your heart?

FLORESTINE   *(Kissing his hand)* You have it entirely, sir. And if
                  I am asked, I will answer that my happiness lies in
                  staying as I am. - Sir, your son may, by marrying
                  (for I am sure that the vows of the knights of
                  Malta will not restrain him now) - Sir, your son by
                  marrying may separate himself from his father.
                  Oh, oh! Let it then be me who cares for you in
                  your old age! It is a duty, sir, I will fulfil with
                  great joy!

COUNT   Don't call me that, don't say "sir"; only the indif-
                  ferent use so formal a title. A child so full of grati-
                  tude would shock nobody if she called me by
                  some gentler name. Call me your father.

BEGEARSS	In all honour, she is worthy of sharing your closest confidences... Miss Florestine, embrace this good, this affectionate guardian. You owe him more than you think. His guardianship is no more than a natural duty. He was once the friend... the secret friend of your mother,... and, to tell you the whole truth in a single word...

SCENE FOUR

Figaro, Countess (in dressing gown), Count, Florestine, Bégearss.

FIGARO	*(Announcing her)* Madame the Countess.
BEGEARSS	*(Aside, throwing a furious look at Figaro)* Devil take the scoundrel!
COUNTESS	*(To Count)* Figaro told me you were not feeling well. I was frightened, I hurried down to you, and now I see...
COUNT	That this officious fellow has been telling you stories again.
FIGARO	Sir, when you met us, you looked so out of sorts ... I am happy there is nothing serious behind it.

Bégearss studies him.

COUNTESS	Good day, Mr Bégearss. There you are, Florestine. You look wonderful... Look how fresh and lovely she is! If God had given me a daughter I would have wished her like you in beauty and in character... You will have to take her place. Would you like that, Florestine?

FLORESTINE   *(Kissing her hand)* Ah! Madame!

COUNTESS   Who has been bringing you flowers then, so early?

FLORESTINE   *(Happily)* Madame, no one has brought me flow-
                  ers. I made these bouquets myself. Is it not the
                  feast of Saint Léon today?

COUNTESS   You are a delightful child, you never forget any-
                  thing! *(She kisses her forehead. The Count reacts
                  with a terrible gesture. Bégearss restrains Figaro.)*
                  Since we are all assembled here, tell my son we
                  will be taking our chocolate in here.

FLORESTINE   While they are preparing it, my godfather, show
                  us that fine bust of Washington they say you have
                  been sent.

COUNT   I have no idea who sent it: I had not asked any-
                  one for it. No doubt it is intended for Léon. It is
                  a handsome piece; I have it here in my study: you
                  must come in and see it.

                  *Bégearss, the last to leave, twice turns round to
                  stare at Figaro, who returns the stare. They seem
                  to be sending each other unspoken threats.*

SCENE FIVE

Figaro, alone, setting the table and laying out cups for breakfast.

FIGARO   Serpent or basilisk! Well may you give me the
                  eye, cast poisoned looks at me! It will be mine
                  which turns out deadly for you!... But where does
                  he get his letters from? Nothing comes for him
                  with the post delivered to the house. Has he risen

straight from hell?... Some other devil is his corre-
spondent! And I can't find anything...

SCENE SIX

Figaro, Suzanne.

SUZANNE   *(Running in, looking round, and gabbling in Figaro's
ear)* He's the one the ward's going to marry. -
The Count has promised it. He's going to cure
Léon of his love. - He's going to peel Florestine
away. - He's going to get the mistress to agree.
He's sending you away. - He's having my mistress
put into a convent while they arrange a divorce. -
Disinheriting the young man and making me
stewardess of the whole household. - That's the
news so far.

She rushes out.

SCENE SEVEN

Figaro, alone.

FIGARO   Excuse me, but no, Major, sir! We have a few
accounts to settle first. I'll teach you that it isn't
only fools who win. Thanks to Suzanne Ariadne,
I hold the thread to your labyrinth, and the mino-
taur is surrounded. I shall snare you in your own
traps, and what an unmasking we shall then have!
But what is he so urgently after with such school-
boy tricks? How can he draw the teeth of a man
like the Count? Is he so sure of himself he thinks
he can...? Foolishness and vanity are inseparable
companions! My schemer babbles and gives his
game away! He's lost. He's missed his shot.

SCENE EIGHT

Guillaume, Figaro.

GUILLAUME   *(Bearing a letter)* Mees-ter Bégearss! I see he iss not here.

FIGARO   *(Laying the table)* You may wait, he will be back.

GUILLAUME   *(Recoiling)* Mein Gott! I vill not vait for Mees-ter hee-yer with you. My master, I svear he this not like vould!

FIGARO   He not vould? Well, give me the letter. I'll pass it on when he returns.

GUILLAUME   *(Recoiling)* Not to you are his letters addressed! Oh Gott! He vill have vords for me soon!

FIGARO   *(Aside)* We must pump this fool. *(Aloud)* You... have come from the post then, I imagine?

GUILLAUME   Gott! No, I not come.

FIGARO   It must be some message from the gentleman... from that Irish relative he's just received his inheritance from? Would that be it, good Guillaume?

GUILLAUME   *(Laughing foolishly)* Letter from a man who has died, Mees-ter? I think not so! Not from him, Himmel! No. It vould have to be from someone else. Maybe it came from one of those man out there ... men not happy men.

FIGARO	There are people with a grudge against this household. One of them, you mean?
GUILLAUME	Ja, but I don't say sure...
FIGARO	*(Aside)* That's very possible. He's got his nose in everyone's business. *(To Guillaume)* We could look at the stamp and check...
GUILLAUME	No need check. Vy? Letters, this one sent by Mees-ter O'Connor. And then, stamp, I don't know how is stamps.
FIGARO	*(Excitedly)* O'Connor? The Irish banker?
GUILLAUME	Ja, Himmel, him!
FIGARO	*(Getting a grip on himself, coldly)* Who lives nearby, behind the house just here?
GUILLAUME	Gott, such a pretty place! Mit the people so ... gracious, if I to say so dare.

He retreats to one side.

FIGARO	*(To himself)* What luck! Excellent!
GUILLAUME	*(Coming back)* Don't mention about this banker, you, not for anyone, you understand? I should not have... Der Teufel!

Stamps his foot.

FIGARO	That's all right. I'll be careful, never fear.
GUILLAUME	My master, he says, Mees-ter... you haf all the vits

and I haf none... Well, it is so.... But maybe I am
angry for saying to you.

FIGARO   And why?
GUILLAUME   I don't know. The valet betray, you see... This is
                  sin which is barbarous, vile and also ... fery stupid.

FIGARO   That is true. But you have said nothing.

GUILLAUME   *(Stricken)* Mein Gott, mein Gott! I do not know
                  what I said haf... or not... *(He retires, sighing.)* Ah!

                  He gawps gormlessly at the books in the library.

FIGARO   *(Aside)* What a discovery! Chance, I kiss you!
                  (He looks for his writing pad.) I must work out how
                  so cunning a man manages to saddle himself with
                  such an imbecile... It's the same as robbers in the
                  night being scared of street lamps... Yes, but a
                  fool is a lantern; light shines through him. *(He
                  speaks as he makes his notes.)* O'Connor, Irish
                  banker. That's where I must set up my little
                  undercover investigative unit. The method is not
                  entirely constitutional; ma, por Dios! It works!
                  And then, I wouldn't be the first! *(Writes)* Four
                  or five gold sovereigns to the servant detailed to
                  sort the post to meet me in a tavern with any letter
                  bearing the handwriting of Honoré-Tartuffe
                  Begearss... Much-honoured Mr Tartuffe! Your
                  days of being so are numbered! A kindly God has
                  put me on your tracks. *(He gathers up his notes.)*
                  Chance, the unacknowledged God! The Ancients
                  used to call you Destiny. We call you by another
                  name.

SCENE NINE

Countess, Count, Florestine, Bégearss, Figaro, Guillaume.

BEGEARSS   *(Catching sight of Guillaume, takes the letter, humorously.)*   Can't you keep these for me in my room?

GUILLAUME   I, ... I think, this one... it's all too...

               Exits.

COUNTESS   *(To Count.)* Sir, the bust is a very fine piece: has your son seen it?

BEGEARSS   *(With the letter open.)* Ah, a letter from Madrid! From the minister's secretary! There's a bit here which concerns you. *(Reads)* "Inform the Count Almaviva that the mail which leaves tomorrow includes the King's consent for the exchange of all his lands."

               Figaro listens, and makes a private gesture of enlightenment.

COUNTESS   Figaro, go and tell my son that we are all break-fasting here.

FIGARO   Madame, I will inform him.

               Exits.

SCENE TEN

Countess, Count, Florestine, Bégearss.

COUNT   *(To Bégearss)* I wish to notify my buyer at once.

Send me some tea in my private office.

FLORESTINE   Dear papa, let me bring it to you.

COUNT   *(Softly, to Florestine)* Think about the few words I said.

He kisses her on the forehead and exits.

<u>SCENE ELEVEN</u>

Léon, Countess, Florestine, Bégearss.

LEON   *(Hurt)* My father leaves whenever I arrive! He has been treating me so sternly...

COUNTESS   *(Severely)* My son, what manner of speech is this? Must I feel for ever blown about by everybody's sense of injustice? Your father needs to write a letter to the person who is organising the exchange of his properties.

FLORESTINE   *(Gaily)* Are you sorry to see your papa go? We are sorry too. However, because he knows today is your name-day, he bade me, sir, present you with this spray.

She sweeps in a low curtsey.

LEON   *(Fixing the flower in his buttonhole)* No other messenger could have made his good wishes more welcome...

He embraces her.

FLORESTINE   *(Struggling free)* You see, madame, it's impossible

to play with him without his taking instant advantage...

COUNTESS   *(Smiling)* My child, on his name-day, we can
                  allow him a little excess.

FLORESTINE   *(Lowering her eyes)* For his punishment, madame,
                  make him recite his speech, which they say won
                  such applause at the club yesterday.

LEON   If madame judges me in the wrong, I shall go and
                  fetch my punishment.

FLORESTINE   Oh, madame, command it!

COUNTESS   My son, bring us your speech. I shall listen to it
                  while I embroider, so as to concentrate better.

FLORESTINE   *(Gaily)* There, you pig-headed thing! I shall hear
                  it in spite of you!

LEON   *(Tenderly)* In spite of me? When you order it so?
                  Ah, Florestine, I rise to such a challenge!

                  Countess and Léon go out through different doors.

SCENE TWELVE

Florestine, Begearss.

BEGEARSS   *(Sotto voce)* Well, Miss Florestine, have you
                  guessed the husband you are to have?

FLORESTINE   *(Joyous)* My dear Mr Bégearss, you are so very
                  much our friend that I will allow myself to think
                  out loud. Who might my eyes be drawn towards?

My godfather quite clearly said: look around you:
choose. I see the meaning of his generosity: who
can it be but Léon? But I, with no money of my
own, how should I take advantage...?

BEGEARSS   *(Terrible)* Who? Léon? His son! Your brother!

FLORESTINE *(With a cry of pain)* Ah! Sir!

BEGEARSS   Did he not say: call me your father? Wake up, my
dear child. Put aside your dreaming delusion, it
could turn into a disaster.

FLORESTINE Ah! Yes, it is a disaster for us both!

BEGEARSS   You realise such secrets must remain buried in
your soul.

He exits, staring hard at her.

SCENE THIRTEEN

Florestine, alone, weeping.

FLORESTINE Oh, my God! He is my brother, and I dare to fall
in love... What a terrible flood of daylight! And
from such dreams, how cruel it is to wake!

She collapses on a chair, stricken.

SCENE FOURTEEN

Léon, a paper in his hand; Florestine.

LEON   *(Aside, joyfully)* Mama is not back, and Mr

Bégearss has left: here's a happy chance.
Florestine, this morning, and always, your beauty
is quite perfect. But you seem so full of joy, you
speak so gaily, my hopes are all reborn.

FLORESTINE   *(In despair)* Ah! Léon!

              She falls back in the chair.

LEON   What is this! Your eyes wet with tears, your face
              distraught! There has been some great catastro-
              phe!

FLORESTINE   A catastrophe! Ah, Léon, only for me!

LEON   Floresta, don't you love me any more? When my
              feelings for you...

FLORESTINE   *(Harshly)* Your feelings? Never mention them to
              me again!

LEON   What! The purest love in the world!...

FLORESTINE   *(In despair)* Stop those cruel words, or I'll run
              away at once.

LEON   Great God, but what has happened? Mr Bégearss
              has been speaking to you. I wish to know what
              that Bégearss told you.

SCENE FIFTEEN

Countess, Florestine, Léon.

LEON   *(Continuing)* Mama, help me! I'm at my wits'
              end! Florestine doesn't love me any more!

FLORESTINE   *(Weeping)* Not love him, madame, me? You, my
                godfather, and him: all that I have ever wanted in
                my life is here!

COUNTESS   My child, I have never doubted it. Your warm
                heart tells me it is so. But why then is your heart
                so grieved?

LEON   Mama, you know I love her desperately: you do
                approve, don't you?

FLORESTINE   *(Throwing herself into the Countess's arms)* Make
                him be quiet! *(Weeping)* It's too painful! He's
                killing me!

COUNTESS   My child, I don't understand you. I am as
                shocked as Léon... She's shaking in my arms.
                What can he have done to make you hate him so?

FLORESTINE   *(Pushing her away)* Madame, he is not hateful to
                me. I love him and respect him as I would a
                brother. But he must ask for nothing more.

LEON   Listen to her, mama! Explain yourself, cruel girl!

FLORESTINE   Go away! Go away! If you don't go away I'll die!

SCENE SIXTEEN

Countess, Florestine, Léon, Figaro (arriving with the tea things),
Suzanne (from the other side, with an embroidery frame).

COUNTESS   Take it all back, Suzanne, there's no question of
                breakfast now, and no speech. You, Figaro, serve
                your master his tea; he is writing in his study.

And you, Florestine, come with me to mine and
tell your friend everything. My darling children, I
love you both very much! Why do you hurt each
other so pitilessly? There are things here it is
important I throw light on.

Countess and Florestine leave.

SCENE SEVENTEEN

Suzanne, Figaro, Léon.

SUZANNE: *(To Figaro)* I haven't the slightest idea what this
is about. But I'd lay a hefty bet it's pure Bégearss.
I insist you let me tell my mistress what we know.

FIGARO   Wait until I know more; we will put our heads
together this evening. Oh! I've made a discovery...

SUZANNE   Don't bother telling me!

Exits.

SCENE EIGHTEEN

Figaro, Léon.

LEON   *(Stricken)* Ah, God!

FIGARO   What is it all about, sir?

LEON   Alas, I don't understand myself. I'd never seen
Florestine in such a happy mood, and I knew she
had been having a talk with my father. I leave her

for a moment with Mr. Bégearss; when I come
back, she's all alone, her eyes streaming tears, and
ordering me to flee her sight for ever. So what
can he have said?

FIGARO   If I was not wary of your impulsiveness, I would
inform you of one or two details you ought to
know. But when caution is so vital, one single
word from you, anything too sudden, and I would
lose the fruits of ten years' watchfulness.

LEON   Oh, if it's a simple matter of caution... So what do
you think he said to her?

FIGARO   That she must accept Honoré Bégearss for a husband; that the whole business has been arranged
between the Count your father and him.

LEON   Between my father and him? I'll pay for the traitor with my life.

FIGARO   If you carry on like that, sir, it's not your life the
traitor will take in payment, but your mistress,
and your fortune along with her.

LEON   Oh, my friend, forgive me. Tell me what I must
do.

FIGARO   Guess the riddle of the Sphinx, or else be
devoured by it. In other words, you must keep
yourself under control, allow him to speak, and
hide your feelings.

LEON   (Furious) Control myself!... Yes, I will control
myself. But in my heart I rage! Steal Florestine
from me! Ah! Here he comes: I will explain
myself... coldly.

FIGARO   All is lost if you forget yourself.

SCENE NINETEEN

Bégearss, Figaro, Léon.

LEON   *(Containing herself with difficulty)* Sir, sir, a word.
                It is important for your peace of mind that you
                answer me straight. Florestine is in a state of
                despair: what have you been saying to her?

BEGEARSS   *(Icily)* And who says I said anything to her? Is
                she not capable of despairing on her own account?

LEON   *(With vigour.)* No avoiding the issue, sir. She
                was in the sunniest of moods; after being with you
                she was found in floods of tears. Wherever her
                sorrows come from, they are shared in my own
                heart. You will tell me their cause, or else I will
                demand some other satisfaction.

BEGEARSS   To moderate tones I am the most acessible of
                men. To threats I am unyielding.

LEON   *(Furious)* In that case, traitor, defend yourself! I
                will have your life, or you mine!

                He puts his hand on his sword.

FIGARO   *(Steps between them.)* Mr. Bégearss! The son of
                your friend! In his own house, where you live!

BEGEARSS   *(Containing himself.)* I am well aware of the duty I
                owe myself... I shall give him his explanations; but

in private. Go, leave us alone together.

LEON   My dear Figaro, you must go. You can see he
                cannot escape me. We must give him no excuse
                to.

FIGARO   I will go - to warn his father at once.

                Exits.

<u>SCENE TWENTY</u>

Léon, Bégearss.

LEON   *(Blocking the doorway)* It may suit you better to
                fight than to explain. The choice is yours. But I
                will have plain dealing either way.

BEGEARSS   *(Coldly)* Léon, a man of honcur does not butcher
                the son of his friend... Did you expect me to
                account for myself in front of a miserable servant,
                a fellow with all the insolence of a lackey control-
                ling his master?

LEON   *(Sitting down)* To business, sir, I am waiting...

BEGEARSS   Ah, you are going to regret this unreasoning rage.

LEON   That is what we shall shortly discover.

BEGEARSS   *(Affecting a cold dignity)* Léon, you love
                Florestine; I have seen that for a long time. While
                your brother was alive, I did not think it my duty
                to assist an unfortunate love affair which was lead-
                ing nowhere. But since a tragic duel, costing him
                his life, has set you in his place, I have had the

vanity to imagine my influence sufficient to persuade the Count your father to unite you with the
woman you love. I assailed him with every
weapon I could muster; an immovable resistance
repulsed my every assault. Grieved to see him
reject a plan which seemed expressly designed to
bring happiness to all... Forgive me, young man, I
am about to wound you; but at this moment I
must, if you are to be saved from an everlasting
error. I forced your father to break silence, to
confide in me his secret. "Oh, my friend!" - the
Count said at last - "I know of my son's love. But
how can I give him Florestine for his wife? The
girl accepted as my ward... she is my daughter,
she is his sister."

LEON: *(Throwing himself violently back)* Florestine! My
            sister!

BEGEARSS: I have spoken the words commanded by stern
            duty... Ah, I owe it to you both. Had I remained
            silent, you might have been lost. So, Léon, do
            you wish to try swords with me?

LEON: My generous friend. I am ungrateful, I am noth-
            ing but a monster! Forget my blind, mad rage...

BEGEARSS: *(Very Tartuffe like)* On the one condition that this
            dreadful secret is never repeated. To strip the veil
            from your father's shame, that would be a crime...

LEON: *(Throwing himself into his arms)* Ah! Never!

SCENE TWENTY-ONE

Count, Figaro, Léon, Bégearss.

FIGARO: *(Rushing in)* There they are! There they are!

COUNT: Embracing! Ah, you're losing your wits!

FIGARO: *(Amazed)* Good God, sir, and not without reason.

COUNT: *(To Figaro)* Will you explain this puzzle?

LEON: *(Overcome)* Ah, father, the explanation is mine. Forgive me! I should die of shame! It was only some trivial matter, and I fear I forgot myself. His generous character not only brings me back to my senses, but his heart is great enough to understand my madness and forgive it. I was demonstrating my gratitude when you came in and saw us.

COUNT: You owe him a hundred other similar debts of gratitude. As, indeed, do we all.

> *Figaro silently punches his forehead. Bégearss stares at him and smiles.*

COUNT: *(To his son)* Withdraw, sir. Your very confession adds fuel to my anger.

BEGEARSS: Ah, sir! All is forgiven.

COUNT: *(To Léon)* Go away and repent on your misjudgement of my friend, of your friend, too, of this most upright of men ...

LEON: *(Leaving)* I don't know which way to turn!

FIGARO: *(Aside, angry)* Here's a complete army of demons
                 stuffed inside a single shirt!

SCENE TWENTY-TWO

Count, Bégearss, Figaro.

COUNT: *(Aside, to Bégearss)* My friend, let us conclude the
                 affairs we have set in motion. *(To Figaro)* You,
                 Mr Witless, with your colourful imagination, let
                 me have that three million in gold brought from
                 Cadiz by yourself in sixty bills made payable to
                 bearer. You had orders to check them off.

FIGARO: I have done so.

COUNT: Then hand over the portfolio.

FIGARO: What portfolio? With the three million in gold?

COUNT: Of course. Well! What's stopping you?

FIGARO: *(Humbly)* I am, sir... I haven't got it any more.

COUNT: What! You haven't got it any more?

FIGARO: *(Proudly)* No, sir.

BEGEARSS: *(Roughly)* What have you done with it?

FIGARO: When my master questions me, it is my duty to
                 account for my actions: but to you I owe no duty
                 whatever.

COUNT:	*(Angrily)* Don't be insolent! What have you done with it?
FIGARO:	*(Coldly)* I have left it in desposit with Mr Fal, your lawyer.
BEGEARSS:	On whose instructions?
FIGARO:	*(Proudly)* On mine. And I maintain I acted properly.
BEGEARSS:	I would be prepared to bet you have done nothing of the sort.
FIGARO:	Since I have his receipt, you're in danger of losing your bet.
BEGEARSS:	Or if he has got it, he'll be using it to speculate. Those sort of people always take their share.
FIGARO:	You might speak more highly of a man who has obliged you.
BEGEARSS:	I owe him nothing.
FIGARO:	I can believe that. When a man has just inherited forty thousand gold doubloons.
COUNT:	*(Angrily)* Have you some observation to share with us on that score as well?
FIGARO:	Who, sir, me? I hardly think so, since I was well acquainted with the relative who has left this gentleman his fortune. A somewhat wild young man, a gambler, a spendthrift, a quarreller, a man of no restraint, no manners, no character, and having nothing of his own, not even the vices that killed

him; a man who became embroiled in the most
miserable of fights...

The Count stamps his foot.

BEGEARSS: *(Enraged)* Enough! Will you tell us why you left
this gold in deposit?

FIGARO   Why, sir, to be rid of it. Might it not have been
stolen? Anything could have happened. Often
the worst sort of rogue manages to worm his way
into people's houses...

BEGEARSS   *(Enraged)* The Count, however, wishes that the
portfolio be delivered to him.

FIGARO   Sir can easily send for it.

BEGEARSS   But will this lawyer let it out of his clutches without a receipt?

FIGARO   I will deliver the receipt to the Count; and when I
have thus done my duty, if any harm should come
to the money, he will not be able to accuse me.

COUNT   Bring it to me in my study.

FIGARO   *(To Count)* I warn you that Mr Fal will only
release the money on your signature; I gave him
instructions.

Exits.

SCENE TWENTY-THREE

Count, Bégearss.

BEGEARSS	*(Enraged)* Let vermin run free, and look where it all ends! Truly, sir, my friendship forces me to speak out: you are becoming too trusting; he has guessed our secrets. From valet, barber, surgeon, you have set him up as treasurer, secretary; a kind of general factotum. It is well known that this gentleman is using you to line his own pockets.
COUN	For his loyalty, I have nothing to reproach him; but it is true that his arrogance...
BEGEARSS:	There is of course one way you can rid yourself of him whilst rewarding him at the same time.
COUNT	I often wish I could.
BEGEARSS	*(Confidential)* When you send your son on his Maltese travels, no doubt you will wish a dependable lieutenant to keep an eye on him? This Figaro, too flattered to be able to refuse such an honoured position, is bound to accept; and there you are, free of him for a good long time.
COUNT	My friend, you are right. And apart from that, I hear he is far from happy with his wife.

Exits.

SCENE TWENTY-FOUR

Bégearss, alone.

BEGEARSS	And there's another step taken!... Ah, you noble little spy, prince of clowns, acting out the good servant while you're trying to grab our dowry,

insulting us with theatrical names! Thanks to the skill of Honoré Tartuffe, you're off to share all the miseries of journeying abroad; and there's an end to your spying on us.

END OF ACT TWO

ACT THREE

SCENE ONE

Countess, Suzanne. The Countess's private rooms, decorated everywhere with flowers.

COUNTESS   I could get nothing out of the child. - It was all tears and choking!... She believes she has wronged me, she insisted on begging my forgiveness. She wants to enter the convent. If I were to connect all this with her behaviour towards my son, I can only assume she blames herself for having listened to his declarations of love, sustaining his hopes, when she thinks herself too lowly a match for him. - There is charm in her delicacy of feeling; she is zealously and lovably virtuous. It appears that Mr Bégearss touched on the subject in a way which has caused her to torture herself with it. For he is a man of such scruples and such refinement when it is a question of honour that he is inclined occasionally to lean too hard, and imagines spectres where others see nothing.

SUZANNE   Where the trouble comes from I don't know; but there are some very strange things going on here. Some demon is fanning a secret fire. Our master is as gloomy as death; he holds all at arm's length. You are constantly in tears; Miss Florestine is choked with misery; you son, desolate... Mr Bégearss alone, imperturbable as a god, seems affected by nothing, gazes on all your sorrows with a dry eye...

COUNTESS   My dear, he shares them in his heart. Alas, without his consoling strength, spreading balm on our wounds, sustaining us with his widsom, soothing all our rough edges, calming my husband's temper, we would be a great deal more sorrowful.

SUZANNE   I hope, madame, you are not deluding yourself.

COUNTESS   There was a time when you spoke of him with more justice. *(Suzanne lowers her eyes.)* In any event, he alone can help me ease the anguish into which this child has cast me. Have someone ask him to visit me.

SUZANNNE   No need, here he comes. I will see to your hair later.

> *Exits.*

SCENE TWO

Countess, Bégearss.

COUNTESS   *(Distressed)* Ah, my poor Major! What is happening here? The crisis I have feared for so long, is this it approaching? I have seen it developing from a long way off. The Count's detachment from my unhappy son seems daily to increase. Has some terrible light dawned on him?

BEGEARSS: Madame, I do not think so.

COUNTESS   Since God punished me with the death of my elder son, I have seen the Count change utterly. Instead of working with the ambassador in Rome to deflect Léon's feelings, I see him insist on this Maltese venture. And I also know, Mr Bégearss, that he is disinheriting the natural successor to his

fortune, and intends to abandon Spain and estab-
lish himself here in France. - The other day at
dinner, in front of thirty guests, he expounded on
the subject of divorce in a way that quite terrified
me.

BEGEARSS   I was there. I remember only too well.

COUNTESS   *(Weeping)* Forgive me, my worthy friend, I can
weep only with you!

BEGEARSS   Lay your sorrows in the bosom of a man of feeling.

COUNTESS   And now, is it him, or is it you, who has rent the
heart of Florestine? I intended her for my son.
Born with no wealth of her own, it is true, but
noble, beautiful and virtuous; brought up amongst
us. My son, as our heir, does he not have wealth
enough for two?

BEGEARSS   Too much so, perhaps. That is where the trouble
lies.

COUNTESS   But it's as if God had only been waiting this long
in order to punish me better for a folly bitterly
repented: everything seems to be combining all at
once to overturn my hopes. My husband hates
my son; Florestine rejects him. Embittered I
know not why, she wishes to flee his sight for ever.
It will kill him, the unhappy boy! That is certain.
(She clasps her hands together.) Vengeful heavens,
after twenty years of tears and repentance, are you
keeping me alive for the final horror of witnessing
my crime brought to light? Ah, Lord, if I were
alone in my misery, I would offer no complaint.
But let my son not bear the penalty for a crime he

did not commit! Mr Bégearss, for so many sorrows, is there any remedy that you know?

BEGEARSS   Yes, virtuous woman! And I was on my way here
              for the very purpose of banishing your fears. For
              when we fear a thing, our gaze is drawn and held
              spellbound by that too horrible subject. Whatever
              we say or do, fear poisons all. Well, I hold the key
              to these mysteries. You can yet be happy.

COUNTESS   How is that ever possible for a soul torn by
              remorse?

BEGEARSS   Your husband does not want to lose Léon. He
              suspects nothing about the secret of his birth.

COUNTESS   *(Eagerly)* Mr Bégearss!

BEGEARSS   And all the stiffness which you take to be hatred is
              in fact no more than the result of a question of
              scruple. Ah, the relief I can bring you!

COUNTESS   *(Passionately)* Mr dear Mr Bégearss!

BEGEARSS   But bury deep in your relieved heart the shocking
              words you are about to hear. Your secret is the
              birth of Léon. His secret is the birth of Florestine.
              (Lowering his voice) She is his issue... He is her
              father.

COUNTESS   (Clasping her hands) Almighty God! Have pity
              on me.

BEGEARSS   Imagine his horror on seeing those children fall in
              love with each other! Unable to reveal his secret
              or stand the idea that their marriage might result
              from his silence, he became dark, strangely

moody. And if he wishes to send his son away, it
is to destroy, if he can, by means of his absence
and the knightly vows he has taken, a disastrous
love affair he believes to be impossible.

COUNTESS   *(On her knees, praying ardently)* Oh God, eternal
fount of all goodness, you have given me a chance
to repair in some part the unwilled error forced on
me by a man out of his senses. You have given
me an error of his own to set against this husband
I offended. Oh, Almaviva! My withered heart,
crippled by twenty years of sorrowing, can at last
open out to you! Florestine is your daugher. She
becomes as dear to me as if my own body had
borne her. Let us, without saying a word,
exchange our forgiveness. Oh, Mr Bégearss, tell
me everything!

BEGEARSS   *(Lifting her to her feet)* My friend, I will not check
the instinctive elation of a goood woman's heart.
The emotions of joy are not dangerous, unlike
those of grief. For the sake of your peace of mind,
hear me to the end.

COUNTESS   Speak, my generous friend. You to whom I owe
everything, speak.

BEGEARSS   Your husband, seeking a way to preserve
Florestine from this love which he believes inces-
tuous, has offered her in marriage to me. This is
separate entirely from the deep and unhappy feelings which my respect for your own sorrows...

COUNTESS   Ah, my friend, if you have any compassion...

BEGEARSS   We will speak of it no more. A few preparatory
words, somewhat ambiguously expressed, led

Florestine to think that he was talking about
Léon. Her young heart was just beginning to
burst out in joy, when a servant announced your
arrival. Without explaining what I knew about her
father's concern, a rapid word from me, bringing
her mind to bear on the harsh subject of brother-
and sister-hood, caused this storm, and the reli-
gious terror for which neither you nor your son
could find the motive.

COUNTESS   He was on quite the wrong track, poor child!

BEGEARSS   Now that you are aware of it, must we pursue this
plan for a marriage which repairs all faults?

COUNTESS   *(Animatedly)* We must insist on it, my friend. My
heart and my mind are at one on that point, and it
is up to me to persuade her. That way our secrets
remain safe. No outsider will penetrate them.
After twenty years of suffering, we shall spend our
days in happiness, and it is to you, my worthy
friend, that my family will owe them all.

BEGEARSS   *(Raising his voice)* In order that nothing shall dis-
turb them further, one more sacrifice is vital, and
my dear friend is noble enough to make it.

COUNTESS   Alas, I want to make them, every last one.

BEGEARSS   Those letters, that evidence of an ill-fated man no
longer with us, they must be reduced to ashes.

COUNTESS   *(Grieving)* Ah, God!

BEGEARSS   When that dying friend charged me with their
delivery, his last order was that your honour must
be saved, leaving no trace which might injure it.

COUNTESS God! God!

BEGEARSS Twenty years have passed, and still I have not found a way to remove from your eyes this sad evidence of your lasting sorrow. But quite apart from the suffering these papers cause you, think of the risks you are running.

COUNTESS Oh! What is there to fear?

BEGEARSS *(Looking around to check he cannot be overheard, and lowering his voice)* I do not suspect Suzanne; but any chambermaid, informed that you keep these papers, might she not find a way of making them into her fortune? A single one passed to your husband, and which might perhaps cost him a great deal to obtain, and then you would be plunged straight into fresh difficulties.

COUNTESS No, Suzanne is too good a soul...

BEGEARSS *(With lofty command)* My virtuous friend, you have paid your debt to love, to sorrow, to your duties of all kinds. And if you are satisfied by the conduct of a friend, I wish to claim its reward. You must burn all these papers, destroy all these memories of an error so deeply expiated! But in order never again to raise so painful a subject, I require that their sacrifice be offered this very minute.

COUNTESS *(Trembling)* I think I hear the voice of God! He is commanding me to forget the man, to tear the black veil with which his death has shrouded my life. Yes, oh Lord, I will obey this man whom you have sent. *(She rings.)* What he demands in your

name, my repentant soul echoed: but my weak
will fought against it.

SCENE THREE

Suzanne, Countess, Bégearss.

COUNTESS   Suzanne, bring me the casket with my diamonds.
            - No, I will go and fetch it myself. You would
            have to find the key...

            Exits.

SCENE FOUR

Suzanne, Bégearss.

SUZANNE   *(Somewhat troubled)* Mr Bégearss, what is this all
            about? Everybody is behaving oddly. This house-
            hold is coming to resemble a home for madmen!
            Madame weeps; Miss Florestine is in anguish;
            Léon talks of drowning himself; the Count is shut
            away and refuses to see anyone. Why is this dia-
            mond case suddenly of such interest to everyone?

BEGEARSS   *(Mysteriously, placing a finger to his lips)* Hush!
            Show no sign of curiosity just yet. You will
            understand soon... It's all going well, everything
            is fine... This day will be worth... Hush...

SCENE FIVE

Countess, Bégearss, Suzanne.

COUNTESS   *(Holding the jewel case)* Suzanne, bring us coals
                  from the brazier in my dressing room.

SUZANNE   If it's for burning papers, the night light is still lit
                  in its stand.

                        She carries it over.

COUNTESS   Watch the door. Don't allow anyone in.

SUZANNE   *(Aside, as she exits)* I must run and tell Figaro.

SCENE SIX

Countess, Bégearss.

BEGEARSS   How I have longed, for your sake, for this moment
                  now upon us!

COUNTESS   *(Overcome)* Oh, my friend. Think what day we
                  have chosen to accomplish this sacrifice, the birth-
                  day of my unhappy son. At this time each year I
                  would give this day over to them, I would ask God
                  for his forgiveness and I would cleanse myself with
                  tears as I read once again those sad letters. I
                  would offer myself the consolation that what
                  passed between us was more error than crime.
                  Ah, must I then burn the only part of him that yet
                  remains?

BEGEARSS   What! Madame, are you destroying the son who
                  is his representative? Do you not owe him the
                  sacrifice which preserves him from so many terri-
                  ble dangers? You owe it to yourself, and the safe-
                  ty of your whole life may very well depend on this
                  majestic deed!

> *He opens the secret compartment of the jewel case and takes out the letters.*

COUNTESS   *(Surprised)* Mr Bégearss, you open it with more skill than I..! Let me read them one last time.

BEGEARSS   *(Sternly)* No, I cannot permit it.

COUNTESS   Just the final one, the one where he traced his sad farewell in the blood he spilled for me, giving me an example of the courage I need so badly today.

BEGEARSS   *(Resisting)* If you read a single word we shall burn none of them at all. Offer to God a sacrifice that is complete, courageous, voluntary, void of all human frailty! Or if you dare not do the deed, it is I who will be strong on your behalf. There they all are, in the flames.

> *He throws the packet of letters into the burning night light.*

COUNTESS   *(Animatedly)* Mr Bégearss! Cruel friend! That is my life you are burning! Let me keep at least one shred.

> *She tries to seize the blazing letters. Bégearss restrains her with an arm round her body.*

BEGEARSS   I will cast the ashes to the winds.

SCENE SEVEN

Suzanne, Count, Figaro, Countess, Bégearss.

COUNT   *(Catching them in this posture)* What do I see here,
                 madame? What is the cause of this disorder?
                 What is this fire, this jewel case, these papers?
                 Why these pleadings, these tears? *(Bégearss and
                 the Countess are trapped in confusion.)* Have you
                 nothing to say?

BEGEARSS   *(Recovering himself, peevishly)* I hope, sir, that you
                 do not require me to account for myself in the
                 presence of your servants. I cannot conceive what
                 intention lay behind your thus bursting in on
                 madame. As for me, I am resolved to stand by my
                 reputation, and serve only the truth, whatever it
                 may be.

COUNT   *(To Figaro and Suzanne)* Leave us, both of you.

FIGARO   But, sir, at least do me the justice of confirming
                 how I have indeed delivered to your keeping the
                 lawyer's receipt concerning the important business
                 we were discussing.

COUNT   I willingly declare it so, since that rights a wrong.
                 (To Bégearss) Rest assured, sir, that I have the
                 receipt in person.

                      *He replaces it in his pocket. Figaro and Suzanne
                      leave by their respective exits.*

FIGARO   *(Aside to Suzanne as they go out)* If he wriggles out
                 of this one!...

SUZANNE   *(Whispered)* The man's a subtle wriggler!

FIGARO   *(Whispered)* I've done for him!

SCENE EIGHT

Countess, Count, Bégearss.

COUNT   *(Gravely)* Madame, we are alone.

BÉGEARSS   *(Still in the grip of emotion)* The explanation shall
               be mind. I will submit myself to this interroga-
               tion. Have you ever known me, sir, to bend the
               truth on any occasion whatsoever?

COUNT   *(Curtly)* Sir, I do not suggest that.

BÉGEARSS   *(Completely in control again)* Although I am far
               from approving this barely decent inquisition, I
               am obliged by honour to reiterate my words to
               madame, offered in answer to her seeking my
               advice: "No repository of secrets must ever pre-
               serve any documents which might compromise a
               friend no longer alive, who once entrusted them to
               our care. Whatever the pain in disposing of them,
               and whatever one might stand to gain by keeping
               them, our religious respect for the departed must
               come before all else." *(He indicates the Count.)*
               Might not some untoward mischance put them in
               the hands of an enemy? *(The Count tugs at his
               sleeve to prevent his explanation going too far.)*
               Would you have said any different, sir, in my posi-
               tion? A person who seeks only weak-minded
               counsel, or connivance at a shameful frailty,
               should not address himself to me! You have each
               of you your proof of that, and yourself especially,
               my lord Count! *(The Count makes him a sign.)* In
               that consideration, and in reply to the Countess's
               question, and without ever seeking to penetrate
               the secrets of these papers, I advised that strict
               course of action for which her courage was lack-

ing. And I did not hesitate to exercise my own, to end her unwise delay. That was the subject of our debate. But however my actions may be judged, I will not regret my words or my deds. *(He raises his arms aloft.)* Holy bonds of friendship! You are but vain posturings if your duties remain unfulfilled. - Allow me to withdraw.

COUNT   *(In exaltation)* Oh, best of men! No, you shall not leave us. - Madame, he is to be attached to us more closely still; I have given him the hand of my Florestine

COUNTESS   *(With animation)* Sir, you could not exercise more worthily the power the law gives you to command her. This choice has my assent if you judge it fitting, and the sooner it is accomplished the better.

COUNT   *(Hesitating)* Well!... In that case this evening... with no fuss...

COUNTESS   *(Ardently)* Let me, who am as a mother to her, prepare her for this noble ceremony. But can you stand apart from your friend's generosity towards the worthy child? It would please me to think not.

COUNT   *(Embarrassed)* Ah, madame!... Believe me...

COUNTESS   *(Joyously)* Yes, sir, I believe you! Today is the feast-day of my son; the two events thus combined, today's celebrations make this the happiest of days for me.

               She goes out.

SCENE NINE

Count, Bégearss.

COUNT   *(Watching her exit)* I cannot get over my astonish-
ment. I was expecting endless discussions, objections; and I find her fair, good and generous
towards my child. "I who am as a mother to her,"
she says... No, this is not an evil woman! In her
actions works a dignity which obliges my own... a
tone of voice to scatter the reproaches I was about
to bring down upon her head. But I think I owe
myself some reproach, my friend, for the surprise
I showed on seeing her burn those papers.

BÉGEARSS   For my part, there was no surprise at all, seeing
who it was who burst in with you. That serpent
whispered in your ear that I was here to betray
your secrets! Such base slanders do not afflict a
man of my high standing. They crawl like worms
at my feet. And even then, sir, what did those
papers matter to you? Had you not already taken,
in spite of me, the ones you wanted to keep? Ah,
would to God she had consulted me earlier! You
would not have had such unanswerable proof
against her!

COUNT   *(Sadly)* Yes, unanswerable! *(Passionately)* I must
take them from their hiding place, they are burning my heart.

        *He removes the letter from inside his coat and puts
        it in his outer pocket.*

BÉGEARSS   *(Continuing gently)* It would have helped me
stand up for your legally recognised son with more
success. For after all, he cannot be held to

account for the sad fate which brought him into
your arms.

COUNT   *(Furious again)* Him in my arms? Never!

BEGEARSS   Nor is he guilty in his love for Florestine. And
yet, for as long as he remains near her, can I be
united with this child, who, possibly infatuated in
similar fashion, will yield only to her respect for
you? My sense of delicacy thus wounded...

COUNT   My friend, I understand you! And your reflections make me resolved that he shall leave at once,
without delay. Yes, I shall be less unhappy when
that fatal object no longer offends my sight. But
how are we to broach the subject with Florestine?
Will she want to be separted from him? Must we
then cause a scandal?

BEGEARSS   A scandal!... No... but the possibility of divorce,
legalised by this flighty nation, will provide you
with a means.

COUNT   What, make my shame public! Some feeble men
may have done so, and it demonstrates the very
pit of degradation to which this century has sunk.
Let the disgrace be the lot of whoever publishes
such a scandal, and of the scoundrels who cause
it!

BEGEARSS   I have acted towards her, and towards you, as
honour dictated. I am not a man to choose vio-
lent means, particularly in the case of a son...

COUNT   Of a stranger, rather, whose speedy departure is
my dearest wish.

BEGEARSS   Don't forget that arrogant valet.

COUNT   I am weary of him and have no desire to retain
              him. You must hurry, my friend, to my lawyer.
              Draw out with my receipt - I have it here - my
              three million in gold. Then you may rightly be
              generous in the contract we must bring to a rapid
              conclusion today... for with this you are indeed a
              man of means... *(He hands over the receipt, takes
              him by the arm, and they exit.)* And tonight at mid-
              night, as quietly as possible, in the Countess's
              chapel...

                   The rest is lost

                   END OF ACT THREE

ACT FOUR

SCENE ONE

The Countess's private rooms again. Figaro, alone, agitated, looking round on all sides.

FIGARO   She told me: "Come to her study at six. It's the safest place to speak..." I rush about my business in town and I come back in a sweat! Where is she? *(He strides up and down, mopping his brow.)* Ah, for heaven's sake, I'm not mad! I saw them leaving this room, the Count taking him by the arm!... Well, do we abandon the game just because of one set-back? Does a speaker weakly climb down from the soap-box just because a single argument is refuted? But what a smooth-tongued villain! *(Vigorously)* Fixing it that all the mistress's papers are burned so that she won't discover one is missing; and getting out of it with an explanation like that!... The man is the very picture of Milton's hell! *(Light-heartedly)* When I was angry earlier, I was right: Honoré Bégearss is that devil the Hebrews call Legion. And if you looked closely you'd see the little demon had a cloven hoof, the only part that demons can't disguise, as my mother used to tell me. *(Laughs)* Ha! Ha! Ha! I can feel my good humour returning. In the first place I've made that Mexican gold safe by depositing it with Fal, which will buy us more time! *(He taps his hand with a letter he is holding.)* And then, Doctor of Hypocrisy, you very model of a modern Major Tartuffe, thanks to fortune which directs us all, thanks also to my cunning, and to a few sovereigns sown here and there, here's what purports to be a letter belong-

ing to you, and in which, I am reliably informed,
you reveal the true face behind the mask. *(He
opens the letter.)* The rascal who read it wants fifty
sovereigns for it, does he? If this letter is worth it,
he'll get them! It would be worth a whole year of
my wages if I can help our master to whom we
owe so much, and pull the veil from his eyes...
But where are you, Suzanne? Come and join the
fun! "*O che piacere*"! ... Well, then, tomorrow is
soon enough, for I can see no immediate danger
tonight.... And yet why waste time? I have always
regretted it... *(Vigorously)* No delays, I'll go and
plant this time bomb, and then we'll so to say
sleep on it. Night brings its own counsel, and in
the morning we'll see which of us blows the other
up.

SCENE TWO

Bégearss. Figaro.

BEGEARSS	*(Mocking)* Aha! It's my Figaro! All the more pleasant to be here for finding Sir present.
FIGARO	*(In the same tone)* If only for the pleasure of finding Sir not here any more presently.
BEGEARSS	Bearing a grudge for so little? It's charming of you to remember. Still, everyone has his own little ways.
FIGARO	And Sir's is to advance his schemes behind closed doors only?
BEGEARSS	*(Clapping him on the shoulder)* But a wise man does not need to be privy to everything, not when

he's so clever at guessing.

FIGARO   Everyone has to use what small talents God has given him.

BEGEARSS   And does our intriguer expect to gain much with such talents as he's shown us so far?

FIGARO   I have the game won without playing a short ... if I merely make sure the other man loses.

BEGEARSS   *(Stung)* We shall soon see your game.

FIGARO   Oh, there'll be no brilliant strokes to dazzle the crowd. *(He affects simple naivety.)* But "every man for himself, and God for all", as King Solomon said.

BEGEARSS   *(Smiling)* A fine phrase. Didn't he also say, "The sun shines down on all and sundry"?

FIGARO   *(Proudly)* Yes, lighting up the snake who waits to bite the hands of his incautious benefactor!

Exits.

SCENE THREE

Bégearss, alone, watching him go.

BEGEARSS   He doesn't bother to hide his plans any more! Is our man proud? A good sign, he knows nothing of mine. He'd have a long face if he found out what's to happen at midnight... *(He searches busily in his pockets.)* Where is it, what have I done with that paper? Here it is. *(Reads)* "Received from

Mr Fal, lawyer, the three millions in gold itemised
in the statement attached. Signed this day, in
Paris, ALMAVIVA." Good work. I have the
ward and I have the money! But it is not enough.
The Count is weak, he'll never complete the job
with the rest of his fortune. The Countess is too
influential. He's afraid of her; he still loves her...
She won't go into the convent unless I force them
to a crisis, force them to reveal everything... bru-
tally. *(Paces up and down.)* My God, I can't risk
such a damaging climax tonight. If you pull the
house down too quickly, you pull it down on top
of yourself as well. Tomorrow morning is soon
enough, by which time I will have thoroughly tied
that sweet and holy knot which will chain them to
me! *(He presses both hands to his chest, holding himself in.)* Now then, damnable joy, bursting in my
heart, can you not contain yourself?... It will
choke me, the hothead, or will give me foolishly
away, unless I allow it to blow off a little pressure
when I am safely alone here. Sweet, holy creduli-
ty! The husband owes you that magnificent
dowry! Pale goddess of the night, soon he will
owe you his cold wife! *(He rubs his hands with
delight.)* Bégearss! Happy Bégearss!... Why do I
call him Bégearss? Is he not already more than
halfway Lord Almaviva? *(Terrible)* One more
step, Bégearss, and you are entirely so! But first
you are going to have to... This Figaro hangs
around my neck. For it was he who sent for the
Count. The slightest trouble would ruin me...
That valet will bring me bad luck... He's a most
perceptive villain!... Come, come, he must be
sent on his way with his knight errant!

SCENE FOUR

Bégearss, Suzanne.

SUZANNE   *(Rushing in, gives a cry of surprise on seeing someone else instead of Figaro)* Ah! *(Aside)* It's not him!!

BEGEARSS   Why the surprise? And who were you expecting then?

SUZANNE   *(Recovering)* No one. I expected to be alone for once.

BEGEARSS   Since we've run into each other, just a word before the committee meets.

SUZANNE   Committee? What's all this committee? Honestly, for the last two years I haven't understood a word of the language they've taken to speaking in this country.

BEGEARSS   *(Laughs sardonically)* Ha! Ha! *(He fiddles in his tin for a pinch of tobacco, pleased with himself.)* This committee, my dear, is a conference between the Countess, her son, our young ward and me, concerning the important matter I told you about.

SUZANNE   After the scene I saw, how can you dare hope for it still?

BEGEARSS   *(Very smug)* Hope for it!... No. It's merely that... I'm marrying her tonight.

SUZANNE   *(Agitated)* But she's in love with Léon.

BEGEARSS   My poor good woman, and weren't you telling me: "If you try that, sir..."?

SUZANNNE   Well! Who could have imagined it?

BEGEARSS   *(Taking several pinches of tobacco)* So, what do
they say? Are they gossiping? You're a member
of the inner household, you enjoy their confi-
dence: do they think well of me, because that's the
important point?

SUZANNNE   The most important point would be to know what
lucky charm you use to control their minds. The
master can only speak of you with the utmost
enthusiasm, my mistress praises you to the skies,
you are the only hope of her son, and our ward
positively worships you...!

BEGEARSS   *(Smug, brushing tobacco from his stock)* And you,
Suzanne, what do you say?

SUZANNE   My word, sir, I admire you! You are the ringmas-
ter of this chaotic circus, and you're the only one
who's calm and collected. It's like a sorcerer making the whole world bend to his will.

BEGEARSS   *(Smug)* My child, nothing is simpler! To start
with, there are but two pivots, around which all
the world's affairs revolve: morality and politics.
Morality, mean thing that it is, consists of being
just and true. It is, they say, the key to a whole
array of humdrum virtues.

SUZANNE   Whereas politics...?

BEGEARSS   *(Warmly, to himself)* Ah! It is the art of creating
facts, of dominating without apparently trying,
both men and their actions. Its goal is self-interest, its method, intrigue: always frugal with the
truth, its vast and rich conceptions are a dazzling

prism. Deep as Mount Etna, it smoulders and rumbles for a long time before erupting on the world outside. But when it does, nothing can resist it. It demands talent of a high order: and its only enemy is scruple. *(Laughs)* But that's the intriguer's secret.

SUZANNE

Morality may not seem to appeal to you, but the other one certainly inspires no small enthusiasm!

BEGEARSS

(Alerted, recovers himself) What?... No, it's not that, it's you! ... Your comparison with a sorcerer... - The young knight is coming. Leave us.

SCENE FIVE

Léon, Bégearss.

LEON

Mr Bégearss, I am in despair!

BEGEARSS

(Protectively) What has happened, my young friend?

LEON

My father has just informed me - and with such harshness - that I have two days to make all preparations for my departure for Malta. With no other retinue, he says, but Figaro who is to accompany me, and a valet to go on ahead.

BEGEARSS

This behaviour is indeed strange for anyone not aware of its secret reasons. But for those who have penetrated them, our duty is to pity him. This journey is the product of an all too forgivable fear. Malta and your knight's vows are no more than the pretext. His real motive is a love affair which terrifies him.

LEON   *(Sorrowfully)* But, my friend, since you are going
                to marry her?

BEGEARSS   *(Confidentially)* If her brother believes it worth-
                while to defer a painful separation... I can see only
                one way out.

LEON   Oh, my friend, tell me!

BEGEARSS   It would be for madame your mother to overcome
                that timidness which prevents her from facing him
                with any opinion of her own. For it is her gentle-
                ness which harms you far more than if she were
                too demanding. - Let us suppose that his mind
                has been unfairly prejudiced by someone: who has
                more right than a mother to recall a father to his
                reason? Make her promise to try ... not today, but
                ... tomorrow, and don't let her fall back into her
                weak ways.

LEON   My friend, you are right. Her fear is really at the
                root of it. There's no doubt, my mother is the
                only one who might make him change his mind.
                Look, here she comes, with the girl I... I dare
                adore no longer. *(Painfully)* Oh, my friend, make
                her happy!

BEGEARSS   *(Soothingly)* By speaking to her every day of her
                brother.

SCENE SIX

*Countess, Florestine, Bégearss, Suzanne, Léon.   Countess, fully coi
fured, wearing her jewels, and a red and black dress, is carrying a bouquet
in the same colours.*

COUNTESS   Suzanne, bring me my diamonds.

        Suzanne goes to fetch them.

BÉGEARSS   *(Affecting great dignity)* Madame, and you, young
lady, I leave you with this friend. I confirm in
advance all he is about to say. Alas, think not of
the happiness it would give me to belong to you as
part of your family; your own peace of mind must
be your only consideration. The only part I wish
to play is the part you yourselves choose for me.
But whether Miss Florestine accepts my offer or
not, accept my promise here made that the entire
fortune I have inherited is by my own will destined for her, either by contract of marriage or by
legacy. I am about to have the deeds drawn up:
Miss Florestine shall choose. In the light of what
I have said, it would not be fitting for my presence
here to affect a decision which she must make of
her own free will. But whatever her decision may
be, oh my friends, know that it is sacred for me: I
adopt it without condition.

        He bows deeply and exits.

SCENE SEVEN

Countess, Léon, Florestine.

COUNTESS *(Watching him go)* He is an angel sent from heaven to right our misfortunes.

LEON *(With passionate grief)* Oh, Florestine! We must give in. When we discovered we could not belong to one another, our first transports of grief made us swear never to belong to anyone. I will fulfil that vow for us both. And it does not mean I must lose you entirely, since where I had hoped to have a wife I have found a sister. We shall still be able to love one another.

SCENE EIGHT

Countess, Florestine, Léon, Suzanne. Suzanne enters with the jewel case.

COUNTESS *(Putting on, without seeing them, her ear-rings, her rings, her bracelet)* Florestine, marry Bégearss, his conduct makes him worthy of it. And since this marriage will make your god-father happy, it must be accomplished today.

Suzanne exits with the jewel case.

SCENE NINE

Countess, Léon, Florestine.

COUNTESS *(To Léon)* Let us never know, my son, the things we are better ignorant of. Florestine, you are weeping!

FLORESTINE   *(Weeping)* Take pity on me, madame. Ah, how
can I bear so many griefs in a single day. I hardly
learn who I really am before I must renounce my
new self and give it away ... I am dying from grief
and terror. Deprived of any reasonable objection
to Mr Bégearss, my heart is in agony to think that
he may become ... And yet I must. I have to sacrifice myself for the good of this cherished brother, for his happiness ... which I can no longer
bring. You say I weep! Ah! For him I do more
than if I were to lay down my life! Mama, have
pity on us ... bless your children, they are so
unhappy!

                  She drops to her knees. Léon does likewise.

COUNTESS   *(Laying her hands on their heads)* I bless you both,
my dearest children. My Florestine, I adopt you
as my own. If you could only know how dear you
are to me! You will be happy, my daughter, with
the happiness virtue brings. It is a happiness
which can compensate for all the others.

FLORESTINE   But do you believe, madame, that my devotion
might bring the Count closer to Léon, his son?
For we must not deceive ourselves: his unjust
prejudice extends at times to outright hatred.

COUNTESS   Dearest daughter, I have hopes of it.

LEON   That is Mr Bégearss's opinion. He told me so.
But he also told me that only Mama could work
that miracle. Will you have the strength, then, to
speak to him on my behalf?

COUNTESS   I have often attempted it, my son, but with no
                apparent success.

LEON   Oh, good mother! It is your gentleness which has
                caused me harm. Your fear of angering him has
                prevented you from wielding the proper influence
                which your virtue and the deep respect that sur-
                rounds you make your right. If you spoke to him
                forcefully, he would not resist you.

COUNTESS   Do you believe so, my son? Then you shall hear
                me try. Your reproaches wound me almost as
                much as his injustice. But you must not undo the
                good words I shall say on your behalf, so go next
                door into my study. You will hear me from there,
                and the cause I plead will be so just you will no
                longer accuse a mother of wanting energy in the
                defence of her son! *(She rings.)* Floresta, decency
                forbids you to remain: go to your room; ask God
                to grant me some success and bring peace at last
                to my despairing family.

                Florestine exits.

SCENE TEN

Suzanne, Countess, Florestine.

SUZANNE   What does madame wish? She rang?

COUNTESS   Ask the Count from me if he will come and see
                me for a moment here.

SUZANNE   *(Alarmed)* Madame! You make me tremble!
                Heavens, what is to happen, then? What, the
                Count, here, where he never comes ... unless...?

COUNTESS   Do as I tell you, Suzanne, and don't worry about
                the rest.

                Suzanne exits, her arms aloft in terror.

SCENE ELEVEN

Countess, Léon.

COUNTESS   You shall see, my son, whether your mother is a
                weak woman when it comes to defending your
                interests! But let me collect my thoughts, prepare
                myself by prayer for this crucial appeal.

                Léon goes into his mother's private study.

SCENE TWELVE

Countess, alone, one knee bent on her chair.

COUNTESS   This moment seems as terrible as the last judge-
                ment! My blood is ready to freeze... Oh Lord,
                give me the strength to pierce a husband's heart!
                (More quietly) You alone know the motives which
                have always kept my lips sealed. Ah, if my son's
                happiness were not at stake, you know, Lord, I
                would utter no word for myself. But now, if it is
                true that a fault wept over for twenty years might
                earn your generous forgiveness, as a wise friend
                assures me, oh Lord, give me the strength to strike
                a husband's heart!

SCENE THIRTEEN

Countess, Count, Léon (hidden).

COUNT	*(Curtly)* Madame, I am told you asked for me?

COUNTESS	*(Timidly)* I thought, sir, we would be more free in my study than in yours.

COUNT	Here I am, madame. Speak.

COUNTESS	*(Trembling)* Sit down, I beg you, sir, and listen to me.

COUNT	No, I shall hear you standing. You know how I can never keep still when we are talking.

COUNTESS	*(Sitting down with a sigh, and speaking in a low voice)* It is about my son, ... sir.

COUNT	*(Brusquely)* About your son, madame?

COUNTESS	And what other interest could make me suppress the repugnance I feel for starting a discussion so studiously avoided? But I have just seen him in a state that would move any human being to compassion. His mind is troubled, his heart is torn by your order that he must leave immediately; and especially by the hard words with which you condemn him to this exile. Oh! How has he incurred such disfavour from a father ... from a man so just? Since that abominable duel stole from us our other son...

COUNT	*(Hands over face in grief)* Ah!...

COUNTESS	This young man, who should never have known such grief, has redoubled his efforts and atten-

tions in order to soften the bitterness of ours.

COUNT

(Pacing more calmly) Ah!...

COUNTESS

The wild character of his brother, his disorderliness, his tastes and his reckless behaviour often caused us cruel suffering. When the Lord above, stern but wise in his dispositions, took that child from us, perhaps he spared us even more bitter suffering to come.

COUNT

(In pain) Ah!... Ah!...

COUNTESS

But consider our remaining son: Has he ever fallen short in his duties? Has he ever done anything to deserve the mildest reproof? He is the example for the man of his age; held in high regard by all. He is loved, his company is sought, his opinions consulted. Only his fa... his natural guardian, only my husband seems to have his eyes closed to such transparent merit, whose radiance is obvious to one and all. *(Count paces quicker, not speaking. Countess, drawing courage from his silence, continues more firmly, and, little by little, more loudly.)* On any other subject , sir, I would hold it the greatest honour to have your thoughts command my own, to model my feelings, my feeble opinions, on yours. But we are talking about... about a son... *(Count paces agitatedly.)* When he had an elder brother, the pride and renown of a great family name condemned him to bachelorhood, and it was his destiny to swear the vows of a knight of Malta. It was convention then which seemed to make this unequal division between two sons... *(Timidly)* equal in rights.

COUNT

(More agitated. Aside, choking.) Equal in rights!

COUNTESS   *(A touch more forcefully)* But since a dreadful acci-
             dent two years ago transferred all those rights to
             him, is it not astonishing that you have done noth-
             ing to release him from his vows? It is only too
             well known that you left Spain in order to sever
             those hereditary links binding you to your posses-
             sions, by selling or by exhanging your lands. If
             you are doing all this just to deprive the young
             man, how much further can hatred go? Then you
             drive him from your house and seem to close the
             door of the paternal... of the home you live in.
             Permit me to tell you, in the eyes of reason, such
             treatment is beyond excuse. What has he ever
             done to deserve it?

COUNT   *(Stops: his voice becomes terrible.)* What has he
             done?

COUNTESS   *(Alarmed)* It is not my intention, sir, to give you
             offence!

COUNT   *(Louder)* What has he done, madame? You ask
             me that?

COUNTESS   *(Confused)* Sir, sir! You are frightning me!

COUNT   *(Furious)* Respect for human decency was keep-
             ing my resentment in check. But since you insist
             on provoking an explosion, you shall hear my
             judgement on him, and on yourself.

COUNTESS   *(More alarmed)* Ah, sir! Ah, sir!

COUNT   You ask me what he has done?

COUNTESS   *(Raising her arms)* No, sir, tell me nothing.

COUNT   *(Beside himself)* Remember, treacherous wife,
                 what you yourself have done! Remember how you
                 welcomed an adulterer into your arms, and
                 brought into my household that foreign child
                 whom you dare to call my son!

COUNTESS   *(Desperate, trying to rise)* Let me flee, I beg you!

COUNT   *(Pinning her to her chair)* No, you shall not flee.
                 You shall not escape the burden of your own
                 knowledge. *(Showing her the letter)* Do you know
                 this writing? The guilty hand is yours! And these
                 blood-stained words of his reply...

COUNTESS   *(Crushed)* I shall die! I shall die!

COUNT   *(Powerfully)* No, no! You will listen to the lines I
                 have marked. *(Reads wildly.)* "Unhappy man, we
                 took leave of our senses, and our fate is sealed.
                 Your crime, mine, receives its just punishment.
                 This day, the feast-day of Saint Léon, patron saint
                 of this place and of your own name, this day I
                 have brought into the world a son, my disgrace
                 and my despair..." *(Speaks out again.)* And this
                 child was born on Saint Léon's day, more than
                 ten months after my departure from Vera-Cruz!

                 *While he reads in a shout, the Countess, beside
                 herself, can be heard stumbling over broken, deliri-
                 ous words.*

COUNTESS   *(Praying, hands clasped)* Almighty God! May not
                 even the most long-hidden of crimes remain
                 unpunished?

COUNT   ... And in the defiler's own hand: *(Reads)* "You

may trust the man who gives you these things
when I am dead."

COUNTESS   *(Praying)* Strike me down, Lord, for a I have
            deserved it!

COUNT   *(Reads)* "If the death of a poor unfortunate were
            to inspire in you some remnant of pity, among the
            names with which the infant heir - heir to anoth-
            er..."

COUNTESS   *(Praying)* Accept this horror I suffer in expiation
            of my error!

COUNT   *(Reads)* "May I hope that the name of Léon..."
            (Speaks out.) And the name of this son is LEON!

COUNTESS   *(Beside herself, eyes closed)* Oh my Lord, my crime
            was great indeed, if it matches my punishment.
            Let your will be done!

COUNT   *(Louder)* And, covered in this disgrace, you dare
            to demand that I account for my lack of fatherly
            feelings!

COUNTESS   *(Still praying)* Who am I to resist, when your
            heavy arm is raised?

COUNT   And when you plead for the child of this wretch,
            you still wear on your arm my likeness!

COUNTESS   *(Removing her bracelet, looks at it.)* Sir, sir you
            must have it back. I know I am unworthy to wear
            it. *(Completely losing control)* My God! What is
            happening to me. Ah! My mind has gone! My
            troubled conscience is seeing ghosts! - A punish-
            ment in advance! - I see what cannot exist ... This

is no longer you ... Léon-Cherubin is signalling
me to follow, he is beckoning me to join him in
the tomb!

COUNT   *(Alarmed)* What? No, you're wrong, it's not ...

COUNTESS   *(Raving)* Terrible phantom, go away!

COUNT   *(With a cry of grief)* It's not what you think!

COUNTESS   *(Hurling the bracelet to the ground)* Wait ... Yes, I
will obey you...

COUNT   *(Becoming more alarmed)* Madame, listen to me...

COUNTESS   I will go ... I obey ... death ...

                She faints.

COUNT   *(Horrified, scoops up the bracelet)* I have gone too
far. She is ill... Ah, God! I must get help.

                He runs from the room. Her convulsions of
                anguish cause the Countess to slide to the floor.

SCENE FOURTEEN

Léon, rushing in; Countess, unconscious.

LEON   *(Shouting)* Oh, my mother! My mother! I have
killed you! *(He picks her up and helps her back on to*
the armchair, still in a faint.) If only I had just
gone away without demanding anyone's help! I
would have prevented this horror!

SCENE FIFTEEN

Count, Suzanne, Léon, Countess (unconscious)

COUNT	*(Entering, shouts)* And now her son!
LEON	*(Wildly)* She is dead! Ah, I shall die too! *(Clasps her as he yells.)*
COUNT	*(Frightened)* Salts! Bring some salts! Suzanne, a million if you save her!
LEON	Oh unhappy mother!
SUZANNE	Madame, try to sniff this bottle. Hold her up, sir. I'll see if I can loosen her clothing to help her breathe.
COUNT	*(Beside himself)* Tear it away, rip the lot! Ah, I should have treated her with more consideration.
LEON	*(Crazed, shouting)* She is dead! She is dead!

SCENE SIXTEEN

Count, Suzanne, Léon, Countess (unconscious), Figaro (rushing in).

FIGARO	Eh? Who's dead? Madame? Stop yelling then! It's the din that's killing her! *(Takes her arm.)* No, she's not dead. She's passed out. It's a rush of blood to the head. But there's no time to lose, we must bring her round. I'll go and get what's needed.
COUNT	*(Beside himself)* Wings on your heels, Figaro! My fortune is yours!

FIGARO	*(Sharply)* Your promises are a big help, when madame's life is in peril.

Runs out.

SCENE SEVENTEEN

Count, Léon, Suzanne, Countess (unconscious).

LEON	*(Holding the bottle of salts under her nose)* If we could only make her breathe! Oh God, give me back my unhappy mother!... She's coming round.
SUZANNE	*(Weeping)* Madame! Come on, madame!...
COUNTESS	*(Coming to her senses)* Ah, it is so hard to die!
LEON	*(Wildly)* No, mama, you shall not die!
COUNTESS	*(Wildly)* Oh, my Lord! Caught between my judges! My husband and my son! Nothing remains hidden... and I have sinned against them both. *(She prostrates herself on the floor.)* Take your vengeance both! There can be no pardon for me! *(In horror)* A guilty mother! Unworthy wife! We are all lost for the sake of a single moment! I have brought horror to my family! I laid the fires of civil war between the father and the children! Just heavens, it was proper that my crime be exposed! May death pay for my wickedness!
COUNT	*(Desperate)* No, come back to us! Your grief has torn my soul! Her chair, Léon! ... my son! *(Léon stops in his tracks.)* Suzanne, her chair.

They lift her back to her armchair.

SCENE EIGHTEEN

As before, plus Figaro.

FIGARO   *(Rushing in)* Has she come round?

SUZANNE   Ah! God! I'm choking too.

              She loosens her clothes.

COUNT   *(Shouts)* Figaro! Help us!

FIGARO   *(Puffing)* Just a moment, calm down. She is
              much better now. And me about my business in
              town, great God! Lucky I returned when I did! ...
              She gave me a terrible fright! Come along,
              madame, take heart!

COUNTESS   *(Praying, slipping sideways in her chair)* God of all
              goodness, make me die!

LEON   *(Seating her more comfortably)* No, mama, you shall
              not die, and we will set our wrongs to rights. Sir,
              I shall offend you no longer with any other name.
              Take back your titles, your possessions. I had no
              right to them: alas, I did not know it. But if you
              have any pity, do not call down public dishonour
              to crush this unhappy woman who was your... An
              error paid for by twenty years of weeping cannot
              still remain a crime when justice is eventually
              served. My mother and I will impose our own
              banishment from your household.

COUNT   *(In a state of elation)* Never! You shall not leave!

LEON   A convent will be her retreat. And I, under my
              plain name of Léon, wearing the simple uniform

of a soldier, will defend the freedom of my new country. I shall die for France as an unknown, or I shall serve her as a faithful citizen.

Suzanne weeps in one corner. Figaro is lost in his own thoughts in the other.

COUNTESS   *(Speaking with difficulty)* Léon! My dearest child! Your courage brings me back to life. It is no longer so unbearable for me since my son has the humanity not to hate his mother. This pride in the midst of misfortune will be your most noble inheritance. He married me when I had nothing; we shall demand nothing of him now. The toil of my own hands will support my frail existence, and you, you shall serve the state.

COUNT   *(Desperate)* No, Rosine! Never! It is I who am truly the guilty one! What goodness I was casting out from my sad old age!

COUNTESS   You will be surrounded by goodness. - You have Florestine and Bégearss with you still. Floresta, your daughter, the cherished child of your heart!...

COUNT   *(Amazed)* What! ... How do you know? ... Who told you? ...

COUNTESS   Sir, give her all your possessions. My son and I raise no objections. Her happiness will be our consolation. But before we part, grant me one favour at least. Tell me how you came to possess a letter which I thought had been burned with the others. Did someone give me away?

FIGARO   *(Calling out)* Yes! The infamous Bégearss! I caught him handing it to the Count earlier today.

COUNT	*(Speaking rapidly)* No, I had it by sheer chance. This morning he and I, looking for something quite different, had your jewel case out, never suspecting it had a double bottom. While we were arguing, and he had the case in his hands, the secret compartment suddenly opened, to his considerable astonishment. He thought he had broken it!
FIGARO	*(Calling out louder)* His astonishment? The secret compartment, the monster! He was the one who had it built in!
COUNT	Is this possible?
COUNTESS	It is all too true.
COUNT	Some papers fell out before our eyes. He didn't know of their existence. And when I wanted to read them out, he refused to listen.
SUZANNE	*(Calling out)* He's read them dozens of times over with madame!
COUNT	Is this true? Did he know them?
COUNTESS	He was the one who delivered them, he brought them back from the regiment, after the death of a certain unhappy man.
COUNT	This loyal friend, the sharer of all our secrets?...
FIGARO COUNTESS SUZANNE	*(All calling together)* It was him!
COUNT	This is the wickedness of the devil himself! He

had me round his little finger! Now I understand
everything.

FIGARO

You think so?

COUNT

I understand his hideous plan. But to make mat-
ters even more certain, let's rip the veil entirely.
Who was it who told you the truth about my
Florestine?

COUNTESS

(Rapidly) He alone confided in me.

LEON

(Rapidly) He told me in secret.

SUZANNE

(Rapidly) He told me too.

COUNT

(Horrified) Ah, the monster! And I was going to
give her to him for his wife! Put my fortune in his
hands.

FIGARO

(With vigour) More than a third of it would be
there already if I hadn't deposited your three million in gold with Mr Fal without telling you. You
were going to make him master of it, but fortunately I suspected. I gave you his receipt...

COUNT

(Agitated) The villain has just retrieved it from
me to go and claim the money.

FIGARO

(Distraught) I am ruined! If the money is handed
over, all my plans are destroyed! I must run to
Mr Fal. God hope it's not too late!

COUNT

(To Figaro) The traitor can't have been there yet.

FIGARO

If he's delayed at all, we've got him. I'm on my
way.

He makes as if to leave.

COUNT   *(Sharply, stopping him)* But, Figaro, the dreadful
         secret you have just discovered, bury it for ever in
         your soul!

FIGARO   *(With great dignity)* Sir, it has been buried in my
         soul for twenty years, and for ten of them I have
         been fighting off a monster's attempts to abuse it.
         But wait until I return before you take any further
         steps.

COUNT   *(Sharply)* But could he plead innocence?

FIGARO   He'll do everything he can to try. *(He takes a letter
         from his pocket.)* But here is your protection.
         Read the contents of this appalling letter; it con-
         tains the secrets of hell. You'll be grateful to me
         for what I did to get it. *(He passes over Bégearss's
         letter.)* Suzanne! Some drops for your mistress.
         You know how I prepare them. *(Gives her a little
         bottle.)* Take her through to her chaise longue.
         And no disturbance whatsoever near her. Sir, I
         beg you, do not start again. She could slip away
         in our very hands!

COUNT   *(Excited)* Start again! I will perpetrate no such
         horrors!

FIGARO   *(To Countess)* Do you hear him, madame? There
         he is, back in his own character. It is my master I
         hear speaking. Ah, I have always said this of him:
         in good heart, the voice of anger is merely the
         sound of the urge to forgive!

         *He runs out. - Count and Léon take Countess by
         the arms, and all exit.*

         END OF ACT FOUR

ACT FIVE

SCENE ONE

The drawing room of the First Act.

Count, Countess, Léon, Suzanne.
(Countess with no make-up, her finery in disarray).

LEON   *(Supporting his mother)* It is too hot in your
              appartment, mama. Suzanne, bring up the wing
              chair.

              They sit Countess down.

COUNT   *(Solicitous, arranging cushions)* Are you comfort-
              able? Now then, crying again?

COUNTESS   *(Overcome)* Ah, let me weep these soothing tears.
              Those dreadful revelations have quite shattered
              me. Especially that wicked letter.

COUNT   *(In a rage)* With a wife in Ireland, he was going to
              marry my daughter! And all my wealth banked in
              London. He'd have made it his hide-out until the
              last one of us was dead!... And, great God! Who
              knows what ways he'd have...

COUNTESS   Unhappy man, try to be calm! But it is time
              Florestine came down. She was so frightened of
              what was to become of her! Go and bring her,
              Suzanne. And tell her none of this.

COUNT   *(With dignity)* What I told Figaro, Suzanne, was
              intended equally for you.

SUZANNE   Sir, anyone who watched the mistress weep and
               pray over twenty years has shared too much of her
               sorrows to do anything to make matters worse!

               Exits.

SCENE TWO

Count, Countess, Léon.

COUNT   *(In a burst of feeling)* Ah, Rosine! Dry your tears.
               And a curse on any man who harms you further!

COUNTESS   My son! Fall at the knees of your generous pro-
               tector and give thanks to him for your mother.

               Léon makes to kneel.

COUNT   *(Raising him)* Let us forget the past, Leon, and
               cover it in silence. Your mother has been moved
               enough. Figaro calls for no disturbance. Ah!
               And let us above all protect Florestine's tender
               years by concealing the causes of this chain of
               events.

SCENE THREE

As before, plus Florestine, Suzanne.

FLORESTINE   *(Running in)* My God! Mama, what has hap-
               pened?

COUNTESS   For you there is only good news to hear, and your
               godfather is going to explain.

COUNT	Alas, my Florestine, I tremble at the danger I was about to bring down on your young head. Thanks to the good Lord, who pulls all veils aside, you will not be marrying Bégearss. No, you shall not be the wife of the most villainous parasite...!
FLORESTINE	Ah, God! Léon!...
LEON	My sister, he has tricked us all!
FLORESTINE	*(To Count)* His sister!
COUNT	He was deceiving us. He was playing us off one against the other, and you were to be the prize of his terrible treachery. I am going to expel him from my household.
COUNTESS	Your instinctive dread served you better than our supposedly reasoned judgements. Loving child, give thanks to the Lord who has saved you from great danger.
LEON	My sister, he tricked us all!
FLORESTINE	*(To Count)* Sir, he keeps calling me his sister!
COUNTESS	*(In exaltation)* Yes, Floresta, you are ours. That was our cherished secret. There is your father, there is your brother; and as for me, while there is life, I am your mother. Ah! And God preserve that you ever forget it! *(She holds her hand out to the Count.)* Almaviva, is it not true, she is MY DAUGHTER?
COUNT	*(In exaltation)* And Léon, MY SON. Here are our two children.

All embrace.

SCENE FOUR

Figaro, Monsieur Fal, lawyer; the others as before.

FIGARO   *(Running in and throwing off his coat)* We are
              cursed! He has the portfolio. I saw the traitor
              carrying it off as I arrived at Mr Fal's office.

COUNT   Oh, Mr Fal! You have been too hasty!

M. FAL   *(With vigour)* No, sir. On the contrary. He was
              with me for more than an hour, insisting I finish
              making out the contract, inserting the donation he
              intends to bestow. Then he handed over my
              receipt, with your note attached saying the money
              belonged to him, it was an inheritance of his own
              which he has entrusted to you in confidence...

COUNT   Ah, the scoundrel! He forgets nothing!

FIGARO   Except to tremble for what the future will bring!

M. FAL   With all that authorisation, could I have refused
              the portfolio he was demanding? It was three mil-
              lion paid to bearer. If you break the marriage
              contract and he wishes to keep the money, it's
              hard to see that anything can be done about it.

COUNT   *(Vehemently)* God rot all the gold in the world,
              and grant that I be rid of the man!

FIGARO   *(Throwing his hat on a chair)* I'll be hanged if he
              keeps a penny of it! *(To Suzanne)* Keep watch
              outside, Suzanne.

She exits.

M. FAL   Do you have some way of getting him to admit in
                front of reliable witnesses that he obtained this
                treasure from the Count? Without that, I defy
                you to get the money back from him.

FIGARO   If his German servant tells him what is happening
                here, we won't see him back again.

COUNT   So much the better! That's all I ask! Ah, let him
                keep the rest.

FIGARO   *(With vigour)* Let him have it by default? It's
                your children's inheritance! That's not being vir-
                tuous, that's being feeble!

LEON   *(Angrily)* Figaro!

FIGARO   *(Loudly)* I stick to what I say. *(To Count.)* What
                are you going to pay for affection if that's what
                you pay for treachery?

COUNT   *(Getting angry)* But to attempt it and fail would
                be handing him his victory ...

SCENE FIVE

As before, plus Suzanne.

SUZANNE   *(Shouting from the doorway)* It's Mr Bégearss
                coming back!

                Exits.

SCENE SIX

As before, minus Suzanne. (Strong reaction all round).

COUNT   *(Beside himself)* Ah! The traitor!

FIGARO   *(Very rapidly)* No time to agree to plan. But if
                 you listen to me and all back me up to make him
                 feel he's completely secure, I promise success or
                 you can have my neck.

M. FAL   Are you going to mention the portfolio and the
                 contract?

FIGARO   *(Very rapidly)* Certainly not. He knows too much
                 about it to be attacked directly. We need to start
                 at a distance and draw him slowly in until he
                 makes his own admission. *(To Count)* Pretend
                 you want to give me the sack.

COUNT   *(Confused)* But, but ... what have you done?

SCENE SEVEN

As before, plus Suzanne, Bégearss.

SUZANNE   *(Rushing in)* Mr Bégeaaaaaaars!

                 *She moves to the Countess's side. Bégearss looks
                 very surprised.*

FIGARO   *(Calling out, on seeing him)* Mr Bégearss!
                 (Humbly) Ah well, it is only one more humilia-
                 tion. Since the pardon I seek depends on the con-
                 fession of all my sins, I hope Sir will not be any
                 less generous.

BEGEARSS	*(Astonished)* What is the matter here? I find you all gathered together!

COUNT	*(Brusquely)* To dismiss an unworthy servant.

BEGEARSS	*(Even more surprised, seeing the lawyer)* And Mr Fal!

M. FAL	*(Showing the contract)* As you can see, we waste no time. Everything here is as you wished.

BEGEARSS	*(Surprised)* Ah! Ah!...

COUNT	*(Impatient, to Figaro)* Get on with it. I'm losing patience.

> *During this scene, Bégearss scrutinises them one after the other, very closely.*

FIGARO	*(Pleading, to Count)* Since pretence is impossible, I must conclude my sorry confession. Yes, in order to damage Mr Bégearss, I repeat, to my embarrassment, that I set out to spy on him, follow him, and dog his footsteps. *(To Count.)* For Sir had indeed not rung for me when I entered madame's study to find out what they were doing with her jewel case, which I discovered had been broken open.

BEGEARSS	Broken indeed, to my profound regret.

COUNT	*(Starting dangerously, aside)* The effrontery of it!

FIGARO	*(Bowing before him, tugging warningly at his coat.)* Ah, my master!

M. FAL	*(Alarmed)* Sir!

BEGEARSS   *(Aside, to Count)* Control yourself, or we will get nothing out of him.

Count stamps his foot. Bégearss stares at him.

FIGARO   *(With a sigh, to Count)* That is why, knowing the mistress was in private conversation with him about burning some papers I knew to be important, I brought you in such haste.

BEGEARSS   *(To Count)* Did I not tell you?

Count chews his hankerchief in fury.

SUZANNE   *(Hisses at Figaro from behind)* Get on with it! Get on with it!

FIGARO   So, seeing that you were all in agreement after all, I confess that I did everything I could to provoke between yourself and madame that terrible scene of revelations ... which did not have the ending I was hoping for...

COUNT   *(Angrily, to Figaro)* Have you finished this pathetic entreaty?

FIGARO   *(Very humbly)* Alas, there is nothing more I can say, since it was that scene which caused Mr Fal to be summoned, to finalise the contract here. Mr Bégearss's guiding star has triumphed over all my tricks ... My master! In consideration of thirty years ...

COUNT   *(With humour)* It's not for me to judge.

He paces rapidly up and down.

FIGARO	Mr Bégearss!
BEGEARSS	*(Who feels he is safe again, ironically)* Who? Me? Dear friend, I hardly thought I owed you so much service! *(Becoming lofty in tone)* To see my happiness brought closer by the very scheme whose villainous intent was to deprive me of it! *(To Léon and Florestine)* Oh, you young people! What a lesson to learn! Let us always walk the path of virtue with heads held high. See how, sooner or later, the scheme brings the downfall of the schemer.
FIGARO	*(Prostrate)* Ah! Yes!
BEGEARSS	*(To Count)* Sir, for just this once, very well. But then he must go!
COUNT	*(To Bégearss, sternly)* That is your judgement? ... I consent.
FIGARO	*(Ardently)* Mr Bégearss! I owe it to you! But I see Mr Fal anxious to finalise his contract ...
COUNT	*(Brusquely)* I am familiar with it stipulations.
M. FAL	Apart from this item. I will read you the article of donation which this gentleman is making. *(Scans the contract.)* M..., M..., M.., Mr James-Honoré Bégearss ... Ah! *(Reads)* "And to give Miss Florestine, his future wife, unequivocal proof of his affection for her, the said future husband makes over to her as an entire gift all the wealth he possesses; consisting on this date *(He leans on the words.)* and as herewith declared and presented to us, lawyer and signatory below, of three million francs in gold here attached in valid bills

payable to bearer."

He holds his hand out as he reads.

BEGEARSS   They are here in this portfolio. *(Gives the portfolio to M.Fal.)* It's just two thousand sovereigns short, which I have just removed in order to make provision for the wedding preparations.

FIGARO   *(With vigour, pointing to Count)* Sir has decided that he will pay for all that. He's given me his orders.

BEGEARSS   *(Taking the bills from his pocket and passing them to the lawyer)* In that case, make a record of them. Let the gift be entire!

            Figaro, turning his back, clasps his hand to his mouth to stifle his laughter. M.Fal opens the portfolio and slips the bills inside.

M. FAL   *(Indicating Figaro)* Mr Figaro will add everything up, whilst we shall complete the formalities.

            He gives the open portfolio to Figaro, who sees the bills.

FIGARO   *(Eyeing the returned bills, elated)* And for my part I find true repentance is like all good actions: it brings its own reward.

BEGEARSS   In what way?

FIGARO   It gives me happiness to know that we are in the presence of not just one generous man. Oh, my God, crown the desires of two such perfect friends. We have no need to write anything down.

(To Count) These are your bills payable to bearer; yes, sir, I recognise them. Between you and Mr Bégearss it's a real battle of generosity. One gives all his wealth to the future husband, the other passes it on to his future wife! *(To Léon and Florestine)* Sir, Miss! Oh, what a munificent protector, and how you are going to cherish him! ... But what am I saying? Could my enthusiasm have caused me to commit some hurtful indiscretion?

Everyone is silent.

BEGEARSS   *(A little surprised, recovers, makes up his mind.)* It need be for no one, if my friend does not contest it; if he puts my conscience at rest by allowing me to confess that these bills come originally from him. It is a hard-hearted man who finds gratitude tiresome, and my satisfaction was incomplete without that admission. *(Indicating Count.)* I owe him my happiness and my fortune. And when I share them with his worthy daughter, I do no more than restore to her what is hers by right. Give me back the portfolio; I want merely the honour of laying it at her feet with my own hands, which I can do now by signing our happy contract.

He makes to take it back.

FIGARO   *(Leaping with joy)* Gentlemen, did you hear that? You will bear witness if necessary. My master, here are your bills. Give them to their bearer, if your heart judges him worthy of them.

He hands portfiolio to Count.

COUNT   *(Rising, to Bégearss)* Great God! Give them to

him! Vicious man, get out of my house! Hell
itself has lesser pits than you! Thanks to this good
old servant, my lack of caution is redeemed.
Leave my house this very second!

BEGEARSS   Oh, my friend, you have been deceived!

COUNT   *(Beside himself, quells him with Bégearss's own letter.)* And this letter, sir? Does this deceive as
well?

BEGEARSS   *(Sees it; furious, snatches letter from Count and
reveals the true man as the mask slips.)* Ah!... I have
been tricked! But I will have satisfaction.

LEON   You have filled this family with your horrors: now
leave it in peace.

BEGEARSS   *(Furious)* Young madman! You shall pay for
them all! I challenge you to fight.

LEON   *(Rapidly)* Ready and willing!

COUNT   *(Rapidly)* Léon!

COUNTESS   *(Rapidly)* My son!

FLORESTINE   *(Rapidly)* My brother!

COUNT   Léon, I forbid you... *(To Bégearss)* You have
made yourself unworthy of the honour you
demand. That is not the way a man like you must
be allowed to lose his life.

Bégearss makes a terrible gesture, speechless.

FIGARO   *(Stopping Léon, sharply)* No, young man, you

shall not go. The Count your father is right, and opinions have altered on that appalling act of frenzy. Here we shall no longer fight anyone but the enemies of the state. Leave him prey to his fury, and if he dares attack you, defend yourself as if cutting down a would-be murderer. No one has anything against putting down mad dogs. But he won't dare: a man capable of such viciousness is bound to be as cowardly as he is vile!

BEGEARSS   *(Beside himself.)* You miserable wretch!

COUNT   *(Stamping his foot)* Now, will you leave us? The very sight of you is a torment.

> *Countess is distraught on her chair. Florestine and Suzanne support her. Léon goes over to join them.*

BEGEARSS   *(Through clenched teeth)* Yes, God blast you, I'll leave you. But I still have the proof of your base treachery! You only sought His Majesty's authorisation for the exchange of your Spanish possessions in order to be able to make trouble on the other side of the Pyrenees without danger to yourself.

COUNT   Oh, monster! What is he saying!

BEGEARSS   That I am going to Madrid to denounce you for it. If all you had amounted to a life-size bust of Washington in your study, I'd still have them confiscate every last thing you own!

FIGARO   *(Shouting)* Naturally you would. One third of everything goes to the denouncer.

BEGEARSS   But in case you try to go ahead with any
                exchange, I am going straight to the Spanish
                ambassador to get him to seize the document of
                consent from His Majesty, which is expected to
                arrive with the next mail.

FIGARO   *(Pulling a packet from his pocket with a shout of tri-*
                umph) The King's consent? Here it is! I knew
                you would; so I have just been to recover the
                packet on your behalf, from the embassy secre-
                tary. The mail from Spain was just arriving!

                The Count eagerly takes the package.

BEGEARSS   *(Furious, strikes his forehead, takes two steps towards*
                the door, then turns back) Farewell, abandoned
                family, a house without morals and without hon-
                our. You will go shamelessly ahead and conclude
                an abominable marriage by uniting a brother with
                his sister: but the whole universe will hear of your
                vile perversion!

                Exits.

SCENE EIGHT

As before, minus Bégearss.

FIGARO   *(Excitedly)* Let him spread his slanders, a cow-
                ard's last resort! He's no danger to us now.
                Completely unmasked, at the end of the road, and
                not twenty-five sovereigns in the world! Ah! Mr
                Fal! I would have put a dagger between my ribs if
                he had kept the two thousand sovereigns he had
                removed from the rest! *(He resumes a serious tone.)*
                Besides, no one knows better than he that both in

nature and in law, these young people here have
nothing in common, that they are strangers to
each other.

COUNT   *(Embracing him, with a shout)* Oh, Figaro! ...
Madame, he is right.

LEON   *(Very rapidly.)* God! Mama! If that were true!

FLORESTINE   *(To Count)* What is that, sir, are you no longer ...?

COUNT   *(Intoxicated with joy)* My children, we will return
to this matter, and we will consult, under another
name, some discreet men of the law, well
informed, full of honour. Oh, my children! We
are at the dawn of an age when honest people forgive each other's faults, their former frailties, and
bring a gentle affection in the wake of those
stormy passions which drove them too far apart.
Rosine, hear once more the name your husband
gives you back again - let us go and rest from the
fatigues of this long day! Mr Fal, stay with us.
Come, my two children! Suzanne, embrace your
husband, and let the subject of our quarrels be
buried for ever! *(To Figaro)* The two thousand
sovereigns which he had extracted, they are yours
to enjoy whilst waiting for the full reward you are
so richly owed.

FIGARO   *(With vigour)* Mine, sir? No, please! A man like
me let a mean payment taint the good service I
have done! My reward is to die in your household. If I often let you down as a young man, let
this day redeem my life! Old age, pardon my
unruly youth. You will become its proud boast!
A single day has changed our world! No more
oppressor; no insolent-tongued hypocrite; each

one has done his duty well. We need never regret
a moment or two of trouble: The family is the
winner when the wicked are expelled.

THE END